W9-DFN-329

9/26

SEPTEMBER

Previous books by the author:

Sleeping Tiger
Another View
Snow in April
The End of Summer
The Empty House
The Day of the Storm
Under Gemini
Wild Mountain Thyme
Voices in Summer
The Blue Bedroom and Other Stories
The Carousel
The Shell Seekers

ROSAMUNDE PILCHER

SEPTEMBER

LARGE PRINT BOOK CLUB EDITION

A Thomas Dunne Book
St. Martin's Press / New York

Volume 1

This Large Print Edition, prepared especially for Doubleday Book & Music Clubs, Inc., contains the complete, unabridged text of the original Publisher's Edition.

This Large Print Book carries the seal of approval of N.A.V.H.

Printed in the U.S.A.

Quality Printing and Binding by:
R.R. Donnelley & Sons Company
1009 Sloan Street
Crawfordsville, IN 47933 U.S.A.

MAY

❦ 1 ❦

Tuesday the Third

IN EARLY MAY, THE SUMMER CAME, at
last, to Scotland. Winter had clung, with
steely fingers, for far too long, refusing to re-
linquish its cruel grip. All through April, bitter winds had blown from the north-west,
tearing the first blossom from the wild
geynes, and burning brown the yellow trum-
pets of the early daffodils. Snow frosted the
hilltops and lay deep in corries, and the farmers, despairing of fresh grazing, tractored the
last of their feed out to the barren fields
where lowing stock huddled in the shelter of
the drystone walls.

Even the wild geese, usually gone by the
end of March, were late in returning to their
Arctic habitats. The last of the skeins had
disappeared around the middle of April,
honking away north into the unknown skies,

flying so high that the arrowhead formations looked no more substantial than cobwebs drifting in the wind.

And then, overnight, the fickle Highland climate relented. The wind veered around to the south, bringing with it the balmy breezes and the soft weather that the rest of the country had been enjoying for weeks, along with the scent of damp earth and growing things. The countryside turned a sweet and verdant green, the wild white cherry trees recovered from their battering, took heart, and spread their branches in a mist of snowflake petals. All at once, cottage gardens burgeoned into colour—yellow winter-flowering jasmine, purple crocus, and the deep blue of grape hyacinths. Birds sang, and the sun, for the first time since last autumn, brought a real warmth with it.

Every morning of her life, rain or shine, Violet Aird walked to the village to collect, from Mrs. Ishak's supermarket, two pints of milk, *The Times,* and any other small groceries and supplies needed for the sustenance of one elderly lady living on her own. Only sometimes, in the depths of winter, when the snow piled in deep drifts, and the ice became treacherous, did she eschew this exercise, on the principle that discretion was the better part of valour.

It was not an easy walk. Half a mile down the steep road, between fields which had once been the parkland of Croy, Archie Balmerino's estate, and then the stiff half-mile climb home again. She had a car, and could perfectly well have made the journey in that, but it was one of her convictions that, as old age crept up on you, once you started to use the car for short journeys, then you were in dire danger of losing the use of your legs.

For all the long months of winter, she had had to bundle up in layers of clothing for this expedition. Thick boots, sweaters, waterproof jacket, scarf, gloves, a woollen hat pulled well down over her ears. This morning, she wore a tweed skirt and a cardigan and her head was bare. The sun lifted her spirits and made her feel energetic and young again, and being uncluttered by extraneous garments reminded her of childhood satisfaction when black woollen stockings were abandoned and one felt the pleasant, draughty sensation of cool air on bare legs.

The village shop, this morning, was busy, and she had to wait for a little to be served. She did not mind, because it meant that there was time to chat with other customers, all of whom were familiar faces; marvel at the weather; ask after somebody's mother; watch a small boy choose, with painful deliberation, a packet of Dolly Mixtures, which he proceeded to pay for with his own money. He was not hurried. Mrs. Ishak stood with gentle patience while he made up his mind. When he had finally done this, she put the Dolly Mixtures into a little paper bag and took the money from him.

"You must not eat them all at once, or you will lose all your teeth," she warned him. "Good morning, Mrs. Aird."

"Good morning, Mrs. Ishak. And what a lovely day it is!"

"I could not believe it when I saw the sun shining." Usually Mrs. Ishak, exiled to these northern climes from the relentless sunshine of Malawi, was bundled in cardigans and kept a paraffin heater behind the counter, over which she huddled whenever there was a moment of quiet. This morning, however, she looked much happier. "I hope it will not become cold again."

"I don't think so. Summer is here. Oh, thank you, my milk and my paper. And Edie wants some furniture polish and a roll of paper towel. And I think I'd better take half a dozen eggs."

"If your basket is too heavy, I can send Mr. Ishak up to your house in his motor car."

"No, I can manage, thank you very much."

"It is a lot of walking you are doing."

Violet smiled. "But just think how good it is for me."

Laden, she set off once more for home, for Pennyburn. Down the pavement, past the rows of low cottages, with windows blinking reflected sunlight, and doors standing open to the fresh warm air; then through the gates of Croy and up the hill again. This was a private road, the back driveway of the big house, and Pennyburn stood half-way up it, to one side and surrounded by steep fields. It was approached by a neat lane bordered in clipped beech hedges, and it was always something of a relief to reach the turning and to know that one did not have to climb any farther.

Violet changed her basket, which was becoming heavy, from one hand to the other, and made plans as to how she would spend the rest of her day. This was one of Edie's mornings for helping Violet, which meant that Violet could abandon her house and instead get busy in the garden. Lately, it had been too cold for even Violet to garden, and things had become neglected. The lawn was looking tired and mossy after the long winter. Perhaps she should run her spiker over it and give it a bit of air. After that, a huge pit of carefully nurtured compost needed to be barrowed and spread over her new rose-bed. The prospect filled her with satisfying joy. She could not wait to get down to work.

Her step quickened. But then, almost at once, she saw the unfamiliar car parked outside her front door, and knew that the garden, for the moment, would have to wait. A visitor. Such irritation. Who had come to call? Who was Violet going to have to sit with and talk to, instead of being allowed to get on with her digging?

The car was a neat little Renault and betrayed no clue as to its owner. Violet went into the house through the kitchen door, and there found Edie at the tap and filling the kettle.

She dumped the basket on the table. "Who is it?" she mouthed, making pointing gestures with her forefinger.

Edie, too, kept her voice down. "Mrs. Steynton. From Corriehill."

"How long has she been here?"

"Only a moment. I told her to wait. She's in the sitting-room. She wants a wee word." Edie resumed her normal voice. "I'm just making you both a cup of coffee. I'll bring it in when it's ready."

With no excuse or possible escape route, Violet went to find her visitor. Verena Steynton stood at the window of the sun-filled sitting-room, gazing out at Violet's garden. As Violet came through the door, she turned.

"Oh, Violet, I am sorry. I feel embarrassed. I told Edie I'd come back another time, but she swore you'd be home from the village in a moment or two."

She was a tall and slender woman around forty, and invariably immaculately and elegantly turned out. Which instantly set her apart from the other local ladies, who were, for the most part, busy country women, with neither the time nor the inclination to bother too much about their personal appearance. Verena and her husband Angus were newcomers to the neighbourhood, having lived at Corriehill for a mere ten years. Before that, Angus had worked as a stockbroker in London, but having made his pile, and tiring of the rat race, he had bought Corriehill, ten miles distant from Strathcroy, moved north with his wife and his daughter Katy, and cast about, locally, for some other, and hopefully less demanding, occupation. He had ended up taking over a run-down timber business in Relkirk, and over the years had built this up into a lucrative and thriving concern.

As for Verena, she, too, was something of a career woman, being heavily involved with an organization called Scottish Country Tours. During the summer months, this company shuttled busloads of American visitors hither and yon, and arranged for them to stay, as paying guests, in a selection of well-vetted private houses. Isobel Balmerino had been roped into this exercise, and hard labour it was, too. Violet could not think of a more exhausting way of making a bit of money.

However, from the social point of view, the Steynton family had proved themselves a true asset to the community, being both friendly and unassuming, generous with their hospitality, and always willing to give time and effort to the running of fêtes, gymkhanas, and various fund-raising events.

Even so, Violet could not begin to imagine why Verena was here.

"I'm glad you stayed. I would have been sorry to miss you. Edie's just making us a cup of coffee."

"I should have telephoned, but I was on my way to Relkirk and suddenly thought, much better to drop in and take my chance. On the spur of the moment. You don't mind?"

"Not in the least," Violet fibbed robustly. "Come and sit down. I'm afraid the fire's not been lighted yet, but . . ."

"Oh, heavens, who needs a fire on a day like this? Isn't it blissful to see the sun?"

She settled herself on the sofa and crossed her long and elegant legs. Violet, less gracefully, lowered herself into her own wide-lapped chair.

She decided to come straight to the point. "Edie said you wanted a word with me."

"I just suddenly thought . . . you'd be the very person to help."

Violet's heart sank, envisaging some bazaar, garden-opening, or charity concert, for which she was about to be asked to knit tea-cosies, declare open, or sell tickets.

"Help?" she said faintly.

"No. Not so much help, as give advice. You see, I'm thinking of throwing a dance."

"A *dance?*"

"Yes. For Katy. She's going to be twenty-one."

"But how can *I* advise you? I haven't done such a thing for longer than I can remember. Surely, you'd be better to ask somebody a little more up-to-date. Peggy Ferguson-Crombie, or Isobel, for instance?"

"It's just that I thought . . . you're so experienced. You've lived here longer than anybody I know. I wanted to get your reactions to the idea."

Violet was nonplussed. Casting about for something to say, she welcomed the appearance of Edie with the coffee tray. Edie set this down on the fireside stool. "Are you wanting biscuits?" she asked.

"No, Edie, I think that will do very nicely. Thank you so much."

Edie departed. In a moment, the vacuum cleaner could be heard roaring away upstairs.

Violet poured the coffee. "What sort of an affair did you have in mind?"

"Oh, you know. Reels and country dances."

Violet thought that she did know. "You mean tapes on the stereo, and eightsomes in the hall?"

"No. Not like that. A really *big* dance. We'd do it in style. With a marquee on the lawn . . ."

"I hope Angus is feeling rich."

Verena ignored this interruption. ". . . and a proper band for the music. We'll use the hall, of course, but for sitting out. And the drawing-room. And I'm sure Katy will want a disco for all her London friends, it seems to be the thing to do. Perhaps the dining-room. We could turn it into a cave, or a grotto. . . ."

Caves and grottoes, thought Violet. Verena had clearly been doing her homework. But then, she was an excellent organizer. Violet said mildly, "You *have* been laying plans."

"And Katy can ask all her friends from the south . . . we'll have to find beds for them, of course. . . ."

"Have you spoken to Katy about your idea?"

"No, I told you. You're the first person to know."

"Perhaps she won't want a dance."

"But of course she will. She's always loved parties."

Violet, knowing Katy, decided that this was probably true. "And when is it to be?"

"I thought September. That's the obvious time. Lots of people up for the shooting, and everybody still on holiday. The sixteenth might be a good date, because by then most of the younger children will have gone back to boarding-school."

"This is only May. September's a long way off."

"I know, but it's never too early to fix a date and start making arrangements. I'll have to book the marquee, and the caterer, and get invitations printed. . . ." She came up with another pleasurable idea. "And, Violet, wouldn't fairy lights be pretty, all the way up the drive to the house?"

It all sounded dreadfully ambitious. "It's going to be a lot of work for you."

"Not really. The Tourist Invasion will be over by then, because the paying guests stop coming at the end of August. I shall be able to concentrate my mind. Do admit, Violet, it is a good idea. And just think of all the people I'll be able to cross off my social-conscience list. We can get everybody off in one fell swoop. Including," she added, "the Barwells."

"I don't think I know the Barwells."

"No, you wouldn't. They're business colleagues of Angus's. We've been to dinner with them twice. Two evenings of jaw-aching boredom. And never asked them back, simply because we couldn't think of anybody who could be asked to endure an evening in such excruciatingly dull company. And there are lots of others," she remembered comfortably. "When I remind Angus about *them,* he's not going to raise any difficulties about signing a few cheques."

Violet felt a little sorry for Angus. "Who else will you ask?"

"Oh, everybody. The Millburns and the Ferguson-Crombies and the Buchanan-Wrights and old Lady Westerdale, and the Brandons. And the Staffords. All their children have grown up now, so they can be invited, too. And the Middletons should be up from Hampshire, and the Luards from Gloucestershire. We'll make a list. I'll pin a sheet of paper to the kitchen notice-board, and every time I think of a new name, I'll write it down. And you, of course, Violet. And Edmund, and Virginia, and Alexa. And the Balmerinos. Isobel will give a dinner party for me, I'm sure. . . ."

Suddenly, it all began to sound rather fun. Violet's concentration drifted back to the past, to forgotten occasions now remembered. One memory led to another. She said without thinking, "You should send Pandora an invitation," and then could not imagine why she had come up with the impulsive suggestion.

"Pandora?"

"Archie Balmerino's sister. One thinks of parties, and one automatically thinks of Pandora. But of course you never knew her."

"But I know *about* her. For some reason, her name always seems to come up at dinner-party conversations. You think she would come? Surely she hasn't been home for over twenty years?"

"That's true. Just a silly thought. But why not give it a try? What a shot in the arm it would be for poor Archie. And if anything would bring that errant creature back to Croy, it would be the lure of a full-blown dance."

"So you're on my side, Violet? You think I should go ahead and do it?"

"Yes, I do. If you have the energy and the wherewithal, I think it's a wonderful and generous idea. It will give us all something splendid to look forward to."

"Don't say anything until I've bearded Angus."

"Not a word."

Verena smiled with satisfaction. And then another happy thought occurred to her. "I shall have a good excuse," she said, "to go and find myself a new dress."

But Violet had no such problem. "I," she told Verena, "shall wear my black velvet."

❧ 2 ❧

Thursday the Twelfth

THE NIGHT WAS SHORT and he did not sleep. Soon it would be dawn.

He had imagined that, for once, he might sleep, since he was tired, exhausted. Drained by three days of an unseasonably hot New York; days filled to the brim with breakfast meetings, business lunches, long afternoons of argument and discussion; too much Coca-Cola and black coffee, too many receptions and late nights, and a miserable dearth of exercise and fresh air.

Finally, successfully, it had been achieved, though not easily. Harvey Klein was a tough nut, and some persuasion was necessary to convince him that this was the very best, and indeed the only way to hook the English market. The creative campaign that Noel had brought with him to New York, complete with a time-schedule, layouts, and photographs, had been approved and agreed upon. With the contract under his belt, Noel could return to London. Pack his bag, make a last-minute telephone call, stuff his briefcase with documents and calculator, take another telephone call (Harvey Klein to say safe journey), get himself downstairs, check out, flag down a yellow cab, and head for Kennedy.

In the evening light Manhattan, as always, looked miraculous—towers of light thrusting upwards into the suffused glow of the sky, and the freeways moving rivers of headlights. Here was a city that offered, in its brash and open-handed way, every conceivable form of delight.

Before, on previous visits, he had taken full advantage of all the fun, but there had been no opportunity, this time, to accept any of them, and he knew a pang of regret at leaving unfulfilled, as though he were being hustled away from a stupendous party long before he had even started to enjoy it.

At Kennedy the cab dropped him at the BA terminal. He duly queued, checked in, rid himself of his suitcase, queued again for

Security, and at last made his way to the departure lounge. He bought a bottle of Scotch in the Duty-Free, a *Newsweek* and *Advertising Age* from the newsstand. Finding a chair he sat, slumped with tiredness, waiting for his flight to be called.

By courtesy of Wenborn & Weinburg, he was traveling Club Class, so at least there was space for his long legs, and he had asked for a seat by the window. He took off his jacket, settled himself, longed for a drink. It occurred to him that it would be fortuitous if no one came to sit beside him, but this faint hope died almost at once as a well-upholstered individual in a navy-blue chalk-stripe suit claimed the seat, stowed various bags and bundles in the overhead bin, and at last collapsed, in an overflowing fashion, alongside.

The man took up a great deal of space. The interior of the aircraft was cool, but this man was hot. He pulled out a silk handkerchief and dabbed his brow, heaved and humped, searched for his seat-belt, and managed to jab Noel, quite painfully, with his elbow.

"Sorry about that. Seems we're a full load this evening."

Noel did not wish to talk. He smiled and nodded, and pointedly opened his *Newsweek*.

They took off. Cocktails were served, and then dinner. He was not hungry, but ate it, because it passed the time and there was nothing else to do. The huge 747 droned on, out over the Atlantic. Dinner was cleared and the movie came on. Noel had already seen it in London, so he asked the flight attendant to bring him a whisky and soda and drank it slowly, cradling it in his hand, making it last. Cabin lights were extinguished and passengers reached for pillows and blankets. The fat man folded his hands over his stomach and snored momentously. Noel closed his eyes, but this made them feel as though they were filled with grit, so he opened them again. His mind raced. It had been working full throttle for three days and refused to slow down. The possibility of oblivion faded.

He wondered why he was not feeling triumphant, because he had won the precious account and was returning home with the whole thing safely sewn up. A suitable metaphor for Saddlebags. Saddlebags. It was one of those words which, the more times you said it, the more ridiculous it sounded. But it wasn't ridiculous. It was immensely important not only to Noel Keeling, but to Wenborn & Weinburg as well.

Saddlebags. A company with its roots in Colorado, where the business had started up some years ago, manufacturing high-class leather goods for the ranching fraternity. Saddles, bridles, straps, reins, and riding boots, all branded with the prestigious trademark of a hoof-print enclosing the letter *S*.

From this modest beginning, the company's reputation and sales had grown nation-wide, outstripping all rivals. They moved into the manufacture of other commodities. Luggage, handbags, fashion accessories, shoes and boots. All constructed from the finest of hide, hand-stitched and hand-finished. The Saddlebag logo became a status symbol, vying with Gucci or Ferragamo, and with a price-tag to match. Their reputation spread, so that visitors to the United States, wishing to return home with a truly impressive piece of loot, chose a Saddlebag satchel, or a hand-tooled, gold-buckled belt.

And then came the rumour that they were moving into the British market, retailing through one or two carefully chosen London stores. Charles Weinburg, Noel's chairman, got wind of this by means of a chance remark dropped at a London dinner party. The next morning Noel, as Senior Vice-President and Creative Director, was called for his briefing.

"I want this account, Noel. At the moment only a handful of people in this country have ever heard of Saddlebags, and they're going to need a top-gear campaign. We've got the headstart and if we land it we can handle it, so I put through a call to New York late last night, and spoke to Saddlebag's President, Harvey Klein. He's agreeable to a meeting but he wants a total presentation . . . layouts, media coverage, slogans, the lot. Top-level stuff, full-page colour spreads. You've got two weeks. Get busy with the Art Department and try to work something out. And for God's sake find a photographer who can make a male model look like a man, not like a shop-window dummy. If necessary, get hold of a genuine polo-player. If he'll do the job, I don't care what we have to pay him. . . ."

It was nine years since Noel Keeling had gone to work for Wenborn & Weinburg. Nine years is a long time in the advertising business for a man to stay with the same firm, and from time to time he found himself astonished by his own uninterrupted progress. Others, his own contemporaries, who had started with him, had moved on—to other companies, or even, like some colleagues, to start their own agencies. But Noel had stayed.

The reasons for the constancy were basically rooted in his personal life. Indeed, after a year or two with the firm, he had considered quite seriously the possibility of leaving. He was restless, unsatisfied, and not even particularly interested in the job. He dreamt of greener fields: setting up on his own, abandoning advertising altogether and moving into property or commodities. With plans for making a million, he knew that it was simply lack of the necessary capital that was holding him back. But he had no capital, and the frustration of lost opportunities and missed chances drove him nearly to distraction.

And then, four years ago, things had dramatically changed. He was thirty, a bachelor, and still resolutely working his way through a string of girl-friends, with no inkling that this irresponsible state of affairs would not last for ever. But his mother quite suddenly died, and for the first time in his life Noel had found himself a man of some means.

Her death had been so totally unexpected that for a little while he was shocked into a state where he found it almost impossible to come to terms with the cold fact that she had gone for ever. He had always been fond of her, in a detached and unsentimental manner, but basically he'd thought of her as his constant source of food, drink, clean clothes, warm beds, and, when he asked for it, moral support. As well, he had respected both her independence of spirit and the fact that she had never interfered, in any way, with Noel's own adult and private life. At the same time, much of her dotty behaviour had maddened him. Worst was her habit of surrounding herself with the most down-at-heel and needy of hangers-on. Everybody was her friend. She

called them all her friends. Noel called them
a lot of bloody spongers. She disregarded his
cynical attitude, and bereaved spinsters,
lonely widows, penniless artists, and unem-
ployed actors were drawn to her side as
moths seek a candle flame. Her generosity to
all and sundry he had considered both mindless and selfish, for there never seemed to be
any money to spare for the things in life that
Noel believed to be of primary importance.

When she died, her will reflected this
thoughtless bounty. A hefty bequest was left
to a young man . . . nothing to do with the
family . . . whom she had taken under her
sheltering wing, and whom, for some reason,
she wished to help.

For Noel, it was a bitter blow. His feelings
—and pocket—deeply hurt, he was consumed by a resentment that was totally impotent. It was no use raging, because she was
gone. He could not have it out with her, ac-
cuse her of disloyalty and demand to know
what the bloody hell she thought she was doing. His mother had moved beyond his reach.
He imagined her, safe from his wrath, across
some chasm or uncrossable river, surrounded
by sunshine, fields, trees, whatever consti-

tuted her own personal conception of Heaven. She was probably, in her mild way, laughing at her son, her dark eyes bright with mischievous amusement, unperturbed as always by his demands and reproaches.

With only his two sisters to make miserable, he turned his back on his family and concentrated instead on the only stable element left in his life—his job. Somewhat to his surprise, and to the astonishment of his superiors, he discovered, just in time, that he was not only interested in advertising but extremely good at it. By the time his mother's estate was cleared, and his share of the loot was safely deposited in the bank, youthful fantasies of enormous gambles and fast profits had faded forever. As well, Noel realized that making money with some other person's hypothetical fortune was actually very different from parting with your own. He felt protective about his bank balance, as though it were a child, and was not about to risk its safety. Instead, in modest fashion, he bought himself a new car and began, tentatively, to put out feelers for some place new to live. . . .

Life moved on. But youth was over, and it

was a different life. Gradually Noel came to terms with this and, at the same time, discovered that he was incapable of sustaining his final grievance against his mother. Nourishing useless resentment was far too exhausting. And at the end of the day he had to admit that he hadn't come out of it all too badly. As well, he missed her. During the last years he had seen little of her, closeted as she was in the depths of Gloucestershire, but still she was always *there*—at the end of a telephone, or at the end of a long drive when you felt you couldn't stand the hot summer streets of London a moment longer. It didn't matter if you went alone or took half a dozen friends for the weekend. There was always space, a relaxed welcome, delicious food, everything or nothing to do. Fires flickering, fragrant flowers, hot baths; warm comfortable beds, fine wines, and easy conversation.

All gone. The house and garden sold to strangers. The warm smell of her kitchen and the good feeling that somebody else was in charge and you didn't have to make a single decision. And gone was the only person in the world with whom you never had to put on an act or pretend. Life without her, maddening and capricious as she had been, was like living a life with a ragged hole in the middle of it, and had taken, he recalled wryly, some getting used to.

He sighed. It all seemed a long time ago. Another world. He had finished his whisky and sat staring out into the darkness. He remembered being four years old and having measles, and how the nights of illness had seemed long as a lifetime, each minute lasting an hour, and the dawn an eternity away.

Now, thirty years later, he watched the dawn. The sky lightened and the sun slid up from beneath the false horizon of cloud, and everything turned pink and the light was dazzling to the eye. He watched the dawn and was grateful, because it had chased away the night, and now it was the next day and he did not have to try to sleep. Around him, people stirred. The cabin crew came around with orange juice and scalding face towels. He wiped his face and felt the stubble on his chin. Others collected themselves, found wash-bags, went to the lavatory for a shave. Noel stayed where he was. He could shave when he reached home.

Which, three hours later, he did. Weary, dirty, and dishevelled, he clambered out of the taxi and paid the driver off. The morning air was cool, blessedly cool after New York, and it was raining lightly, a dampening drizzle. In Pembroke Square the trees were greening, the pavements wet. He smelt the freshness and, as the taxi drove away, stood for a moment and thought of spending this day on his own, recovering. Having a nap, taking a long walk. But this was not to be. There was work to be done. The office and his chairman waited. Noel picked up his bag and his brief-case, went down the area steps and opened his own front door.

It was called a garden flat because at the back of it French windows opened out onto a tiny patio, his share of the larger garden of the tall house. In the evening the sun fell upon it, but at this early hour it lay in shadow, and the upstairs cat was comfortably ensconced in one of his canvas chairs, having apparently spent the night there.

It was not a large flat but the rooms were spacious. A living-room and a bedroom, a small kitchen and a bathroom. Overnight guests had to sleep on the sofa, a tricky piece of equipment which, if resolutely approached, folded down into a second double bed. Mrs. Muspratt, who did for him, had been in while he was away and so all was neat and clean, but airless and stuffy.

He opened the French windows and chased the cat away. In his bedroom, he unzipped his suitcase and took out his washbag. He undressed and dropped his soiled and crumpled clothes onto the floor. In the bathroom he cleaned his teeth, took a scalding shower, shaved. By now he needed, more than anything, black coffee. In his towel robe and barefooted, he padded into the kitchen, filled the kettle and switched it on, spooned coffee into his French coffee-pot. The smell of this was heartening and delicious. While the coffee filtered, he collected his mail, sat at the kitchen table and leafed through the envelopes. Nothing looked too urgent. There was, however, a garish picture postcard of Gibraltar. He turned it over. It had been posted in London and was from the wife of Hugh Pennington, an old school friend of Noel's, who lived in Ovington Street.

Noel, I've been trying to ring you, but no reply. Unless we hear to the contrary, we'll expect you for dinner the thirteenth. Seven-thirty for eight. No black tie. Love, Delia.

He sighed. This evening. Unless we hear to the contrary. Oh well, by then he'd probably have got his second wind. And it would be more amusing than watching television. He dropped the postcard onto the table, heaved himself to his feet, and went to pour his coffee.

Shut in the office, in conference for most of the day, Noel lost track and sight of what was happening out of doors. Finally emerging and driving home through rush-hour traffic that did not rush but moved at the pace of an arthritic snail, he saw that the rain of the morning had been blown away by the breeze and it was a perfect May evening. By now he had reached that state beyond exhaustion when all is light and clear and strangely disembodied, and the prospect of sleep seemed as far away as death. Instead, another shower, a change of clothes, and a drink. And then he would not take his car but walk to Ovington Street. The fresh air and exercise would whet his appetite for the excellent meal that he hoped was waiting for him. He could scarcely remember when he had last sat at a table and eaten something that was not a sandwich.

The walk was a good idea. He went by leafy back roads, residential terraces, and gardens where magnolias opened and wistaria clung to the faces of expensive London houses. Coming out into the Brompton Road, he crossed over by the Michelin Building and turned down into Walton Street. Here his steps slowed as he paused to look in at the delectable shop windows, the interior decorators and the art gallery that sold sport-

ing prints, hunting scenes, and oil paintings
of faithful Labradors bounding through the
snow with pheasants in their mouths. There
was a Thorburn that he craved. He stood
longer than he intended, simply looking at it.
Perhaps tomorrow he would ring the gallery
and discover its price. After a little, he
walked on.

By the time he reached Ovington Street, it
was twenty-five to eight. The pavements were
lined with the cars of the residents, and some
older children were riding their bicycles up
and down the middle of the road. The Penningtons' house was half-way down the terrace. As he approached it, a girl came down
the pavement towards him. She had with her,
on a lead, a small white Highland terrier and
was apparently on her way to the post-box,
for she carried a letter in her hand. He
looked at her. She wore jeans and a grey
sweat-shirt and had hair the colour of the
very best sort of marmalade, and she was neither tall nor particularly slender. In fact, not
Noel's type at all. And yet, as she passed
him, he gave her a second glance because
there was something vaguely familiar about
her, and it was difficult to think where they

might once have met. Some party, perhaps. The hair was distinctive. . . .

The walk had tired him and he found himself sorely in need of a drink. With better things to think about, he put the girl out of his mind, went up the steps, and gave the bell a token push. He turned the handle to open the door, with a greeting ready and waiting. Hi. Delia, it's me. I've arrived.

But nothing happened. The door remained firmly closed, which was odd and out of character. Knowing that he was on his way, Delia should surely have left it on the latch. He rang the bell again. And waited.

More silence. He told himself that they had to be there, but already knew with hideous certainty that nobody was going to answer the bell and the Penningtons, damn their bloody eyes, were not at home.

"Hello."

He turned from the inhospitable door. Below, on the pavement, stood the dumpy girl and her dog, back from posting the letter.

"Hi."

"Did you want the Penningtons?"

"They're meant to be giving me dinner."

"They've gone out. I saw them going off in their car."

Noel digested, in gloomy silence, this unwelcome confirmation of what he already knew. Disappointed and let down, he felt very much ill-disposed towards the girl, as one usually does when told something perfectly horrible by another person. It occurred to him that it couldn't have been much fun being a medieval messenger. There was every chance you'd end up without a head, or else employed as a human cannon-ball for some monstrous catapult.

He waited for her to go away. She didn't. He thought, shit. And then, resigned, put his hands in his pockets and descended the steps to join her.

She bit her lip. "What a shame. It's miserable when something like this happens."

"I can't think what's gone wrong."

"What's worse," she told him, in the tones of one determined to look on the bright side, "is when you arrive on the wrong night, and they're not expecting you. I did that once, and it was dreadfully embarrassing. I'd got the dates mixed up."

This did not help. "I suppose you think I've got the dates mixed up."

"It's easily done."

"Not this time. I only got the postcard this morning. The thirteenth."

She said, "But this is the twelfth."

"No, it isn't." He was quite firm. "It's the thirteenth."

"I'm terribly sorry, but it's the twelfth. Thursday, the twelfth of May." She sounded deeply apologetic, as though the mix-up were all her fault. "Tomorrow's the thirteenth."

Slowly, his punch-drunk brain worked this out. Tuesday, Wednesday . . . damn her eyes, she was right. The days had run into each other, and somewhere he had lost track of them. He felt shamefully foolish, and because of this he instantly began to come up with excuses for his own stupidity.

"I've been working. Flying. I've been in New York. Got back this morning. Jet lag does ghastly things to your brain."

She made a sympathetic face. Her dog smelled at his trousers and he moved aside, not wishing to be peed upon. Her hair in the evening sunlight was astonishing. She had grey eyes flecked with green and milkmaid skin, bloomy as a peach.

Somewhere. But where?

He frowned. "Have we met before?"

She smiled. "Well, yes, actually. About six months ago. At the Hathaways' cocktail party, in Lincoln Street. But there were about a million people there, so there's no reason why you should remember."

No, he wouldn't remember. Because she was not the sort of girl that he would register, would want to stay with, or even talk to. Besides, he had gone to that party with Vanessa, and spent most of his time trying to keep track of her, and stop her from finding some other man to have dinner with.

He said, "How extraordinary. I am sorry. And how clever of you to remember me."

"Actually, there was another time." His heart sank, fearing to be faced with yet another social gaffe. "You're with Wenborn and Weinburg, aren't you? I cooked a directors' lunch for them about six weeks ago. But you wouldn't even have noticed, because I was wearing a white overall, and handing round plates. Nobody ever looks at cooks and waitresses. It's a funny feeling, as though you are invisible."

He realized that this was true. By now feeling more friendly towards her, he asked her name.

"Alexa Aird."

"I'm Noel Keeling."

"I know. I remembered from the Hathaways' party, and then for the lunch, I had to do a placement, and write names on cards."

Noel cast his mind back to that particular day and recalled in satisfying detail the meal she had produced. Smoked salmon, a perfectly grilled fillet steak, watercress salad, and a lemon sorbet. The very thought of these delights caused his mouth to water. Which reminded him that he was ravenously hungry.

"Who do you work for?"

"Myself. I'm free-lance." She said this quite proudly. Noel hoped that she was not about to embark upon the history of her career. He did not feel strong enough to stand and listen. He needed food, but, more importantly, he needed a drink. He must make some excuse, take his leave, and be rid of her.

He opened his mouth to do this, but she spoke first.

"I suppose you wouldn't like to come and have a drink with me?"

The invitation was so unexpected that he did not immediately reply. He looked at her and met her anxious gaze, and realized that she was, in fact, extremely shy, and to come out with such a suggestion had caused her some courageous effort. As well, he found himself uncertain as to whether she was inviting him to the nearest pub or to some grotty attic pad filled with cohabiting colleagues, one of whom would doubtless just have finished washing her hair.

No point in committing himself. He was cautious. "Where?"

"I live two doors down from the Penningtons. And you look as though you could do with a drink."

He stopped being cautious. "I do."

"There's nothing worse than arriving in the wrong place at the wrong time, and knowing that it's all your own fault."

Which could have been more tactfully put. But she was kind. "You're very kind." He made up his mind. "I'd like that very much."

⋦ 3 ⋧

THE HOUSE WAS IDENTICAL to the Penningtons', except that the front door was not
black, but dark blue, and a bay tree stood in
a tub beside it. She went ahead of him,
opened it with her key, and he followed her
indoors. She shut the door behind them and
then stooped to unfasten the little dog's lead.
The dog instantly went to drink copiously
from a round dish that stood, handily, near
the foot of the stairs. The dish had DOG written on it.

She said, "He always does that when he
comes in. He seems to think that he's been
for a long, long walk."

"What's his name?"

"Larry."

The dog lapped noisily, filling the silence,
because, for once in his life, Noel Keeling
found himself at a loss for words. He had

been caught on the hop. He was not certain what he had expected, but certainly not this —an instant impression of warm opulence, loaded with evidence of wealth and good taste. This was a grand London residence, but on a miniature scale. He saw the narrow hallway, the steep staircase, the polished bannister rail. Honey-coloured carpeting, thick to the wall; an antique console table upon which stood a pink-flowering azalea; an ornately framed oval mirror. As well, and this is what really threw him, the smell. Poignantly familiar. Wax polish, apples, a suggestion of fresh coffee. Pot-pourri, perhaps, and summery flowers. The smell of nostalgia, of youth. The smell of the homes that his mother had created for her children.

Who was responsible for this assault of memory? And who was Alexa Aird? It was an occasion to fall back on small talk, but Noel couldn't think of a mortal thing to say. Perhaps that was best. He stood waiting for what was going to happen next, fully expecting to be led upstairs to some rented bedsitter or tiny attic apartment. But she laid the dog's lead on the table and said in hostessly fashion, "Do come in," and led him into the room that lay beyond the open door.

The house was a twin of the Penningtons' but about a thousand times more impressive. Narrow and long, this room stretched from the front of the house to the back. The street end was the drawing-room—too grand to be called a sitting-room—and the other end was set up for dining. Here, French windows led out onto a wrought-iron balcony, bright with geraniums in terracotta pots.

All was gold and pink. Curtains, padded thick as eiderdowns, hung in swags and folds. Sofas and chairs were loose-covered in the best sort of country chintz, and scattered haphazardly with needlepoint cushions. Recessed alcoves were filled with blue-and-white porcelain, and a bulging *bombé* bureau stood open, stacked with the letters and paperwork of an industrious owner.

It was all very elegant and grown-up, and did not match up in the very least with this quite ordinary and not particularly attractive girl in her jeans and sweat-shirt.

Noel cleared his throat.

"What a charming room."

"Yes, it is pretty, isn't it? You must be exhausted." Now that she was safe, in her own territory, she did not seem so diffident. "Jet lag's a killer. When my father flies in from New York he comes by Concorde because he hates those night flights."

"I'll be all right."

"What would you like to drink?"

"Have you any whisky?"

"Of course. Grouse or Haig's?"

He could scarcely believe his luck. "Grouse!"

"Ice?"

"If you have some."

"I'll go down to the kitchen and get it. If you'd like to help yourself . . . there are glasses . . . everything's there. I won't be a moment. . . ."

She left him. He heard her talking to the little dog, and then light footsteps as she ran down the stairs to the basement. All quiet. Presumably the dog had gone with her. A drink. He moved to the other end of the room, where stood an enviable sideboard, satisfactorily loaded with bottles and decanters.

Here hung charming oil-paintings, still lifes and country scenes. His eyes, roaming, assessing, took in the silver pheasant in the centre of the oval table, the beautiful Georgian coasters. He went to the window and looked down into the garden—a small paved courtyard, with roses climbing the brick wall and a raised bed of wallflowers. There was a white wrought-iron table with four matching chairs, conjuring up visions of alfresco meals, summer supper parties, cool wine.

A drink. On the sideboard were six heavy tumblers, neatly lined up. He reached for the bottle of Grouse, poured himself a slug, added soda, and then returned to the other room. Alone, and still curious as a cat, he prowled. He lifted the fine net curtain and glanced down into the street, then moved to shelves of books, glancing at the titles, endeavouring to find some clue as to the personality of the owner of this delectable house. Novels, biographies, a book on gardens, another on growing roses.

He paused to mull things over. Putting two and two together, he came to the obvious conclusion. Ovington Street belonged to Alexa's parents. Father in some sort of business, sufficiently prestigious to fly Concorde as a matter of course and, moreover, to take his wife with him. He decided that they were, at this moment, in New York. In all probability, once the hard work was over and the conferences finished with, they would fly down to Barbados or the Virgin Islands for a restorative week in the sun. It all clicked logically into place.

As for Alexa, she was house-sitting for them, keeping bandits at bay. This explained why she was on her own, and able to be generous with her father's whisky. When they returned, sun-tanned and bearing gifts, she would go back to her own abode. A shared flat or terraced cottage in Wandsworth or Clapham.

With all this tidily settled in his mind Noel felt better, and strong enough to continue his investigative circuit. The blue-and-white porcelain was Dresden. By one of the armchairs a basket stood on the floor, brimming with bright wools and a half-worked tapestry. On top of the bureau were a number of photographs. People getting married, holding babies, having a picnic with thermos flasks and dogs. Nobody recognizable. One photograph caught his attention, and he picked it up the better to inspect it. A large Edwardian mansion of some bulk, smothered in Virginia creeper. A conservatory bulged from one side, and there were sash windows and a row of dormer windows in the roof. Steps led up to an open front door, and on top of these sat two stately springer spaniels, obediently posed. In the background were winter trees, a church tower, and a rising hill.

The family's country house.

She was coming back. He heard her light footsteps ascending the stair, carefully replaced the photograph, and turned to meet her. She came through the door, carrying a tray loaded with an ice-bucket, a wineglass, an opened bottle of white wine, and a dish of cashew nuts.

"Oh, good, you've got a drink." She set the tray down on the table behind the sofa, edging some magazines aside to make space for it. The little terrier, apparently devoted, dogged her heels. "I'm afraid I could only find a few nuts. . . ."

"At the moment"—he raised his glass—"this is really all I need."

"Poor man." She fished for a handful of cubes and dropped them into his drink.

He said, "I've been standing here coming

to terms with the fact that I've made a complete fool of myself."

"Oh, don't be stupid." She poured the wine. "It could happen to anybody. And just think, now you've got a lovely party to look forward to tomorrow evening. And you'll have had a good night's rest, and be the life and soul. Why don't you sit down? This chair's the best, it's large and comfortable. . . ."

It was. And bliss, at last, to be off his aching feet, buffered by soft cushions, and with a drink in his hand. Alexa settled herself in the other chair, opposite him, and with her back to the window. The dog instantly jumped into her lap, made a nest, and went to sleep.

"How long were you in New York?"

"Three days."

"Do you like going?"

"Usually. It's getting back that's so exhausting."

"What were you doing there?"

He told her. He explained about Saddlebags and Harvey Klein. She was impressed. "I've got a Saddlebag belt. My father brought it back for me last year. It's beautiful. Very thick and soft and handsome."

"Well, soon you'll be able to buy one in London. If you don't mind paying an arm and a leg."

"Who plans an advertising campaign?"

"I do. That's my job. I'm Creative Director."

"It sounds frightfully important. You must be very good at it. Do you enjoy it?"

Noel thought about this. "If I didn't enjoy it, I wouldn't be good at it."

"That's absolutely true. I can't think of anything worse than having to do a job one hates."

"Do you like cooking?"

"Yes, I love it. Just as well, because it's just about the only thing I can do. I was dreadfully thick at school. I only got three O levels. My father made noises about me going to do a secretarial training, or a design course, but in the end he agreed it would be a total waste of time and money, and let me be a cook."

"Did you do a training?"

"Oh, yes. I can produce all sorts of exotic dishes."

"Have you always worked on your own?"

"No, I started with an agency. Then, we

worked in pairs. But it's more fun on my own. I've built up quite a good little business. Not just directors' lunches, but private dinner parties, and wedding receptions, or just filling people's deep-freezes. I've got a little minivan. I cart everything about in that."

"You do the cooking here?"

"Most of it. Private dinner parties are a bit more complicated, because you have to work in other people's kitchens. And other people's kitchens are always a total enigma. I always take my own sharp knives."

"Sounds bloodthirsty."

She laughed. "For chopping vegetables, not for murdering the hostess. Your glass is empty. Would you like another drink?"

Noel realized that it was, and said that he would, but before he could shift himself, Alexa was on her feet, spilling the little dog gently onto the floor. She took his glass from his hand and disappeared behind him. Comforting clinking sounds reached his ears. A splash of soda. It was all very peaceful. The evening breeze, stirring through the open window, moved the filmy net curtains. Outside, a car started up and drove away, but the children who played on their bicycles had apparently been called indoors and told to go to bed. The abortive dinner party had ceased to be of any importance, and Noel felt a little like a man who, trudging across a barren desert, had inadvertently stumbled upon a lush, palm-fringed oasis.

The cold glass was slipped back into his hand. He said, "I always thought that this was one of the nicest streets in London."

Alexa returned to her chair, curling up with her feet tucked beneath her.

"Where do you live?"

"Pembroke Gardens."

"Oh, but that's lovely, too. Do you live alone?"

He found himself taken off guard, but as well amused by her directness. She was probably remembering the Hathaways' party, and his dogged pursuit of the sensational Vanessa. He smiled. "Most of the time."

His oblique reply went over the top of her head. "Have you got a flat there?"

"Yes. A basement, so it doesn't get much sun. However, I don't spend much time there, so it doesn't really matter. And I usually manage to avoid London weekends."

"Do you go home?"

"No. But I have convenient friends."

"What about brothers and sisters?"

"Two sisters. One lives in London and one in Gloucestershire."

"I expect you go and stay with her."

"Not if I can help it." Enough. He had answered enough questions. It was time to turn the tables. "And you? Do you go home for weekends?"

"No. I'm very often working. People tend to throw dinner parties on Saturday evenings, or Sunday lunches. Besides, it's hardly worth going to Scotland just for a weekend."

Scotland.

"You mean . . . you live in Scotland?"

"No. I live here. But my family home is in Relkirkshire."

I live here.

"But I thought your father—" He stopped, because what he had thought had been pure conjecture. Was it possible that he had been barking up entirely the wrong tree? ". . . I'm sorry, but I got the impression . . ."

"He works in Edinburgh. With Sanford Cubben. He's the head of their Scottish Office."

Sanford Cubben, the vast International Trust Company. Noel made a few mental adjustments. "I see. How stupid of me. I imagined him in London."

"Oh, you mean the New York bit. That's nothing. He flies all over the world. Tokyo, Hong Kong. He's not in this country very much."

"So you don't see much of him?"

"Sometimes when he's passing through London. He doesn't stay here, because he goes to the Company flat, but he usually rings, and if there's time, he takes me out for dinner at the Connaught or Claridges. It's a great treat. I pick up all sorts of cooking ideas."

"I suppose that's as good a reason as any to go to Claridges. But . . ." *He doesn't stay here.* ". . . who owns this house?"

Alexa smiled with total innocence. "I do," she told him.

"Oh . . ." It was impossible to keep the disbelief from his voice. The dog was back in her lap. She stroked his head, played with the furry pricked ears.

"How long have you lived here?"

"About five years. It was my grandmother's house. My mother's mother. We were always very close. I used to spend some part of all my school holidays with her. By the time I came to London to do my cooking course, she was a widow and on her own. So I came to stay with her. And then, last year, she died, and she left the house to me."

"She must have been very fond of you."

"I was terribly fond of her. It all caused a bit of family ill-feeling. My living with her, I mean. My father didn't think it was a good idea at all. He was quite fond of her, but he thought I should be more independent. Make friends of my own age, move into a flat with some other girl. But I didn't really want to. I'm dreadfully lazy about things like that, and Granny Cheriton . . ." Abruptly she stopped. Across the space that divided them their eyes met. Noel said nothing, and after a pause she continued, speaking casually, as though it were of no importance. ". . . she was getting old. It wouldn't have been kind to leave her."

Another silence. Then Noel said, "Cheriton?"

Alexa sighed. "Yes." She sounded as

though she were admitting to some heinous crime.

"An unusual name."

"Yes."

"Also well-known."

"Yes."

"Sir Rodney Cheriton?"

"He was my grandfather. I didn't mean to tell you. The name just slipped out."

So that was it. The puzzle solved. That explained the money, the opulence, the precious possessions. Sir Rodney Cheriton, now deceased, founder of a financial empire that stretched world-wide, who, during the sixties and the seventies, had been associated with so many take-over bids and conglomerates that his name was scarcely ever out of the *Financial Times*. This house had been the home of Lady Cheriton, and the sweet-faced, unsophisticated little cook who sat, curled in her chair like a schoolgirl, was her granddaughter.

He was flabbergasted. "Well, who'd have thought it?"

"I don't usually tell people, because I'm not all that proud of it."

"You should be proud. He was a great man."

"It isn't that I didn't like him. He was always very sweet to me. It's just that I don't really approve of huge take-overs and companies getting bigger and bigger. I'd like them to get smaller and smaller. I like corner shops and butchers where the nice man knows your name. I don't like the thought of people getting swallowed up, or lost, or made redundant."

"We can scarcely move backwards."

"I know. That's what my father keeps telling me. But it breaks my heart when a little row of houses gets demolished, and all that goes up in their place is another horrible office block with black windows, like a hen battery. That's what I love about Scotland. Strathcroy, the village we live in, never seems to change. Except that Mrs. McTaggart, who ran the newsagent's, decided that her legs couldn't take the standing any longer and retired, and her shop was bought by Pakistanis. They're called Ishak, and they're terribly nice, and the women wear lovely bright silky clothes. Have you ever been to Scotland?"

"I've been to Sutherland, to fish on the Oykel."

"Would you like to see a picture of our house?"

He did not let on that he had already taken a good look. "I'd love to."

Once more, Alexa set the dog on the floor and got to her feet. The dog, bored by all this activity, sat on the hearthrug and looked fed up. She fetched the photograph and handed it to Noel.

After an appropriate pause he said, "It looks very comfortable."

"It's lovely. Those are my father's dogs."

"What's your father's name?"

"Edmund. Edmund Aird." She went to replace the photograph. Turning, she caught sight of the gold carriage clock which stood in the middle of the mantelpiece. She said, "It's nearly half past eight."

"Good heavens." He checked the time with his watch. "So it is. I must go."

"You don't have to. I mean, I could cook you something, give you supper."

The suggestion was so splendid and so tempting that Noel felt bound to make some

small noises of refusal. "You're too kind,
but . . ."

"I'm sure you haven't got any food at
Pembroke Gardens. Not if you've just come
home from New York. And it's no trouble.
I'd like it." He could tell from her expression
that she was yearning for him to stay. As
well, he was painfully hungry. "I've got some
lamb chops."

That did it. "I can't think of anything I'd
like more."

Alexa's face lit up. She was as transparent
as clear spring water. "Oh, good. I'd have
felt really inhospitable letting you go without
something inside you. Do you want to stay
here, or do you want to come down to the
kitchen and watch me?"

If he stayed in this chair, he would fall
asleep. As well, he wanted to see more of the
house. He heaved himself out of the chair.
"I'll come and watch you."

Alexa's kitchen was predictable, not modern at all, but quite homely and haphazard,

as though it had not been planned, but simply come together over the years. It had a stone-tiled floor with a rush mat or two, and pine cupboards. A deep clay sink faced out over the window and the little area with its steps leading up into the street. The sink was backed with blue-and-white Dutch tiles and the same tiles lined the walls between the cupboards. The tools of her trade were very evident: a thick chopping board, a line of copper saucepans, a marble slab for rolling pastry. There were racks of herbs and bunches of onions and fresh parsley in a mug.

She reached for a blue-and-white butcher's apron and tied it around her waist. Over the thick sweat-shirt this made her look more shapeless than ever and accentuated her rounded, blue-jeaned bottom.

Noel asked if there was anything he could do to help.

"No, not really." She was already busy, turning on the grill, opening drawers. "Unless you'd like to open a bottle of wine. Would you like some?"

"Where would I find a bottle of wine?"

"There's a rack through there. . . ." She

indicated with her head, her hands being occupied. "On the floor. I haven't got a cellar, and that's the coolest spot there is."

Noel went to look. At the back of the kitchen an archway led into what had probably once been a small scullery. This too was stone-floored, and here stood a number of shining white electrical appliances. A dishwasher, a clothes washer, a tall refrigerator, and a huge chest deep-freeze. At the far end, a half-glassed door led directly out into the little garden. By the door, in country fashion, stood a pair of rubber boots and a wooden tub of gardening tools. An ancient raincoat and a battered felt hat hung from a hook.

He found the wine-rack beyond the deep-freeze. Crouching, he inspected a few bottles. She had an excellent selection. He chose a Beaujolais, went back to the kitchen.

"How about this?"

She glanced at it. "Perfect. That was a good year. There's a corkscrew in that drawer. If you open it now, that'll give it time to breathe."

He found the corkscrew and drew the cork. It came, sweetly and cleanly, and he set the open bottle on the table. With nothing more to be done, he drew back a chair and settled himself at the table to enjoy the last of his whisky.

She had taken the chops from the refrigerator, assembled the makings of a salad, found a stick of French bread. Now she was arranging the chops on the grill-pan, reaching for a jar of rosemary. All this was accomplished deftly and with the greatest economy of effort, and it occurred to Noel that, working, she had become quite assured and confident, probably because she was engaged in doing the one thing she knew that she was really good at.

He said, "You look very professional."

"I am."

"Do you garden as well?"

"Why do you ask that?"

"All the clobber by the back door."

"I see. Yes, I do garden, but it's so tiny that it's not *really* gardening. At Balnaid, the garden's enormous, and there's always something needing to be done."

"Balnaid?"

"That's the name of our house in Scotland."

"My mother was a manic gardener." Having said this, Noel could not think why he had mentioned the fact. He did not usually talk about his mother unless somebody asked him a direct question. "Perpetually digging, or barrowing great loads of manure."

"Doesn't she garden any longer?"

"She's dead. She died four years ago."

"Oh, I am sorry. Where did she do her gardening?"

"In Gloucestershire. She bought a house with a couple of acres of wilderness. By the time she died, she'd transformed it into some thing very special. You know . . . the sort of garden people walk around in after lunch parties."

Alexa smiled. "She sounds rather like my other grandmother, Vi. She lives in Strath-croy. Her name's Violet Aird, but we all call her Vi." The chops were grilling, the bread put to warm, the plates to heat. "My moth-er's dead, too. She was killed in a car acci-dent when I was six."

"It's my turn to be sorry."

"I remember her, of course, but not really very well. I remember her mostly coming to say good night before she went out for a dinner party. Lovely airy dresses, and furs, and smelling of scent."

"Six is very young to lose your mother."

"It wasn't as bad as it might have been. I had a darling Nanny called Edie Findhorn. And after Mummy died we went back to Scotland and lived with Vi at Balnaid. So I was luckier than most."

"Did your father marry again?"

"Yes. Ten years ago. She's called Virginia. She's not much older than I am."

"A wicked stepmother?"

"No. She's sweet. A bit like a sister. She's terribly pretty. And I've got a half-brother called Henry. He's nearly eight."

Now she was making the salad. With a sharp knife she chopped and shredded. Tomatoes and celery, tiny fresh mushrooms. Her hands were brown and capable, the nails short and unvarnished. There was something very satisfactory about them. He tried to recall the last time he had sat thus, slightly woozy with hunger and drink, and peacefully watched while a woman prepared a meal for him. He couldn't.

The trouble was that he had never gone for domesticated females. His girl-friends were usually models, or young aspiring actresses with immense ambition and little brain. All they had in common was their general appearance, for he liked them very young and very thin with tiny breasts and long, attenuated legs. Which was great for his own personal amusement and satisfaction, but not much use when it came to being good about the house. Besides, they were nearly all . . . however skinny . . . on some sort of diet, and while able to down enormous and expensive restaurant meals, were disinterested in producing even the simplest of snacks in the privacy of either their own flats, or Noel's.

"Oh, darling, it's such a bore. Besides, I'm not hungry. Have an apple."

From time to time there had come into Noel's life a girl so besotted that she wished only to spend the rest of her days with him. Then much effort—perhaps too much—had been made. Intimate dinners by gas-fired logs, and invitations to the country and doggy weekends. But Noel, wary of commitment, had backed away, and the girls in question, after a painful period of abortive telephone calls and tearful accusations, had found other men and married them. So he had reached thirty-four and was still a bachelor. Brooding over his empty whisky glass, Noel could not decide whether this left him feeling triumphant or defeated.

"There." The salad was ready. Now she began to mix a dressing with beautiful green olive oil and pale wine vinegar. Various herbs and seasonings were added, and the smell of these made his mouth water. With this done, she started to lay the table. A red-and-white-checked cloth, wineglasses, wooden mills for pepper and salt, a pottery butter dish. She took forks and knives from a drawer and handed them to Noel and he set the two places. It seemed an appropriate moment to pour the wine, so he did, and handed Alexa her glass.

She took it from him. In her apron and bulky sweat-shirt, and with her cheeks glowing from the heat of the grill, she said, "Here's to Saddlebags."

He found himself, for some reason, much touched. "And here's to you, Alexa. And thank you."

It was a simple but splendid meal, living up to all Noel's greedy expectations. The chops were tender, the salad crisp; warm bread to mop up juices and dressings, and all washed down by fine wine. After a bit, his stomach stopped groaning, and he felt infinitely better.

"I can't remember food ever tasting so good."

"It's not anything very special."

"But perfect." He took more salad. "Any time you need a recommendation, let me know."

"Don't you ever cook for yourself?"

"No. I can fry bacon and eggs, but if pushed I buy gourmet dishes from Marks and Spencer and heat them up. Every now and then, if I'm desperate, I go and spend an evening with Olivia, my London sister, but she's as useless in the kitchen as I am, and we usually finish up eating something exotic, like quails' eggs or caviar. A treat, but not very filling."

"Is she married?"

"No. She's a career lady."

"What does she do?"

"She's Editor-in-Chief of *Venus*."

"Goodness." She smiled. "What illustrious relations we both seem to have."

Having devoured everything on the table, Noel found himself still peckish, and so Alexa produced cheese and a bunch of pale-green seedless grapes. With these, they finished the last of the wine. Alexa suggested coffee.

By now it was growing dark. Outside, in the dusky blue street, the lights had come on. Their glow penetrated the basement kitchen, but mostly all was shadowy. Noel was, all at once, overcome by a mammoth yawn. When he had dealt with this, he apologized. "I'm sorry. I really must get home."

"Have some coffee first. It'll keep you awake until you reach your bed. I tell you what—why don't you go upstairs and relax, and I'll bring your coffee up to you. And then I'll phone for a taxi."

Which sounded an eminently sensible idea. "Right."

But even saying the word took much conscious effort. He was aware of arranging his tongue and his lips in the correct position to make the appropriate sound, and knew that he was either drunk or on the point of flaking out from lack of sleep. Coffee was an excellent idea. He put his hands on the table and levered himself to his feet. Going up the basement stairs, headed for the drawing-room, was even more of a trial. Half-way up he stumbled but somehow managed to keep his balance and not to fall flat on his face.

Upstairs, the empty room waited, quiet in the bloomy twilight. The only illumination came from the street lights, and these were reflected from the brass fender and the facets of the crystal chandelier that hung from the middle of the ceiling. It seemed a pity to dispel the peaceful dusk by turning on switches, so he didn't. The dog was asleep on the chair that Noel had previously occupied, so he sank down in a corner of the sofa. The dog, disturbed, awoke and raised his head, and stared at Noel. Noel stared back. The dog turned into two dogs. He was drunk. He had not slept for ever. He would not sleep now. He was not sleeping.

He was dozing. Sleeping and waking at the same time. He was in the 747, droning back over the Atlantic, with his fat neighbour snoring alongside. His chairman was telling him to go to Edinburgh, to sell Saddlebags to a man called Edmund Aird. There were voices, calling and shouting; the children playing in the street on their bicycles. No, they were not in the street, they were outside, in some garden. He was in a cramped and steeply ceilinged room, peering from the peep-hole of a window. Honeysuckle fronds tapped on the glass. His old room, in his mother's house in Gloucestershire. Outside on the lawn, a game was in progress. Children and adults played cricket. Or was it rounders? Or baseball? They looked up and saw his face through the glass. "Come down," they told him. "Come down and play." He was pleased that they wanted him. It was good to be home. He went out of the room and downstairs; stepped out into the garden, but the cricket game was over, and they had all disappeared. He did not mind. He lay on the grass and stared at the bright sky, and everything was all right. None of the bad things had happened after all, and nothing had changed. He was alone, but soon somebody would come. He could wait.

Another sound. A clock ticking. He opened his eyes. The street lamps no longer shone, and the darkness had gone. It was not his mother's garden, not his mother's house, but some strange room. He had no idea where he was. He lay flat on his back on a sofa, with a rug over him. The fringe of the rug tickled his chin, and he pushed it away. Staring upwards, he saw the glittering droplets of the chandelier, and then remembered. Moving his head, he saw the armchair, with its back to the window; a girl sat there, her bright hair an aureole against the morning light beyond the uncurtained window. He stirred. She stayed silent. He said her name. "Alexa?"

"Yes." She was awake.

"What time is it?"

"Just after seven."

"Seven in the morning?"

"Yes."

"I've been here all night." He stretched, easing his long legs. "I fell asleep."

"You were asleep by the time I came up with the coffee. I thought about waking you, but then I decided against it."

He blinked, clearing the sleep from his eyes. He saw that she was no longer wearing her jeans and sweat-shirt, but a white towelling robe, wrapped closely about her. She had bundled herself up in a blanket, but her legs and feet, protruding, were bare.

"Have you been there all night?"

"Yes."

"You should have gone to bed."

"I didn't like to leave you. I didn't want you to wake up and feel you had to go, and not be able to find a taxi in the middle of the night. I made up my spare bed, but then I thought, what's the point? So I just left you to sleep."

He caught the tail end of his dream before it faded into oblivion. He had lain in his mother's garden in Gloucestershire, and known that someone was coming. Not his mother. Penelope was dead. Somebody else. Then the dream was gone for good, leaving him with Alexa.

He felt, surprisingly, enormously well, energetic and refreshed. Decisive. "I must go home."

"Shall I call you a taxi?"

"No. I'll walk. It'll do me good."

"It's a lovely morning. Do you want something to eat before you go?"

"No, I'm fine." He pushed aside the rug and sat up, smoothing back his hair and running his hand over his stubbly chin. "I must go." He got to his feet.

Alexa made no effort to persuade him to stay, but simply came with him into the hall, opened her front door onto a pearly, pristine May morning. The distant rumble of traffic was already audible, though a bird was singing from some tree, and the air was fresh. He imagined that he could smell lilac.

"Goodbye, Noel."

He turned to her. "I'll ring you."

"You don't need to."

"Don't I?"

"You don't owe me anything."

"You're very sweet." He stooped and kissed her peachy cheek. "Thank you."

"I've liked it."

He left her. Went down the steps and set off, at a brisk clip, down the pavement. At the end of the street he turned and looked back. She was gone, and the blue front door stood closed. But it seemed to Noel that the house with the bay tree had a special look about it.

He smiled to himself and went on his way.

JUNE

∿ 1 ∿

Tuesday the Seventh

ISOBEL BALMERINO, AT THE WHEEL of her minibus, drove the ten miles to Corriehill. It was nearly four o'clock in the afternoon and the beginning of June, but although the trees were heavy with leaf and the fields green with growing crops, there had, so far, been no summer at all. It was not exactly cold, but it was dank and drizzling, and all the way from Croy her windscreen wipers had been working. Clouds hung low over the hills and all was drowned in greyness. She felt sorry for the foreign visitors, come so far to see the glories of Scotland, only to find them shrouded in murk and almost invisible.

Not that this troubled her. She had made the complicated journey, cross-country and by back roads, so many times before that she sometimes thought that if she were to dispatch the minibus on its own it would manage very nicely, getting itself to Corriehill and back with no human assistance, reliable as a faithful horse.

Now she had come to the familiar junction and was nearly there. She changed down and swung the minibus into a single-track lane hedged with hawthorn. This lane led up and onto the hill, and as she climbed, the mist grew thicker; prudently she switched on the headlights. To her right appeared the tall stone wall, the march boundary of the Corriehill estate. Another quarter of a mile, and she had reached the great entrance gates, the two lodges. She turned between these and bumped her way up the rutted drive lined with historic beeches and deep verges of rough grass which, in spring, were gold with daffodils. The daffodils had long since died back, and their withered heads and dying leaves were all that remained of their former glory. Some time, some day, Verena's handyman would cut the verges with his garden tractor, and that would be the end of the daffodils. Until next spring.

It occurred to her, sadly, and not for the first time, that as you grew older you became busier, and time went faster and faster, the months pushing each other rudely out of the way, and the years slipping off the calendar and into the past. Once, there had been time. Time to stand, or sit, and just *look* at daffodils. Or to abandon housekeeping, on the spur of the moment, walk out of the back door and up the hill, into the lark-song emptiness of a summer morning. Or to take off for a self-indulgent day in Relkirk, shopping for frivolities, meeting a girl-friend for lunch, the wine bar warm with humanity and conversation, smelling of coffee and the sort of food that one never cooked for oneself.

All treats that for a number of reasons didn't seem to happen any longer.

The driveway levelled off. Beneath the wheels of the minibus, gravel scrunched. The house loomed up at her through the mist. There were no other cars, which meant that probably all the other hostesses had been, collected their guests, and gone. So Verena would be waiting for her. Isobel hoped that she would not have become impatient.

She drew up, switched off her engine, and got out into the soft, drizzly air. The main door stood open, giving onto a large paved porch, with an inner glass door beyond. This porch was stacked with an enormous amount of expensive luggage. Isobel quailed, because it seemed to be even more lavish than usual. Suitcases (hugely big), garment bags, small grips, golf bags, boxes and parcels and carriers, emblazoned with the familiar names of large stores. (They'd obviously been shopping.) All of these were tagged with distinctive yellow labels: SCOTTISH COUNTRY TOURS.

Diverted, she paused to read the names on the labels. Mr. Joe Hardwicke. Mr. Arnold Franco. Mrs. Myra Hardwicke. Mrs. Susan Franco. The suitcases were heavily monogrammed, and the golf bags had prestigious club labels hanging from their handles.

She sighed. Here we go again. She opened the inner door.

"Verena!"

The hallway at Corriehill was immense, with a carved oak stairway rising to the upper floors, and much panelling. The floor was scattered with rugs, some quite ordinary and others probably priceless, and in the middle of the floor stood a table bearing a varied collection of objects: a potted geranium, a dog's lead, a brass tray for letters, and a massive leather-bound visitors' book.

"Verena?"

A door, distantly, shut. Footsteps came up the passage from the direction of the kitchen. Verena Steynton presently appeared, looking, as always, tall, slender, unfussed, and perfectly turned out. She was one of those women who, maddeningly, always appear coordinated, as though she spent much time each day selecting and matching her various garments. This skirt, this shirt; that cashmere cardigan, these shoes. Even the damp and muggy weather, which ruined the hairdos of most right-minded women, didn't stand a chance with Verena's coiffure, which never wilted under the most adverse of circumstances, and always appeared as neat and glamorous as if she had just come out from under the dryer. Isobel had no illusions about her own appearance. Stocky and sturdy as a highland pony, her complexion rosy and shining, her hands roughened by work, she had long stopped bothering about the way she looked. But, seeing Verena, she all at once wished that she had taken the time to change out of her corduroy trousers

and the quilted sludge-coloured waistcoat
that was her oldest friend.

"Isobel."

"I hope I'm not late."

"No. You're the last but you're not late.
Your guests are ready and waiting for you in
the drawing-room. Mr. and Mrs. Hardwicke,
and Mr. and Mrs. Franco. From the look of
them slightly more robust than our usual run
of clients." Isobel knew some relief. Perhaps
the men would be able to hump their own
golf bags. "Where's Archie? Are you on your
own?"

"He had to go to a church meeting at
Balnaid."

"Will you manage?"

"Of course."

"Well, look, before you whisk them away,
there's been a slight change of plan. I'll explain. We'd better go into the library."

Obediently, Isobel followed her, prepared
to take orders. The library at Corriehill was a
pleasant room, smaller than most of the
other apartments, and smelled comfortably
masculine—of pipe smoke and wood-smoke,
of old books and old dogs. The old-dog smell
emanated from an elderly Labrador snoozing

on its cushion by the ashy remains of a fire. It raised its head, saw the two ladies, blinked in a superior fashion and went back to sleep.

"The thing is . . ." Verena started, and at once the telephone on the desk began to ring. She said, "Damn. Sorry, I won't be a moment," and went to answer it. "Hello, Verena Steynton . . . Yes." Her voice changed. "Mr. Abberley. Thank you for calling back." She pulled the chair from the desk and sat down, reaching for her ball-point pen and a pad of paper. She looked as though she was settling in for a long session and Isobel's heart sank, because she wanted to get home.

"Yes. Oh, splendid. Now, we shall need your largest marquee, and I think the pale-yellow-and-white lining. And a dance floor." Isobel pricked up her ears, stopped feeling impatient and eavesdropped shamelessly. "The date? We thought the sixteenth of September. That's a Friday. Yes, I think you'd better come and see me, and we'll talk it over. Next week would be fine. Wednesday morning. Right. I'll see you then. Goodbye, Mr. Abberley." She rang off and leaned back in her chair, wearing the satisfied expression of one with a job well done. "Well, that's the first thing settled."

"What on earth are you planning now?"

"Well, Angus and I have been talking about it for ages, and we've finally decided to take the plunge. Katy's twenty-one this year, and we're going to have a dance for her."

"Heavens above, you must be feeling rich."

"No, not particularly, but it is something of an event, and we owe about a million people hospitality, so we'll get them all off in one smashing do."

"But September's ages away, and it's only the beginning of June."

"I know, but one can't start too early. You know what September's like." Isobel did know. The Scottish season, with a mass exodus from the south to the north for the grouse shooting. Every large house filled with house parties, dances, cricket matches, Highland games, and every sort of social activity, all finally culminating in an exhausting week of hunt balls.

"We have to have a marquee because there's really not space for dancing indoors, but Katy insists we must fix up some corner

as a night-club so that all her yuppie friends
from London can have their little smooch.
Then I'll have to find a really good country
dance band, and a competent caterer. But at
least I've got the tent. You'll all get invitations, of course." She gave Isobel a stern
look. "I hope Lucilla will be here."

It was hard not to feel a little envious of
Verena, sitting there planning a dance for her
daughter, knowing that that daughter would
be helpful and co-operative and enjoy every
moment of her party. Her own Lucilla and
Katy Steynton had been at school together,
and friends in the lack-lustre fashion of children thrown together by their parents. For
Lucilla was two years younger than Katy,
and had a very different personality, and as
soon as school was behind them, their ways
had parted.

Katy, any mother's dream, had dutifully
conformed. A year in Switzerland, and then
a secretarial course in London. Graduated,
she'd found herself a worthwhile job . . .
something to do with funding for charity
. . . and shared a small house in Wandsworth with three eminently suitable friends.
Before long, she would doubtless become en-

gaged to an excellent young man called either Nigel, Jeremy, or Christopher, her blameless face would appear on the front page of *Country Life,* and the wedding would be predictably traditional with a white dress, a great number of small bridesmaids, and "Praise My Soul the King of Heaven."

Isobel did not want Lucilla to be like Katy, but sometimes, as at this moment, she could not help wishing that her darling, dreamy daughter had turned out to be just a little more ordinary. But even as a child, Lucilla had shown signs of individuality and gentle rebellion. Her political tendencies were strongly Left Wing, and at the drop of a hat she would involve herself, with much passion, in any cause that caught her attention. She was against nuclear power, fox-hunting, the culling of baby seals, the cutting of student grants, and the planting of tracts of horrible conifers in order to provide pop stars with tax-deductible incomes. At the same time, she voiced much concern over the plight of the homeless, the down-and-outs, the drug addicts, and the poor unfortunates who found themselves dying of AIDS.

From an early age, she had always been

intensely creative and artistic, and after six months in Paris working as an au pair, she was accepted at the College of Art in Edinburgh. Here, she made friends with the most extraordinary people, whom, from time to time, she brought to Croy to stay. They were a funny-looking lot, but no funnier than Lucilla, who dressed from the Oxfam shop and thought nothing of wearing a lace evening dress with a man's tweed jacket and a pair of Edwardian lace-up boots.

With Art School behind her, she had failed entirely to find any sort of a way in which to earn her keep. No person seemed inclined to buy her incomprehensible paintings, and no gallery wished to exhibit them. Living in an attic in India Street, she had kept herself by going out to clean other people's houses. This had proved strangely lucrative, and as soon as she had saved up enough to pay her fare across the Channel, she had taken off for France with a backpack and her painting gear. Last heard of she was in Paris, staying with some couple she had met on the road. It was all very worrying.

Would she come home? Isobel could write, of course, to the Poste Restante address her daughter had given her. *Darling Lucilla, be here in September because you have been asked to Katy Steynton's dance.* But it was unlikely that Lucilla would pay much attention. She had never enjoyed formal parties, and could think of nothing to say to the well-connected young men she had met at them. *Mummy, they're quite gruesomely square. And they've all got hair like tweed.*

She was impossible. She was also sweet, kind, funny, and overflowing with love. Isobel missed her quite dreadfully.

She sighed and said, "I don't know. I don't suppose so."

"Oh dear." Verena was sympathetic, which didn't make it any better. "Well, never mind, I'll send her an invitation. Katy would so love to see her again."

Privately, Isobel doubted this. She said, "Is your dance a secret, or can I talk about it?"

"No, of course it's not a secret. The more people who know, the better. Perhaps they'll offer to have dinner parties."

"I'll have a dinner party."

"You are a saint." They might have sat there making plans for ever had not Verena, all at once, remembered the business in hand. "Heavens above, I've forgotten those poor Americans. They'll be wondering what's happened to us. Now, look . . . the thing is"—she rummaged on her desk and produced some sheets of typed instructions—"that the two men have spent most of their time playing golf, and they want to play tomorrow, so they're going to give the trip to Glamis a miss. Instead, I've fixed for a car to come and fetch them from Croy at nine o'clock tomorrow morning and take them to Gleneagles. And the same car will bring them back sometime during the afternoon when they've finished their game. But the ladies want to go to Glamis, so if you could have them back here at about ten o'clock, they can join the others in the coach."

Isobel nodded, hoping that she would forget none of this. Verena was so efficient and, to all intents and purposes, Isobel's boss. Scottish Country Tours was run from a central office in Edinburgh, but Verena was the local co-ordinating agent. It was Verena who telephoned Isobel each week to let her know how many guests she could expect (six was the limit, as she had no room for more) and as well fill her in with any small idiosyncrasies or personality problems of her guests.

The tours started in May and continued until the end of August. Each one lasted a week and followed a regular pattern. The group, arriving from Kennedy, began their stay in Edinburgh, where they spent two days sightseeing in the Borders and in the City itself. On Tuesday their coach brought them to Relkirk, where they dutifully plodded around the Auld Kirk, the local Castle, and a National Trust garden. They were then transported to Corriehill, to be welcomed and sorted out by Verena. From Corriehill they were collected by the various hostesses. Wednesday was the day for Glamis Castle and a scenic drive to Pitlochry, and on Thursday they set off yet again in the coach to view the Highlands and to visit Deeside and Inverness. On Friday they returned to Edinburgh, and on Saturday they flew home, back to Kennedy and all points west.

Isobel was certain that by then they must all be in a state of total exhaustion.

It was Verena who, five years ago, had roped Isobel into the business. She explained what was involved and gave Isobel the firm's hand-out to read. It was effusive.

Stay as a private guest in a private
house. Experience for yourself the
hospitality and historic grandeur of
some of Scotland's loveliest homes, and
meet, as friends, the ancient families
who live in them. . . .

Such hyperbole took a bit of living up to.

"We're not an ancient family," she'd pointed out to Verena.

"Ancient enough."

"And Croy's not exactly historic."

"Bits of it are. And you've got lots of bed-rooms. That's what really counts. And think of all that lovely lolly. . . ."

It was this that had finally decided Isobel. Verena's proposition came at a time when the Balmerino fortunes, in every sense of the word, were at a low ebb. Archie's father, the second Lord Balmerino, and the most charming and impractical of men, had died leaving the estate in some disarray. His unexpected demise took him, and most other people, quite by surprise, and because of this, stupendous death duties creamed off most of the inherited family wealth. With the two children, Lucilla and Hamish, in the throes of their education, the large and inconvenient house to keep going, and the lands to be maintained in some sort of order, the young Balmerinos found themselves faced with certain problems. Archie, at that time, was still a regular soldier. But he had joined the Queen's Loyal Highlanders at the age of nineteen simply because he could think of nothing else he particularly wanted to do, and although he had thoroughly enjoyed his years with the Regiment, he was not blessed with a driving ambition to succeed and knew that he would never make Major-General.

Keeping Croy, living there, come hell or high water, became their first priority. Optimistically, they laid plans. Archie would retire from the Army, and while he was young enough to do so, find himself some sort of a job. But before this could happen he was committed to a last tour of duty with his Regiment, and went with them to Northern Ireland.

The Regiment returned home four months

later, but it was eight months before Archie came back to Croy, and it took Isobel about eight days to realize that any sort of a job was, for the time being, out of the question. In some desperation, through long and sleepless nights, she reviewed their plight.

But they had friends, in particular Edmund Aird. Realizing the gravity of the situation, Edmund moved in and took control. It was Edmund who found a tenant for the home farm, and Edmund who assumed responsibility for the grouse moor. Together with Gordon Gillock, the game-keeper, he saw to the burning of the heather and the maintenance of the butts, and then let the entire concern out to a syndicate of businessmen from the south, retaining a gun for himself and a half-gun for Archie.

For Isobel, to be shed of at least some of her anxieties was an enormous relief, but income remained a vexing problem. There was still some inherited capital, but this was tied up in stocks and bonds, and was all that Archie had to leave to his children. Isobel had a little money of her own, but this, even added to Archie's Army pension and his sixty-percent disability pension, did not amount to

very much. The day-to-day expenses of simply running the house and keeping the family
fed and clothed remained a constant source
of worry, so that Verena's suggestion, ini-
tially daunting, was in fact the answer to a
prayer.

"Oh, come on, Isobel. You can do it standing on your head."

And Isobel realized that she could. After
all, she was well used to managing the big
house, and accustomed to having people to
stay. When Archie's father was alive there
were always house parties to be arranged for
the shooting, and the dances in September.
During the school holidays, Croy filled up
with the children's friends, and Christmas
and Easter never passed without entire families coming to share the festivities.

Compared to all this, Verena's proposition
did not sound at all arduous. It would only
take up two days a week throughout the four
months of summer. Surely that could not be
too demanding. And . . . cheering thought
. . . it would be stimulation for Archie, people coming and going. Helping to entertain
them would give him an interest and bolster
his morale, sadly in need of a boost.

a rush mat or two

once been a small scullery

What she hadn't realized, and what she had painfully learned, was that entertaining paying guests was a very different kettle of fish to having one's own friends about the place. You couldn't argue with them, any more than you could sit about in a companionable silence. Nor could you allow them to slope into the kitchen to peel a pot of potatoes or concoct a salad. The real rub was that they were paying. This put hospitality on a totally different level because it meant that everything had to be perfect. The tour was not cheap and, as Verena forthrightly insisted, the clients must be given value for their dollars.

There were certain guide-lines, printed out on a special instruction sheet for hostesses. Every bedroom must have its own bathroom, preferably adjoining. Beds must have electric blankets, and the rooms must be centrally heated. Also, if possible, there should be supplementary heating . . . preferably a real fire but, failing this, then an electric or gas fire. Fresh flowers must be arranged in the bedrooms.

(Reading this, Isobel had known some annoyance. Who did they think they were? She had never in her life put a guest in a room without seeing that there were fresh flowers on the dressing-table.)

Then there were more rules about breakfast and dinner. Breakfast must be robust and hearty. Orange juice, coffee, and tea, all available. In the evenings, a cocktail must be offered, and wine at dinner-time. This meal had to be formally served, with candles, crystal, and silver on the table, and consist of at least three courses, to be followed by coffee and conversation. Other diversions, however unlikely, could be offered. A little music . . . perhaps bagpipe-playing . . . ?

The overseas visitors awaited them in Verena's drawing-room. Verena flung open the door. "I am sorry we've been so long. Just one or two ends that needed to be tied up," she told them in her best committee-meeting voice, which brooked no question nor argument. "Here we are, and here is your hostess, come to take you to Croy."

The drawing-room at Corriehill was large

and light, palely decorated and little used. Today, however, because of the inclement weather, a small fire flickered in the grate, and around this, disposed on armchairs and sofas, sat the four Americans. To while away the time, they had switched on the television and were watching, in a bemused fashion, cricket. Disturbed, they rose to their feet, turning smiling faces, and one of the men stooped and politely turned the television off.

"Now, introductions. Mr. and Mrs. Hardwicke, and Mr. and Mrs. Franco, this is your hostess for the next two days. Lady Balmerino."

Shaking hands, Isobel understood what Verena had meant when she described this week's guests as being slightly more robust than usual. Scottish Country Tours seemed, for some reason, to attract clients of an extremely advanced age, and sometimes they were not only geriatric but in a dicey state of health—short of breath and uncertain about the legs. These two couples, however, were scarcely beyond middle age. Grey-haired, certainly, but apparently bursting with energy, and all of them enviably tanned. The Francos were small of stature, and Mr.

Franco very bald, and the Hardwickes were tall and muscled and slim, and looked as though they spent their lives out of doors and taking a great deal of exercise.

"I'm afraid I'm a little late," Isobel found herself saying, although she knew perfectly well that she was not. "But we can go whenever you're ready."

They were ready right now. The ladies collected their handbags and their beautiful new Burberry raincoats, and the little party all trooped through the hall and out into the porch. Isobel went to open the back doors of the minibus, and by the time she had done this, the men were humping and heaving the big suitcases across the gravel, and helped her to load them. (This, too, was novel. She and Verena usually had to do the job by themselves.) When all were safely aboard, she shut the doors and fastened them. The Hardwickes and the Francos were saying goodbye to Verena. "But," Verena said, "I'll see you ladies tomorrow. And I hope the golf's a great success. You'll love Gleneagles."

Doors were opened and they all climbed in. Isobel took her place behind the wheel, fastened her seat-belt, turned on the ignition, and they were away.

"I do apologize for the weather. We've had no summer at all yet."

"Oh, it hasn't bothered us in the least. We're just sorry you had to come out on such a day to come and collect us. Hope it wasn't too much trouble."

"No, not at all. That's my job."

"Have we far to go to your home, Lady Balmerino?"

"About ten miles. And I wish you'd call me Isobel."

"Why, thank you, we will. And I am Susan and my husband is Arnold, and the Hardwickes are Joe and Myra."

"Ten miles," said one of the men. "That's quite a distance."

"Yes. Actually my husband usually comes with me on these trips. But he had to go to a meeting. He'll be home for tea, though, so you'll meet him then."

"Is Lord Balmerino in business?"

"No. No, it's not a business meeting. It's a church meeting. Our village church. We have to raise some money. It's rather a shoe-string affair. But my husband's grandfather built it, so he feels a sort of family responsibility."

It was raining again. The windscreen wipers swung to and fro. Perhaps conversation would divert their attention from the misery of it all.

"Is this your first visit to Scotland?"

The two ladies, chipping in on each other like a close-harmony duo, told her. The men had been there before, to play golf, but this was the first time their wives had accompanied them. And they just loved every inch of the place, and had gone crazy in the shops in Edinburrow. It had rained, of course, but that hadn't bothered them. They had their new Burberries to wear, and both decided that the rain made Edinburrow look just so historic and romantic that they had been able to picture Mary and Bothwell riding together up the Royal Mile.

When they had finished, Isobel asked them what part of the States they came from.

"New York State. Rye."

"Are you by the sea there?"

"Oh, sure. Our kids sail every weekend."

Isobel could imagine it. Could imagine those kids, tanned and windblown, bursting with vitamins and fresh orange juice and health, scudding over starch-blue seas beneath the curving wing of a snow-white mainsail. And sunshine. Blue skies and sunshine. Day after day of it, so that you could plan tennis matches and picnics and evening barbecues and know that it wasn't going to rain.

That was how summers, in memory, used to be. The endless, aimless summers of childhood. What had happened to those long, light days, sweet with the scent of roses, when one had to come indoors only to eat, and sometimes not even then? Swimming in the river, lazing in the garden, playing tennis, having tea in the shade of some tree because it was too hot anywhere else. She remembered picnics on moors that simmered in the sunlight, the heather too dry to light a campfire, and the larks flying high. What had happened to her world? What cosmic disaster had transformed those bright days into week after week of dark and soggy gloom?

It wasn't just the weather, it was just that

the weather made everything so much worse. Like Archie getting his leg shot off, and having to be nice to people you didn't know because they were paying you money to sleep in your spare bedrooms. And being tired all the time, and never buying new clothes, and worrying about Hamish's school fees, and missing Lucilla.

She heard herself saying, with some force, "It's the one horrible thing about living in Scotland."

For a moment, perhaps surprised by her outburst, nobody commented on this announcement. Then one of the ladies spoke. "I beg your pardon?"

"I'm sorry. I meant the rain. We get so tired of the rain. I meant these horrible summers."

2

THE PRESBYTERIAN CHURCH in Strathcroy, the established Church of Scotland, stood, impressive, ancient, and venerable, on the south bank of the river Croy. It was reached from the main road that ran through the village by a curved stone bridge, and its setting was pastoral. Glebe lands sloped to the water's edge, a grassy pasture where, each September, the Strathcroy Games were held. The churchyard, shaded by a mammoth beech, was filled with time-worn, leaning gravestones, and a grassy path led between these to the gates of the Manse. This as well was solid and imposing, built to contain the large families of bygone ministers and boasting an enviable garden burgeoning with gnarled but productive fruit trees and old-fashioned roses, for these flourished behind the protection of a high stone wall. All of this, so charmingly disposed, exuded an ambience of timelessness, domestic security, and God-fearing piety.

In contrast, the little Episcopal church, like a poor relation, crouched directly across the bridge, totally overshadowed, both literally and metaphorically, by its rival. The main road ran close by, and between the church and the road was a strip of grass which the rector, the Reverend Julian Gloxby, himself cut each week. A small lane led up a slope to the back of the church and to the rectory that stood behind it. Both were modest in size and whitewashed. The church had a little tower with a single bell, and a wooden porchway enclosed its main door. Inside, it was equally unassuming. No handsome pews, no flagged floors, no historic relics. A worn drugget led to the altar, and a breathless harmonium did duty as an organ. There was always a faint smell of damp.

Both church and rectory had been erected at the turn of the century by the first Lord Balmerino and handed over to the Diocese with a small endowment for maintenance. The income this produced had long since trickled to nothing, the congregation was tiny, and the Vestry, endeavouring to make ends meet, found themselves perpetually strapped for cash.

When the electric wiring was discovered to be not only faulty but downright dangerous, it was very nearly the last straw. But Archie Balmerino rallied his meagre troops, chaired committees, visited the Bishop and wangled a grant. Even so, some fund-raising was going to be necessary. Various suggestions were put forward, discussed, and eventually turned down. In the end, it was decided to fall back on that old dependable, a church sale. This would take place in July, and in the Village Hall. There would be a Jumble stall, a Plant and Vegetable stall, a White Elephant and Handwork stall, and, of course, teas.

A committee was duly appointed and met, on that grey and damp June afternoon, around the dining-room table at Balnaid, home of Virginia and Edmund Aird. By half past four the meeting was over, with business satisfactorily concluded and modest plans laid. These included the printing of eye-catching posters, the borrowing of a number of trestle-tables, and the organizing of a raffle.

The rector and Mrs. Gloxby, and Toddy Buchanan, who ran the Strathcroy Arms, had already taken their leave and driven away in their cars. Dermot Honeycombe, busy with his antique shop, had been unable to attend. In his absence, he had been given the job of running the White Elephant stall.

Now only three people remained. Virginia and Violet, her mother-in-law, sat at one end of the long mahogany table and Archie Balmerino at the other. As soon as the others had gone, Virginia had disappeared into the kitchen to make tea, and brought it to them on a tray, without ceremony. Three mugs, a brown teapot, a jug of milk, and a bowl of sugar. It was both refreshing and welcome, and it was pleasant to relax after the concentrated discussions of the afternoon and to be able to chat without restriction, enjoying the easy closeness of family and old friends.

They were still mulling over the church sale.

"I just hope Dermot won't mind being told he has to run the White Elephant stall. Perhaps I should ring him and give him the opportunity to say he doesn't want to do it." Archie was always cautious about other people's feelings, terrified of it being thought that he was throwing his weight about.

Violet pooh-poohed the very idea. "Of course he won't. Dear man, he never minds pitching in. He'd probably be far more hurt if we gave the job to somebody else. After all, he knows the value of everything. . . ."

She was a tall lady in her late seventies and very large, dressed in a much-worn coat and skirt and shod in sensible brogues. Her hair was grey and wispy, skewered to the back of her head in a small bun, and her face, with its long top lip and wide-set eyes, resembled that of a kindly sheep. And yet she was neither plain nor dowdy. Wonderfully upright, she had presence, and those eyes were both merry and intelligent, dispelling any suggestion of haughtiness. Now they twinkled with amusement. "Even pottery doggies with bones in their mouths, and table lamps made out of old whisky bottles plastered in shells."

Virginia laughed. "He'll probably pick up some wonderful bargain for twenty-five pence and sell it for some incredible price in his shop next day."

She leaned back in her chair and stretched, like a lazy girl. In her early thirties, Virginia

Aird was as blonde and as slender as the day she had married Edmund. Today, making no concession to the formality of the occasion, she wore her usual uniform of jeans, a navy-blue Guernsey sweater, and polished leather loafers. She was pretty in a pert and catlike way, but this prettiness was elevated to beauty by her eyes, which were enormous and of a glittering sapphire blueness. Her skin was fine, innocent of make-up, and the colour of a delectable brown egg. A fine tracing of lines fanned out from the corners of those eyes, and these alone betrayed her age.

Now she flexed her long fingers and circled her wrists, as though performing some prescribed exercise.

"And Isobel will be the tea-lady." She stopped stretching. "Why didn't Isobel come today, Archie?"

"I told you . . . or perhaps you were out of the room. She had to go to Corriehill to pick up this week's batch of visitors."

"Yes, of course, how stupid of me. Sorry . . ."

"That reminds me." Violet held out her mug. "Pour me a little more tea, would you, dear? I can drink it till it comes out of my ears. . . . I met Verena Steynton in Relkirk yesterday, and she told me that I didn't have to keep it a secret any longer. She and Angus are going to throw a party for Katy in September."

Virginia frowned. "What do you mean, keep it a secret?"

"Well, she confided in me a few weeks ago, but she said I wasn't to say anything until she'd spoken to Angus about it. It seems that he has finally been persuaded."

"Goodness, how enterprising! A little hop, or a full-blown affair?"

"Oh, full-blown. Marquees and fairy lights and copperplate invitations and everybody dressed to the nines."

"What *fun*." Virginia was filled with enthusiasm, as Violet had known she would be. "It's lovely when people throw private parties, because then you don't have to pay for your ticket. Instead I'll have a good excuse to go and buy myself a new dress. We'll all have to rally round and have people to stay. I'll have to be certain that Edmund's not planning to go to Tokyo that week."

"Where is he now?" asked Edmund's mother.

"Oh, in Edinburgh. He'll be back about six."

"And Henry? What's happened to Henry? Shouldn't he be back from school?"

"No. He's stopped off to have his tea with Edie."

"That'll cheer her up."

Virginia frowned, puzzled, as well she might be. The boot was usually on the other foot, and Edie the person who did the cheering. "What's happened?"

Violet looked at Archie. "Do you remember that cousin of Edie's, Lottie Carstairs? She was housemaid at Strathcroy the year you married Isobel?"

"Do I *remember* her?" His expression was one of horror. "Dreadful female. Nutty as a fruit-cake. She broke most of the Rockingham tea-set, and she was always creeping around the place, just where you least expected to find her. I never knew what induced my mother to employ her."

"I think it was a case of any port in a storm. It was a busy summer and she was desperate for help. Anyway, Lottie only lasted about four months, and then she went back home to Tullochard to live with her aged parents. She never married . . ."

"That's no surprise . . ."

". . . and now, of course, they're dead, and she's been on her own. Becoming, apparently, odder by the day. Finally, she went over the top and was wheeled off to the nearest mental hospital. Edie's her next of kin. She's been visiting the poor creature every week. And now the doctors say that she's well enough to be discharged, but of course she can't live alone again. At least, not just yet."

"Don't tell me Edie's going to have her?"

"She says she has to. There's nobody else. And you know how kind Edie is . . . she's always had a great sense of family responsibility. Blood is thicker than water and all that nonsense."

"And a great deal nastier," Archie commented drily. "Lottie Carstairs. I can't think of anything worse. When is all this going to happen?"

Violet shrugged. "I don't know. Next month maybe. Or August."

Virginia was horrified. "She's surely not going to *live* with Edie?"

"Let's hope not. Let's hope it's just a temporary measure."

"And where on earth will Edie put her? She's only got two rooms in that little cottage of hers."

"I didn't ask."

"When did she tell you this?"

"This morning. When she was Hoovering my dining-room carpet. I thought she was looking a bit down in the mouth, so I asked her what was the matter. I heard all about it over a cup of coffee."

"Oh, poor Edie. I can't bear it for her. . . ."

Archie said, "Edie is a saint."

"She certainly is." Violet finished her tea, glanced at her watch, and began to gather her belongings. Her large handbag, her papers, her spectacles. "That was very nice, dear. Most refreshing. And now I must take myself home."

"Me too," said Archie. "Back to Croy to drink more tea with the Americans."

"You'll be awash. Who have you got this week?"

"No idea. Just hope they're not too elderly. Last week I thought one old boy was going to die of angina right there, in the middle of the soup. Mercifully, however, he survived."

"It's such a responsibility."

"Not really. The worst are the ones who've signed a pledge and take no drink. Bible Belt Baptists. Orange juice makes for sticky conversation. Have you got your car, Vi, or do you want a lift home?"

"I walked down, but I'd like a lift back up the hill."

"I'll take you then."

He too gathered together his papers and heaved himself to his feet. For an instant he paused and then, when certain of his balance, made his way towards them down the length of the thickly carpeted room. He limped only slightly, which was a miracle because his right leg, from a stump of thigh downwards, was made of aluminum.

He had come to the meeting today straight from his garden and apologized for his attire, but nobody took much notice because this was the way he looked most of the time. Shapeless corduroy trousers, a checked shirt with a patched collar, and a threadbare tweed jacket that he called his gardening coat, though in truth no self-respecting gardener would be seen dead in it.

Virginia pushed back her chair and stood up and Violet did the same, but much more slowly, matching her movements to Archie's painful gait. She was in no way impatient to be gone, but even if she were would never show it, for her feelings towards him were sympathetic and fiercely protective. She had, after all, known him all his life. Remembered him as a boy, as a wild young man, as a soldier. Always laughing, and an enthusiasm—almost a lust for life—that was as catching as the measles. She remembered him endlessly active. Playing tennis; dancing at the Regimental Ball, swinging his partners nearly off their feet; leading a line of guns up the hill behind Croy, his long legs covering the heather with an easy stride that left all the others behind.

Then, he had been Archie Blair. Now, he was Lord Balmerino. The Lord and the Laird. Fine titles for a man thin as a stick, with a tin leg to boot. The black hair was now flecked with white, the skin of his face netted with lines, his dark eyes deep-set and shadowed by the jutting brows.

He reached her side and smiled. "Ready, Vi?"

"All set."

"In that case, we'll go. . . ." And then, in mid-step, he stopped again. "Oh, God, I've just remembered. Virginia, did Edmund give you an envelope to give me? I called him last night. It's rather urgent. Some document from the Forestry Commission?"

Violet was instantly suspicious. "You're not going to start planting conifers, are you?"

"No, it's about some access road they're wanting to build at the edge of the moor."

Virginia shook her head. "He didn't say anything about it. Perhaps he forgot. Let's go and look on his desk in the library. It's probably there. . . ."

"Right. I'd like to take it with me if I can."

They moved at a leisurely pace out of the dining-room and into the hall. This was even larger, panelled in pine with a massive staircase, heavily balustraded, rising in three short flights to the upstairs landing. Various items of undistinguished furniture stood about. A carved oak chest, a gate-leg table, and a chaise longue that had seen better days. This was quite often occupied by dogs, but at the moment was empty.

"I shall not come and look for Forestry Commission documents," Violet announced. "I shall sit here until you have found them." And she settled herself majestically on the dogs' bed to wait.

They left her. "We shan't be a moment." She watched them go down the wide passage that led to the library and on to the drawing-room, and on again through glassed doors to the soaring conservatory.

Alone, Violet savoured her momentary solitude, with the old house around her. She knew it so well, had known it all her life. Its every mood was comfortably familiar. Every creak of the stair, every evocative smell. The hall was draughty, but the draughts did not bother her. No longer Violet's home, but Virginia's. And yet it felt much the same as it ever had, as though, over the years, it had assumed a strength of character all its own. Perhaps because so much had happened here. Because it had been the haven and the touchstone of a single family.

Not that Balnaid was a very old house. In fact, it was younger than Violet by a few years, and built by her father, then Sir Hector Akenside, and a man of considerable means. She always thought that Balnaid was a little like Sir Hector. Large, kindly, and lavish, and yet totally unassuming. At a time when men of newly acquired wealth were constructing for themselves huge monuments to their pride of startling hideousness, castellated and turreted, Sir Hector had concentrated his able mind on less glamorous but infinitely more important features.

Central heating, efficient plumbing, plenty of bathrooms, and kitchens filled with sunlight, so that servants (and there were plenty of them) would work in pleasant surroundings. And from the day it was finally completed, Balnaid never looked out of place. Built from local stone on the south side of the Croy, with its back to the village and the river, the face of the house smiled out over a view both domestic and magnificent.

The garden was large, rich with shrubs and mature trees. Sir Hector's passion, he had planned and landscaped it himself, so that formal lawns flowed into drifts of unmown grass, daffodils, and bluebells. Azaleas, coral and yellow, grew in fragrant masses, and mown paths twisted away invitingly out of sight between tall stands of pink- and scarlet-blossomed rhododendrons.

Beyond the garden, and separated from it by a steep ha-ha wall, was an acre or so of parkland, grazing for the hill ponies; and, beyond again, the stone-dyked fields of the neighbouring sheep farmer. Then, in the distance, the hills. They swelled to meet the sky, dramatic as a stage-drop. Constant, and yet continually changing, as the seasons and the light changed: snow-clad, purple with heather, green with spring bracken, swept by gales . . . whatever. They were always beautiful.

Had always been beautiful.

Violet knew all this because Balnaid had been her childhood home, and so her world. She had grown up within these walls, played solitary games in that magic garden, guddled for trout in the river, ridden her stubby Shetland pony through the village and up onto the lonely hills of Croy. At the age of twenty-two, she had been married from Balnaid.

She remembered driving the little distance to the Episcopalian church in the back of her father's stately Rolls-Royce, with Sir Hector, top-hatted, beside her. The Rolls had been decked out for the occasion with white silk ribbons. These somehow lessened its dignity, and it looked almost as incongruous as Violet felt, with her ample frame laced into a cream satin dress of quite hideous uncomfortableness and a mist of inherited Limerick lace veiling her homely features. She remembered returning to Balnaid in the same opulent vehicle, but on that journey even the agonizing tightness of her stays had ceased to matter, because she was, at long last, the triumphant wife of Geordie Aird.

She had lived at Balnaid, on and off, ever since, and had not finally moved out until ten years ago, when Edmund married Virginia. He brought Virginia back to Balnaid to live, and Violet knew then that the time had come for her to bow out and allow the old place to welcome its new young mistress. She made the property over to Edmund and bought a gardener's derelict cottage from Archie Balmerino. This house was called Pennyburn, and there, within the estate walls of Croy, she made a new home for herself. The restoration and refurbishment of the little house had kept her happy for a year, and she was still not finished with the garden.

I am, she told herself, a fortunate woman.

Sitting there, on the dog-smelling chaise longue, Violet looked about her. Saw the worn Turkey rug, the old bits of furniture that she had known all her life. It was pleasant when things did not change too much. When she said goodbye to Balnaid, Violet had never imagined that so little would change. Edmund's new wife, she decided, would be the new broom, come to sweep away all the dusty old traditions, and she was indeed quite interested to see what Virginia —as young and vital as a breath of fresh air —would achieve. But, apart from completely revamping the big bedroom, freshening up the drawing-room with a lick of paint, and turning an old pantry into a utility room that fairly hummed with deep-freezes, washing machines, drying machines, and attendant luxuries, Virginia did nothing. Violet accepted this, but found it puzzling. There was, after all, no lack of money, and to her it seemed strange that Virginia should be content to live with the worn rugs and the faded velvet curtains and the old Edwardian wall-papers.

Perhaps it had something to do with the arrival of Henry. Because after Henry was born, Virginia abandoned all other interests and immersed herself in her baby son. This was very nice, but came as something of a shock to Violet. She had no idea that her daughter-in-law would prove so deeply maternal. With Edmund away so much, and mother and child left on their own, Violet had secret reservations about this overwhelming devotion, and it was a constant source of astonishment to her that despite his upbringing, Henry had grown into such a delightful little boy. A bit too dependent on his mother, perhaps, but still, not spoiled, and a charming child. Perhaps . . .

"Sorry, Vi, to keep you waiting."

Surprise made her start. She turned and saw Archie and Virginia coming towards her, Archie holding up the long buff envelope as though it were a hard-won banner. ". . . took a bit of searching for. Come along now, and I'll drive you home."

❧ 3 ❧

HENRY AIRD, EIGHT YEARS OLD, banged
with some importance at Edie Findhorn's
front door, using her brass knocker shaped
like a pixie. The house was one of a line of
single-storey cottages that lined the main
street of Strathcroy, but Edie's was nicer
than anybody else's because it had a mossy
thatched roof and forget-me-nots grew in the
little strip of earth between the pavement and
the wall. Standing there, he heard her footsteps; she unsnibbed the door and threw it
open.

"Well, here you are, turned up like a bad
penny."

She was always laughing. He loved her,
and when people asked him who his best
friends were, Edie came on top of the list.
She was not only jolly, but fat, white-haired,
and rosy-cheeked, and appetizing as a fresh
and floury scone.

"Did you have a good day?"

She always asked this, despite the fact that she saw him every lunch-time, because she was the school dinner-lady and served out the midday meal. It was handy having Edie doing this because it meant that she stinted on helpings of things he hated, like curried mince and stodgy custard, and was lavish with the mashed potatoes and chocolate shape.

"Yes, it was all right." He went into her sitting-room, dumped his anorak and his school-bag on the couch. "We had drawing. We had to draw something."

"What did you have to draw?"

"We had to draw a *song.*" He began to undo the buckles of his satchel. He had a problem and thought that probably Edie could help to solve it for him. "We sang 'Speed Bonnie Boat Like a Bird on the Wing over the Sea to Skye,' and we had to draw a picture of it. And everybody else drew rowing boats and islands, and I drew *this.*" He produced it, slightly crumpled from contact with his gym shoes and his pencil box. "And Mr. McLintock *laughed,* and I don't know why."

"He laughed?" She took it from him, went to find her spectacles, and put them on. "And did he not tell you why he laughed?"

"No. The bell rang and it was the end of class."

Edie sat on the couch and he sat beside her. Together they gazed in silence at his work. He thought it was one of his best pictures. A beautiful speedboat slicing through blue waters, with white water pouring up at its bow and a snowy wake at the stern. There were sea-gulls in the sky and, on the front of the boat, a baby wrapped in a shawl. The baby had been difficult to draw, because babies have such funny faces. No noses or chins. Also, this baby looked a bit precarious and as though at any moment it might slip off the boat and into the sea. But still, it was there.

Edie did not say anything. Henry explained to her. "It's a speedboat. And that's the lad that's been born."

"Yes, I can see that."

"But why did Mr. McLintock laugh? It's not funny."

"No, it's not funny. It's a lovely picture. It's just that . . . well . . . speed doesn't mean a speedboat in the song. It means that the boat's going very fast over the water, but it's not a speedboat. And the lad that was born to be king was Bonnie Prince Charlie, and he was grown up by then."

All was now explained. "Oh," said Henry, "I see."

She gave him back the drawing. "But it's still a good picture, and I think it was very rude of Mr. McLintock to laugh. Put it in your bag and take it home for your mother to see, and Edie will go and start getting your tea."

While he did this, she heaved herself to her feet, put her spectacles back on the mantelpiece, and went out of the room through a door at the back that led to her kitchen and bathroom. These were modern additions, for when Edie was a little girl, the cottage had consisted solely of two rooms. A but and ben it was called. The living room, which was the kitchen as well, and the bedroom. No running water, and a wooden lavatory at the end of the garden. What was more astonishing was that Edie had been one of five children, and so seven people had once lived in these rooms. Her parents had slept in a box-bed in the kitchen, with a shelf over their heads for the baby, and the rest of the children had been crowded into the other room. For water, Mrs. Findhorn had made the long walk each day to the village pump, and baths were a weekly affair, taken in a tin tub in front of the kitchen fire.

"But however did five of you get into the bedroom, Edie?" Henry would ask, fascinated by the logistics of sheer space. Even with just Edie's bed and her wardrobe, it still seemed dreadfully small.

"Oh, mind, we weren't all in there at the same time. By the time the youngest was born, my eldest brother was out working on the land, and living in a bothy with the other farm-hands. And then, when the girls were old enough, they went into service in some big house or other. It was a sore wrench when we had to leave, tears all over the place, but there was no space for us all here, and too many mouths to feed, and my mother needed the extra money."

She told him other things, too. How, on winter evenings, they would bank up the fire with potato peelings and sit around it, listening to their father reading aloud the stories of

Rudyard Kipling, or *Pilgrim's Progress*. The little girls would work at their knitting, making socks for the menfolk. And when it came to turning the heels, the sock was given to an older sister or their mother because that bit of the knitting was too complicated for them to do.

It all sounded very poor, but somehow quite cosy too. Looking about him, Henry found it hard to imagine Edie's cottage the way it had been in olden days. For now it was as bright and cheerful as it could be, the box-bed gone and lovely swirly carpets on the floor. The old kitchen fire had gone too, and a beautiful green tile fireplace stood in its place, and there were flowery curtains and a television set and lots of nice china ornaments.

With his drawing safely stowed, he buckled up his satchel once more. Speed Bonnie Boat. He had got it wrong. He often got things wrong. There was another song they had learned at school. "Ho Ro My Nut Brown Maiden." Henry, singing lustily with the rest of the class, could just imagine the maiden. A little Pakistani, like Kedejah

Ishak, with her dark skin and her shining pigtail, rowing like mad across a windy loch.

His mother had had to explain that one to him.

As well, ordinary words could be confusing. People said things to him, and he heard them, but heard them just the way they sounded. And the word, or the image conjured up by the word, stuck in his mind. Grown-ups went on holiday to "My Yorker" or "Portjiggal." Or "Grease." Grease sounded a horrid place. Edie once told him about a lady who was very cut up because her daughter had married some fly-by-night who was not good enough for her. The poor lady, all cut up, had haunted his nightmares for weeks.

But the worst was the misunderstanding that had happened with his grandmother, and which might have come between them for ever and caused a lasting rift, had not Henry's mother finally found out what was bothering him and put it right.

He had gone to Pennyburn one day after school to have tea with his grandmother, Vi. A gale was blowing and the wind howled around the little house. Sitting by the fire, Vi had suddenly made an exclamation of annoyance, got to her feet and fetched from somewhere a folding screen, which she set up in front of the glass door that led out into the garden. Henry asked her why she was doing this, and when she told him he was so horrified that he scarcely spoke for the rest of the afternoon. When his mother came to fetch him, he had never been so glad to see her and could not wait to scramble into his anorak and be out of the house, almost forgetting to thank Vi for his tea.

It was horrible. He felt that he never wanted to go back to Pennyburn, and yet knew that he ought to, if only to protect Vi. Every time his mother suggested another visit, he made some excuse or said he would rather go to Edie's. Finally, one night while he was having his bath, she came and sat on the lavatory and talked to him . . . she brought the conversation gently around to the touchy subject and at last asked him straight if there was any reason why he no longer wanted to go to Vi's.

"You always used to love it so. Did something happen?"

It was a relief at last to talk about it.

"It's frightening."

"Darling, what's frightening?"

"It comes in, out of the garden, and it comes into the sitting-room. Vi put a screen up but it could easily knock the screen over. It might hurt her. I don't think she should live there any more."

"For heaven's sake! What comes in?"

He could see it. With great tall spotted legs, and a long thin spotted neck, and great big yellow teeth with its lips curled back, ready to pounce, or bite.

"A horrible *giraffe.*"

His mother was confounded. "Henry, have you gone out of your mind? Giraffes live in Africa, or zoos. There aren't any giraffes in Strathcroy."

"There are!" He shouted at her stupidity. "She said so. She said there was a horrible giraffe that came out of the garden, and through the door and into her sitting-room. She *told* me so."

There was a long silence. He stared at his mother and she stared back at him with her bright blue eyes, but she never smiled.

At last she said, "She wasn't telling you that there was a giraffe, Henry. She was telling you that there was a draught. You know, a horrid, shivery draught."

A draught. Not a giraffe but a draught. All that fuss about a stupid draught. He had made a fool of himself, but was so relieved that his grandmother was safe from monsters that it didn't matter.

"Don't tell anybody," he pleaded.

"I'll have to explain to Vi. But she won't say a word."

"All right. You can tell Vi. But not anybody else."

And his mother had promised, and he had jumped out of the bath, all dripping wet, and been gathered up into a great fluffy towel and his mother's arms, and she had hugged him and told him that she was going to eat him alive and she loved him so, and they had sung "Camptown Races," and there was macaroni and cheese for supper.

Edie had cooked sausages for his tea and made potato scones, and opened a can of baked beans. While he ploughed his way through this, sitting at her kitchen table, Edie sat opposite him, drinking a cup of tea. Her own meal she would eat later.

Munching, he realized that she was quieter than usual. Normally on such occasions they never stopped talking, and he was the willing recipient of all the gossip in the glen. Who had died and how much they had left; who had abandoned his father on the farm and hightailed it off to Relkirk to work in a garage; who had started a baby and was no better than she should be. But today no such snippets of information came his way. Instead Edie sat with her dimpled elbows on the table and gazed out of the window at her long, thin back garden.

He said, "Penny for your thoughts, Edie," which was what she always said to him when he had something on his mind.

She sighed deeply. "Oh, Henry, I don't know, and that's for certain."

Which told him nothing. However, when pressed, she explained her predicament. She had a cousin who had lived in Tullochard. She was called Lottie Carstairs and had never been bright. Never married. Gone into domestic service, but had proved useless even at that. She had lived with her mother and father until the old folks had died, and then turned very strange and had had to go to hospital. Edie said it was a nervous breakdown. But she was recovering. One day she would come out of hospital, and she was coming to stay with Edie because there was no other place for the poor soul to go.

Henry thought this a rotten idea. He liked having Edie to himself. "But you haven't got a spare room."

"She'll have to have my bedroom."

He was indignant. "But where will *you* sleep?"

"On the Put-U-Up in the sitting-room."

She was far too fat for the Put-U-Up. "Why can't Dotty sleep there?"

"Because she will be the guest, and her name's Lottie."

"Will she stay for long?"

"We'll have to see."

Henry thought about this. "Will you go on being dinner-lady, and helping Mummy, and helping Vi at Pennyburn?"

"For heaven's sake, Henry, Lottie's not bedridden."

"Will I like her?" This was important.

Edie found herself at a loss for words. "Oh, Henry, I don't know. She's a sad creature. Nineteen shillings in the pound, my father always called her. Screamed like a wet hen if a man showed his face around the door, and *clumsy!* Years ago, she worked for a wee while for old Lady Balmerino at Croy, but she smashed so much china that they had to give her the sack. She never worked again after that."

Henry was horrified. "You mustn't let her do the washing-up or she'll break all your pretty things."

"It's not just my china she'll be breaking . . ." Edie prophesied gloomily, but before Henry could follow up this interesting line of conversation she took a hold of herself, put a more cheerful expression on her face, and pointedly changed the subject. "Do you want another potato scone, or are you ready for your Choc Bar?"

ৡ 4 ৢ

EMERGING WITH ARCHIE AND VIRGINIA from the front door of Balnaid, and descending the steps to the gravel sweep, Violet saw that the rain had stopped. It was still damp but now much warmer, and lifting her head she felt the breeze on her cheek, blowing freshly from the west. Low clouds were slowly being rolled aside, revealing here and there a patch of blue sky and a piercing, biblical, ray of sunshine. It would turn into a beautiful summer evening—too late to be of much use to anybody.

Archie's old Land Rover stood waiting for them. They said goodbye to Virginia, Violet with a peck on her daughter-in-law's cheek.

"Love to Edmund."

"I'll tell him."

They clambered up into the Land Rover, both with some effort, Violet because she was elderly, and Archie because of his tin leg. Doors were slammed shut, Archie started up the engine, and they were off. Down the curving driveway to the gate, out onto the narrow lane that led past the Presbyterian church, and so across the bridge. At the main road, Archie paused, but there was no traffic, and he swung out and into the street which ran through Strathcroy from end to end.

The little Episcopal church squatted humbly. Mr. Gloxby was out in front of it, cutting the grass.

"He works so hard," Archie observed. "I do hope we can raise a decent bit of cash with a church sale. It was good of you to come today, Vi. I'm sure you'd much rather have been gardening."

"It was such disheartening weather, I had no desire to get at my weeds," Vi said. "So one might as well spend the day doing something worthy." She thought about this. "Rather like when one is worried sick about a child or a grandchild, but you can't do anything, so you go and scrub the scullery floor. At the end of the day you're still worried sick, but at least you've got a clean scullery."

"You're not worried about your family, are

you, Vi? What could you possibly have to worry about?"

"All women worry about their families," Violet told him flatly.

The Land Rover trundled down the road, past the petrol station, which had once been the blacksmith's forge, and the Ishaks' super-market. Beyond this stood the open gates that led to the back drive of Croy. Archie changed down and drove through these, and at once they were climbing steeply. Once, and not so long ago, the surrounding lands had all been park, smooth green pastures grazed by pedigree cattle, but now these had been ploughed for crops, barley, and turnips. Only a few broad-leaved trees still stood, wit-ness to the splendour of former years.

"Why do you worry?"

Violet hesitated. She knew that she could talk to Archie. She had known him all his life, watched him grow up. Indeed, she was as close to him as if he had been her own son, for although he was five years younger than Edmund, the two boys had been brought up together, spent all their time together, and become the closest of friends.

If Edmund was not at Croy, then Archie

was at Balnaid; and if they were at neither house, then they were walking the hills with guns and dogs, potting at hares and rabbits, helping Gordon Gillock burn the heather and repair the butts. Or else they were out in the boat on the loch, or casting for trout in the brown pools of the Croy, or playing tennis, or skating on frozen flood-water. Inseparable, everybody had said. Like brothers.

But they were not brothers, and they had parted. Edmund was bright. Twice as bright as either of his not unintelligent parents. Archie, on the other hand, was totally unacademic.

Edmund, sailing through University, emerged from Cambridge with an Honours Degree in Economics, and was instantly employed by a prestigious merchant bank in the City.

Archie, unable to think of any other career that he might successfully follow, decided to have a try for the Army. He duly appeared before a Regular Commission Board and somehow managed to bluff his way through the interview, for the four senior officers apparently decided that a modest scholastic record was outweighed by Archie's outgoing and friendly personality and his enormous enthusiasm for life.

He went through Sandhurst, joined the Regiment, and was posted to Germany. Edmund stayed in London. He became, to no person's surprise, enormously successful, and within five years had been head-hunted by Sanford Cubben. In the fullness of time he married, but even this romantic event added glitter to his image. Violet recalled pacing up the long aisle of St. Margaret's, Westminster, arm in arm with Sir Rodney Cheriton, and finding time to hope in her heart that Edmund was marrying Caroline because he truly loved her, and not because he had been seduced by the aura of riches that surrounded her.

And now the wheel had gone full circle, and both men were back in Strathcroy. Archie at Croy, and Edmund at Balnaid. Grown men in their middle years, still friends, but no longer intimate. Too much had happened to both of them, and not all of it good. Too many years had slipped by, like water under a bridge. They were different people: one a very wealthy man of business, the other strapped for cash and perpetually struggling to make ends meet. But it was not because of this that a certain formality, a politeness lay between them.

They were no longer close as brothers.

She sighed gustily. Archie smiled. "Oh, come on, Vi, it can't be as bad as that."

"Of course not." He had troubles enough of his own. She would make light of hers. "But I do worry about Alexa, because she seems so alone. I know she's doing a job she enjoys, and that she has that charming little house in which to live, and Lady Cheriton left her enough to give her security for the rest of her life. But I am afraid that her social life is a disaster. I think she truly believes that she's plain and dull and unattractive to men. She has no confidence in herself. When she went to London, I so hoped that she would make a life for herself, make friends of her own age. But she just stayed at Ovington Street with her grandmother, like a sort of companion. If only she could meet some dear kind man who would marry her. She should have a husband to take care of, and children. Alexa was born to have children."

Archie listened sympathetically to all this. He was as fond of Alexa as any of them. He said, "Losing her mother when she was so little . . . perhaps that was a more traumatic experience than any of us realized. Perhaps it made her feel different from other girls. Incomplete in some way."

Violet thought about this. "Yes. Perhaps. Except that Caroline was never a very demonstrative nor loving mother. She never spent much time with Alexa. It was Edie who provided all Alexa's security and affection. And Edie was always there."

"But you liked Caroline."

"Oh yes, I liked her. There was nothing to dislike. We had a good relationship, and I think she was a good wife to Edmund. But she was a strangely reserved girl. Sometimes I went south, to stay for a few days with them all in London. Caroline would invite me, very charmingly, knowing that I would enjoy being with Alexa and Edie. And of course I did, but I never felt totally at home. I hate cities, anyway. Streets and houses and traffic make me feel beleaguered. Claustrophobic. But, quite apart from that, Caroline was never a relaxed hostess. I always felt a bit in the way, and she was an impossible girl to chat with. Left alone with her I had to struggle, sometimes, to make conversation, and you know perfectly well that, if pressed, I can talk the hind legs off a donkey. But pauses would fall, and they were silences that were not companionable. And I would try to fill those silences in, stitching furiously at my tapestry." She looked across at Archie. "Does that sound ridiculous, or do you understand what I'm trying to say?"

"Yes, I do understand. I hardly knew Caroline, but the few times I met her I always felt my hands and my feet were too big."

But even this mild attempt at levity did not raise a smile with Violet, preoccupied as she was with Alexa's problems. She fell silent, brooding about her granddaughter.

By now they had climbed half-way up the hill that led to Croy and were approaching the turning for Pennyburn. There were no gates, simply an opening that broke the fence to the left of the road. The Land Rover turned into this, and Archie drove the hundred yards or so along a neatly Tarmacked lane bordered on either side by mown grass verges and a trimly clipped beech hedge. At the end of this the lane opened up into a sizable yard, with the small white house on one side and a double garage on the other. The doors of this were open, revealing Violet's car, and, as well, her wheelbarrow and lawn-mower and a plethora of garden tools. Between the garage and the beech hedge was her drying-green. She had done a wash this morning, and a line of laundry stirred in the rising breeze. Wooden tubs, planted with hydrangeas the colour of pink blotting paper, flanked the entrance to the house, and a hedge of lavender grew close to its walls.

Archie drew up and switched off the engine, but Violet made no move to alight. Having started this discussion, she had no wish to end it before it was finished.

"So I don't really believe that losing her mother in that tragic way is the root cause of Alexa's lack of confidence. Nor the fact that Edmund married again and presented her with a stepmother. Nobody could have been sweeter or more understanding than Virginia, and the arrival of Henry brought nothing but joy. Not a hint of sibling rivalry." The mention of Henry's name reminded Violet of yet another tiresome worry. "And now I'm fretting about Henry. Because I'm afraid that Edmund is going to insist on sending him to Templehall as a boarder. And I think he's not ready for that yet. And if he does go, I'm anxious for Virginia, because her life *is* Henry, and if he is torn away from her against her will, I'm afraid that she and Edmund might drift apart. He is away so much. Sometimes in Edinburgh for the entire week, sometimes on the other side of the world. It's not good for a marriage."

"But when Virginia married Edmund, she knew how it would be. Don't get too worked up about it, Vi. Templehall's a good school, and Colin Henderson's a sympathetic headmaster. I've got great faith in the place. Hamish has loved it there, enjoyed every moment."

"Yes, but your Hamish is very different from Henry. At eight years old, Hamish was quite capable of taking care of himself."

"Yes." Archie, not without pride, had to admit this. "He's a tough little bugger."

Violet was visited by another dreadful thought. "Archie, they don't hit the little boys, do they? They don't beat them?"

"Heavens, no. The worst punishment is to be sent to sit on the wooden chair in the hall.

For some reason this puts the fear of God into the most recalcitrant infant."

"Well, I suppose that's something to be thankful for. So barbaric to beat little children. And so stupid. Getting hit by someone you dislike can only fill you with hatred and fear. Being sent to sit on a hard chair by a man you respect and even like is infinitely more sensible."

"Hamish spent most of his first year sitting on it."

"Wicked boy. Oh dear, it doesn't bear thinking about. And Edie doesn't bear thinking about either. Now I've got Edie to worry over, saddling herself with that dreadful lunatic cousin. We've all depended on Edie for so long, we forgot that she's no longer young. I just hope it's not all going to be too much for her."

"Well, it hasn't happened yet. Maybe it'll never happen."

"We can scarcely wish poor Lottie Carstairs dead, which seems the only alternative."

She looked at Archie and saw, somewhat to her surprise, that he was near to laughter.

"You know something, Vi? You're depressing me."

"Oh, I am sorry." She struck him a friendly blow on the knee. "What a miserable old gasbag I am. Take no notice. Tell me, what news of Lucilla?"

"Last heard of, roosting in some Paris garret."

"They always say that children are a joy. But at times they can be the most appalling headaches. Now, I must let you get home and not keep you chattering. Isobel will be waiting for you."

"You wouldn't like to come back to Croy and have more tea?" He sounded wistful. "Help amuse the Americans?"

Violet's heart sank at the prospect. "Archie, I don't think I feel quite up to doing that. Am I being selfish?"

"Not a bit. Just a thought. Sometimes I find all this barking and wagging tails daunting. But it's nothing compared with what poor Isobel has to do."

"It must be the most dreadfully hard work. All that fetching and carrying and cooking and table-laying and bed-making. And then having to make conversation. I know it's only for two nights each week, but couldn't you chuck your hands in and think of some other way to make money?"

"Can you?"

"Not immediately. But I wish things could be different for you both. I know one can't put the clock back, but sometimes I think how nice it would be if nothing had changed at Croy. If your precious parents could still be alive, and all of you young again. Coming and going, and cars buzzing up and down the drive, and voices. And laughter."

She turned to Archie, but his face was averted. He gazed out over her washing-green, as though Violet's tea-towels and pillowcases and her sturdy brassieres and silk knickers were the most absorbing sight in the world.

She thought, *And you and Edmund the closest of friends,* but she did not say this.

"And Pandora there. That naughty, darling child. I always felt that when she left she took so much of the laughter with her."

Archie stayed silent. And then he said "Yes," and nothing more.

A small constraint lay between them. To fill it, Violet busied herself, gathering up her

belongings. "I mustn't keep you any longer."
She opened the door and clambered down
from the bulky old vehicle.

"Thank you for the ride, Archie."

"A pleasure, Vi."

"Love to Isobel."

"Of course. See you soon."

She waited while he turned the Land
Rover, and watched him drive away, along
the lane, and on up the hill. She felt guilty,
because she should have gone with him, and
drunk tea with Isobel, and made polite chat
to the unknown Americans. But too late
now, because he was gone. She searched in
her handbag for her key and let herself into
her house.

Alone, Archie continued on his way. The
road grew steeper. Now there were trees
ahead, Scots pine and tall beeches. Beyond
and above these, the face of the hillside
thrust skywards, cliffs of rock and scree,
sprouting tufts of whin and bracken and determined saplings of silver birch. He reached

the trees; and the road, having climbed as high as it could, swept around to the left and levelled out. Ahead, the beech avenue led the way to the house. A burn tumbled down from the hilltops in a series of pools and waterfalls and flowed on down the hill under an arched stone bridge. This stream was Pennyburn, and lower down the slope it made its way through the garden of Violet Aird's house.

Beneath the beeches all was shaded, the light diffused, limpid and greenish. The leafy branches arched thickly overhead, and it felt a little like driving down the centre aisle of some enormous cathedral. And then, abruptly, the avenue fell behind him and the house came into view, set four-square on the brow of the hill, with the whole panoramic vista of the glen spread out at its feet. The evening breeze had done its work, tearing the clouds to tatters, lifting the mist. The distant hills, the peaceful acres of farmland were washed in golden sunlight.

All at once, it became essential to have a moment or two to himself. This was selfish. He was already late, and Isobel was waiting for him, in need of his moral support. But he pushed guilt out of his mind, drew up out of earshot of the house, and switched off the engine.

It was very quiet, just the sough of the wind in the trees, the cry of curlews. He listened to the silence, from some distant field heard the bleat of sheep. And Violet's voice: *All of you young again. Coming and going . . . And Pandora there . . .*

She shouldn't have said that. He did not want his memories stirred. He did not wish to be consumed by this yearning nostalgia.

All of you young again.

He thought about Croy the way it had once been. He thought about coming home as a schoolboy, as a young soldier on leave. Roaring up the hill in his supercharged sports car with the roof down and the wind burning his cheeks. Knowing, with all the confidence of youth, that all would be just as he had left it. Drawing up with a screech of brakes at the front of the house; the family dogs spilling out of the open door, barking, coming to greet him, and their clamour alerting the household, so that by the time he was indoors, they were all converging. His mother and father, Harris the butler, and

Mrs. Harris the cook, and any other housemaid or daily lady who happened to be helping out at the time.

"Archie. Oh, darling, welcome home."

And then, Pandora. *I always felt that when
she left she took so much of the laughter with
her.* His young sister. In memory, she was
about thirteen and already beautiful. He saw
her flying, long-legged, down the stairs, to
leap into his waiting embrace. He saw her,
with her full, curving mouth and her woman's provocative, slanting eyes. He felt the
lightness of her body as he swung her
around, off her feet. He heard her voice.

"You're back, you brute, and you've got a
new car. I saw it out of the nursery window.
Take me for a ride, Archie. Let's go a hundred miles an hour."

Pandora. He found himself smiling. Always, even as a child, she had been a life-
enhancer, an injector of vitality and laughter
to the most stuffy of occasions. Where she
had sprung from he had never quite worked
out. She was a Blair born and bred, yet so
different in every way from the rest of them
that she might have been a changeling.

He remembered her as a baby, as a little

girl, as that delicious leggy teenager, for she had never suffered from puppy fat, spots, or lack of confidence. At sixteen, she looked twenty. Every friend he brought to the house had been, if not in love with her, then certainly mesmerized.

Life had hummed with activity for the young Blairs. House parties, shooting parties, tennis in the summer, August picnics on the sunlit, purple-heathered hills. He recalled one picnic when Pandora, complaining of the heat, had stripped off all her clothes and plunged naked, with no thought for astonished spectators, into the loch. He remembered dances, and Pandora in a white chiffon dress, with her brown shoulders bare, whirling from man to man through Strip the Willow and The Duke of Perth.

She was gone. Had been gone for over twenty years. At eighteen, a few months after Archie's wedding, she had eloped with an American, some other woman's husband, whom she had met in Scotland during the summer. With this man she flew to California, and in the fullness of time became his wife. Waves of shock and horror reverberated around the county, but the Balmerinos were

so loved and respected that they were treated
with much sympathy and understanding.
Perhaps, said people hopefully, she will come
back. But Pandora did not come back. She
did not return even for her parents' funerals.
Instead, as though engaged in an endless
Strip the Willow, she flung herself, wayward
as always, from one disastrous love affair to
another. Divorced from her American husband, she moved to New York, and later to
France, where she lived for some years in
Paris. She kept in touch with Archie by
means of rare and sporadic postcards, sending a scrawled address, a scrap of information, and a huge straggling cross for a kiss.
Now she seemed to have ended up in a villa
in Majorca. God knew who was her current
companion.

Long since, Archie and Isobel had de-
spaired of her, and yet, from time to time, he
found himself missing her more than anybody else. For youth was over, and his father's household dispersed. Harris and Mrs.
Harris had long retired, and domestic help
was reduced to Agnes Cooper who, two days
a week, climbed the hill from the village to
give Isobel a hand in the kitchen.

As for the estate, matters were hardly better. Gordon Gillock, the keeper, was still in situ in his small stone house with the kennels at the back, but the grouse moor was let to a syndicate, and Edmund Aird paid the keeper's salary. The farm, as well, had gone, and the parkland was ploughed for crops. The old gardener—a weathered stick of a man and an important part of Archie's childhood —had finally died, and not been replaced. His precious walled garden was put down to grass; unpruned, the rhododendrons grew massive, and the hard tennis court was green with moss. Archie now was officially the gardener, with the sporadic assistance of Willy Snoddy, who lived in a grubby cottage at the end of the village, trapped rabbits and poached salmon, and was pleased from time to time to earn a little drinking money.

And he himself? Archie took stock. An ex-Lieutenant-Colonel in the Queen's Loyal Highlanders, invalided out with a tin leg, a sixty-per-cent disability pension, and too many nightmares. But still, thanks to Isobel, in possession of his inheritance. Croy was still his and would, God willing, belong to

Hamish. Crippled, struggling to make ends meet, he was still Balmerino of Croy.

Suddenly, it was funny. Balmerino of Croy. Such a fine-sounding title, and such a ludicrous situation. It was no good trying to work out why everything had gone so wrong because there was nothing much he could do about it anyway. No more harking back. Duty called and the Lady Balmerino waited.

For some obscure reason he felt more cheerful. He started up the engine and drove the short distance across the gravel to the front of the house.

5

IT HAD DRIZZLED MOST OF THE DAY but now it was fine, so after his tea Henry went out into Edie's garden with her. This ran down to the river, and her washing line was strung between two apple trees. He helped her to unpeg the washing and put it into the wicker basket, and they folded the sheets together with a snap and a crack to get all the creases out of them. With this accomplished, they went back into the house and Edie set up the ironing board and began ironing her pillowcases and her pinafore and a blouse. Henry watched, liking the smell and the way the hot iron made the crunchy damp linen all smooth and shiny and crisp.

He said, "You're very good at ironing."

"I'd need to be after all these years at it."

"How many years, Edie?"

"Well . . ." She dumped the iron down

on its end and folded the pillowcase with her dimpled red hands. "I'm sixty-eight now, and I was eighteen when I first went to work for Mrs. Aird. Work that one out."

Even Henry could do that sum. "Fifty years."

"Fifty years is a long way to look ahead, but looking back it doesn't seem any time at all. Makes you wonder what life's all about."

"Tell me about Alexa and London." Henry had never been to London, but Edie had lived there once.

"Oh, Henry, I've told you these stories a thousand times."

"I like to hear them *again.*"

"Well . . ." She pressed a crease, sharp as a knife edge. "When your daddy was much younger, he was married to a lady called Caroline. They were married in London, at St. Margaret's, Westminster, and we all went down for the occasion, and stayed at a hotel called the Berkeley. And what a wedding that was! Ten lovely bridesmaids, all in white dresses, like a flock of swans. And after the wedding we all went to another very grand hotel called the Ritz, and there were waiters in tailcoats and so grand you've have thought they were wedding guests themselves. And there was champagne and such a spread of food you didn't know where to start."

"Were there jellies?"

"Jellies in every colour. Yellow and red and green. And there was cold salmon and wee sandwiches you could eat with your fingers, and frosted grapes all sparkling with sugar. And Caroline wore a dress of wild silk with a great long train, and on her head was a diamond tiara that her father had given her for a wedding present, and she looked like a queen."

"Was she pretty?"

"Oh, Henry, all brides are beautiful."

"Was she as pretty as my mother?"

But Edie was not to be drawn. "She was good-looking in a different sort of way. Very tall, she was, with lovely black hair."

"Did you like her?"

"Of course I liked her. I wouldn't have gone to London to look after Alexa if I hadn't liked her."

"Tell me about that bit."

Edie set aside her pillowcases and started in on a blue-and-white-checked table-cloth.

"Well, it was just after your Grandfather

Geordie died. I was still living at Balnaid, and working for your Granny Vi. It was just the two of us in the house, keeping each other company. We knew that Alexa was on the way, because Edmund had come up for his father's funeral and he told us then. 'Caroline is having a baby,' he told us, and it was a wonderful comfort to your Granny Vi to know that even if Geordie was with her no longer, there was a new wee life on the way. And then we heard that Caroline was looking for a Nanny to take care of the bairn. Your Granny Vi was up to high doh. The truth of the matter was that she couldn't bide the thought of some uninformed bisom having the care of her grandchild, filling her wee head with all the wrong ideas, and not taking the time to talk to the child, nor read to her. I never thought about going until your Granny Vi asked me to. I didn't want to leave Balnaid and Strathcroy. But . . . we talked it over and in the end decided that there was nothing else to be done. So I went to London. . . ."

"I bet Daddy was pleased to see you."

"Och, yes, he was pleased enough. And at the end of the day, it was a mercy I went.

Alexa was born safe and sound, but after the baby arrived, Caroline became very, very ill."

"Did she have measles?"

"No, it wasn't measles."

"Whooping cough?"

"No. It wasn't that sort of illness. It was more nervous. Post-natal depression they call it, and it's a horrible thing to see. She had to go to hospital for treatment, and when she was allowed home she was really not good for anything, let alone take care of a baby. But eventually she recovered a wee bit and her mother, Lady Cheriton, took her off on a cruise to a lovely island called Madeira. And after a month or two there, she was better again."

"Were you left all alone in London?"

"Not *all* alone. There was a nice lady who came in every day to clean the house, and then your father was in and out."

"Why didn't you come back to Scotland and stay with Vi?"

"There was a time when we thought we might. Just for a visit. It was the week of Lord and Lady Balmerino's wedding . . . only then of course he was Archie Blair, and such a handsome young officer. Caroline was still in Madeira and Edmund said we'd all come north together for the occasion and stay at Balnaid. Your Granny Vi was so excited when she heard the news that we were coming to visit. She got the cot down from the attic and washed the baby blankets and dusted up the old pram. And then Alexa started teething . . . she was only a wee thing and what a time she had of it. Crying all night and not a mortal thing I could do to quieten her. I think I went two weeks without a proper night's sleep, and in the end Edmund said he thought the long journey north would be too much for the pair of us. He was right, of course, but I could have cried from disappointment."

"And Vi must have been disappointed too."

"Yes, I think she was."

"Did Daddy come to the wedding?"

"Oh, yes, he came. He and Archie were old, old friends. He had to be there. But he came on his own."

She had finished the table-cloth. Now she was onto her best blouse, easing the point of the iron into the gathered bit on the shoulder. That looked even more difficult than ironing pillowcases.

"Tell me about the house in London."

"Oh, Henry, do you not weary of all these old tales?"

"I like hearing about the house."

"All right. It was in Kensington, in a row. Very tall and thin, and what a work. The kitchens in the basement and the nurseries right up at the top of the house. It seemed to me that I never stopped climbing stairs. But it was a beautiful house, filled with precious things. And there was always something going on—people calling, or dinner parties, and guests arriving through the front door in their fine clothes. Alexa and I used to sit on the turn of the stairs and watch it all through the bannisters."

"But nobody saw you."

"No. Nobody saw us. It was like playing hide-and-seek."

"And you used to go to Buckingham Palace . . ."

"Yes, to watch the Changing of the Guard. And sometimes we took a taxi to Regent's Park Zoo and looked at the lions. And when Alexa was old enough, I walked her to school and dancing class. Some of the other children were little Lords and Ladies, and what a toffee-nosed lot *their* Nannies were!"

Little Lords and Ladies and a house filled with precious things. Edie, Henry decided, had had some marvellous experiences. "Were you sad to leave London?"

"Oh, Henry, I was sad because it was a sad time, and the reason for leaving was so sad. A terrible tragedy. Just think, one man driving his car far too fast and without thinking of any other body on the road, and in a single instant Edmund had lost his wife and Alexa her mother. And poor Lady Cheriton her only child, her only daughter. Dead."

Dead. It was a terrible word. Like the snap of a pair of scissors cutting a piece of string in two and knowing that you could never, ever put the piece of string together again.

"Did Alexa mind?"

" 'Mind' is not the word for such a time of bereavement."

"But it meant that you could come back to Scotland."

"Yes." Edie sighed and folded her blouse. "Yes, we came back. We all did. Your father to work in Edinburgh and Alexa and I to live at Balnaid. And things gradually got better. Grief is a funny thing because you don't have to carry it with you for the rest of your life. After a bit you set it down by the roadside and walk on and leave it resting there. As for Alexa, it was a new life. She went to Strathcroy Primary, just as you do, and made friends with all the village children. And your Granny Vi gave her a bicycle and a wee Shetland pony. Before very long you'd never have known she ever lived in London. And yet every holiday, when she was old enough to travel on her own, back she went to stay a little while with Lady Cheriton. It was the least we could do for the poor lady."

Her ironing was finished. She turned off the iron and set it in the grate to cool, and then folded up her ironing board. But Henry did not want to stop this fascinating conversation.

"Before Alexa, you looked after Daddy, didn't you?"

"That's what I did. Right up to the day when he was eight years old and went away to boarding-school."

Henry said, "I don't want to go to boarding-school."

"Oh, come away." Edie's voice turned brisk. She was not about to have any teary nonsense. "And why not? Lots of other boys your own age, and football and cricket and high jinks."

"I won't know anybody. I won't have a friend. And I shan't be able to take Moo with me."

Edie knew all about Moo. Moo was a piece of satin and wool, remains of Henry's cot blanket. It lived under his pillow and helped him to get to sleep at nights. Without Moo he would not sleep. Moo was very important to him.

"No," she admitted. "You won't be able to take Moo, that's for certain. But nobody would object if you took a teddy."

"Teddies don't work. And Hamish Blair says only babies take teddies."

"Hamish Blair talks a lot of nonsense."

"And you won't be there to give me my dinner."

Edie stopped being brisk. She put out a hand and ruffled his hair. "Wee man. We all have to grow up, move on. The world would come to a standstill if we all stayed in the same place. Now"—she looked at her clock

—"it's time you were away home. I promised your mother you'd be back by six. Will you be all right on your own, or do you want me to come a bit of the way with you?"

"No," he told her. "I'll be all right on my own."

❧ 6 ❧

EDMUND AIRD WAS NEARLY FORTY when he married for the second time, and his new wife Virginia was twenty-three. She hailed not from Scotland but from Devon, the daughter of an officer in the Devon and Dorset Regiment who had retired from the Army in order to run an inherited farm, a considerable spread of land between Dartmoor and the sea. She had been brought up in Devon, but her mother was American, and every summer she and Virginia crossed the Atlantic in order to spend the hot months of July and August in her old family home. This was in Leesport on the south shore of Long Island, a village facing out over the blue waters of the Great South Bay to the dunes of Fire Island.

The grandparents' house was old, clapboard, large and airy. Sea breezes blew through it, stirring filmy curtains and bringing indoors the scents of the garden. This garden was spacious and separated from the quiet, tree-shaded street by a white picket fence. There were decks furnished for outdoor living, and wide porches screened for coolness and sanctuary from bugs. But its greatest charm was that it adjoined the country club, that hub of social activity with its restaurants and bars, golf course, tennis courts, and enormous turquoise swimming pool.

It was a world away from damp and misty Devon, and the annual experience gave the young Virginia a polish and sophistication that set her apart from her English contemporaries. Her clothes, purchased during mammoth Fifth Avenue shopping sprees, were both sleek and trendy. Her voice held a trace of her mother's charming drawl, and returning to school with her groomed blonde head and her long, slender American legs, she was a source of much wonder and admiration and, inevitably, on the receiving end of a good deal of malicious envy.

Early on she learned to cope with this.

Not particularly scholastic, her passion was the open air and any sort of outdoor activity. In Long Island she played tennis, sailed, and swam. In Devon she rode, hunting every winter with the local foxhounds. As she grew up, young men flocked to her side, pole-axed by the sight of her in hunting gear astride some enviable horse, or flying expertly about the tennis court in a white skirt that barely covered her bottom. At Christmas dances they clustered like bees around the proverbial honey-pot. When she was home, the telephone constantly rang, was constantly for her. Her father complained but secretly he was proud. In time, he stopped complaining, and installed a second telephone.

Leaving school, she went to London and learned to work an electric typewriter. This was extremely dull, but as she had no particular talent nor ambition, it seemed to be the only thing to do. She shared a flat in Fulham and did temporary jobs, because that way she was free to come and go whenever a pleasant invitation came her way. The men were still there but now they were different men: older, richer, and sometimes married to other women. She allowed them to spend enormous sums of money on her, take her out to dinner and give her expensive presents. And then, when they were at their wit's end with unrequited lust and devotion, she would without warning disappear from London—to spend another blissful summer with her grandparents, or head for a house party in Ibiza, or a yacht on the west coast of Scotland, or Christmas in Devon.

On one of these impetuous jaunts she had met Edmund Aird. It was September and at a house party in Relkirkshire for the Hunt Ball, where she was staying with the family of a girl with whom she had been at school. Before the ball, there was a lavish dinner party and all the guests—those staying in the house and others who had been invited— gathered in the great library.

Virginia was the last to make her entrance. She wore a dress of so pale a green that it was almost white, strapless but caught over one shoulder by a spray of ivy, the dark leaves fashioned of gleaming satin.

She saw him instantly. He was standing

with his back to the fireplace, and he was tall. Across the room their eyes met and held. He had black hair streaked with white, like silver-fox fur. She was accustomed to men in all the peacock glory of Highland dress but she had never seen one who looked so easy and so well in his finery, the diced hose and the kilt, and the sombre bottle-green jacket sparked with silver buttons.

". . . Virginia dear, there you are." This was her hostess. "Now who do you know and who do you not know?" Unknown faces, new names. She scarcely heard them spoken. Finally, ". . . and this is Edmund Aird. Edmund, this is Virginia, who is staying with us. All the way from Devon. And you mustn't talk to her now because I've put you next to each other at dinner, and you can talk to her then. . . ."

She had never before fallen so instantly and totally in love. There had, of course, been affairs, mad infatuations in the high old days of the Leesport Country Club, but never anything that lasted longer than a few weeks. That evening was very different, and Virginia knew, without question, that she had met the only man with whom she had ever wanted to share the rest of her life. It did not take very long to realize that the incredible miracle was actually happening and that Edmund felt exactly the same way about her.

The world became brilliant and beautiful. Nothing could go wrong. Dazzled by happiness, she was ready to throw in her lot with Edmund, abandon all common sense and any tiresome principle. Give him her life. Live in the back of beyond if necessary; on the top of a mountain; in blatant sin. It didn't matter. Nothing mattered.

But Edmund, having lost his heart, kept a tight rein on his head. He went to some lengths to explain his position. He was, after all, head of the Scottish branch of Sanford Cubben, a man of some prominence and very much in the eye of the media. Edinburgh was a small city, and he had many friends and business colleagues, and their respect and trust he valued. To step too blatantly out of line and end up with his name plastered over the gossip columns of the tabloid newspapers would be not only foolish but possibly disastrous.

As well, he had to consider his family. "Family?"

"Yes, family. I have been married before."

"I should think it very strange if you hadn't been."

"My wife was killed in a car accident. But I have Alexa. She's ten. She lives with my mother in Strathcroy."

"I like little girls. I would be very careful of her."

But there were still other hurdles to be faced.

"Virginia, I'm seventeen years older than you. Does forty seem so very decrepit?"

"Years don't matter."

"It would mean your living in the wilds of Relkirkshire."

"I shall drape myself in tartan and wear a hat with a feather."

He laughed, but wryly. "Unfortunately, it's not September all the year round. All our friends live miles apart and the winters are long and dark. Everybody hibernates. I am so afraid that you would find it very dull."

"Edmund, it sounds a little as though you're having second thoughts and are trying to put me off."

"It's not that. Never that. But you have to

know all the truths. No illusions. You are so young, and so beautiful, and so vital, and you have all of life in front of you. . . ."

"To be with you."

"That's another thing. My job. It's demanding. I'm away so much. Abroad so often, sometimes for two or three weeks at a time."

"But you'll come back to me."

She was adamant, and he adored her. He sighed. "I wish for both our sakes that it could be different. I wish that I were young again, and without responsibilities. Free to behave any way I wanted. Then we could live together and have time to get to know each other. And be totally sure."

"I am totally sure."

She was. Undeviating. He took her in his arms and said, "Then there's nothing for it. I shall have to marry you."

"You poor man."

"You will be happy? I want so much to make you happy."

"Oh, Edmund. Darling Edmund. How could I be anything else?"

They were married two months later, at

the end of November, in Devon. It was a quiet wedding in the tiny church where Virginia had been christened.

The end of her beginning. No regrets. The casual, indiscriminate affairs were over and she let them go without a backward glance. She was Mrs. Edmund Aird.

After their honeymoon they travelled north to Balnaid, Virginia's new home, and her new and ready-made family: Violet, Edie, and Alexa. Life in Scotland was a new and very different experience from anything that Virginia had previously known, but she made every effort to adjust, if only because others, very obviously, were doing the same thing. Violet had already moved firmly out and gone to Pennyburn. She proved a mistress of non-interference. Edie was equally tactful. The time had come, she announced, for her to leave as well and settle herself in the cottage in the village where she had been brought up and which she had inherited from her mother. She was retiring from resident work but instead would continue on a daily basis, sharing her time between Virginia and Violet.

Edie was, in those early days, a tower of strength, a source of excellent advice, and a fund of cosy gossip. It was she who, for Alexa's sake, filled in for Virginia some details of Edmund's previous marriage, but once this was done, never mentioned it again. It was over, finished. Water under the bridge. Virginia was grateful. Edie, the old servant who had seen and heard everything, could well have proved to be the fly in the ointment. Instead she became one of Virginia's closest friends.

Alexa took a little longer. Sweet-natured and self-contained, she was inclined to be shy and withdrawn. She was not a beautiful child, with a dumpy shape and pale-red hair and the white skin that goes with this colouring, and was at first uncertain of her position in the family, yet almost touchingly anxious to please. Virginia responded to the best of her ability. This little girl was, after all, Edmund's child and an important part of their marriage. She could never be a mother, but she could be a sister. Unobtrusively, she eased Alexa out of her shell, speaking to her as though they were the same age, taking much care not to tread on any tender toes. She showed interest in Alexa's ploys, her drawing and her dolls, and included her in every possible activity and occasion. This was not always convenient, but the most important thing was that Alexa should never feel abandoned.

It took about six months, but it was worth it. She was rewarded by Alexa's spontaneous confidences, and a touching admiration and devotion.

So there was family, but there were friends too. Liking her for her youth, for their affection for Edmund, for the fact that Edmund had chosen to marry her, they made her welcome. The Balmerinos, of course, but others too. Virginia was a gregarious girl who did not relish solitude and found herself surrounded by people who seemed to want her. When Edmund was away on business, which he was right from the start, more often than not, everybody was enormously kind and attentive, asking her out on her own, constantly phoning to be certain that she was neither lonely nor unhappy.

Which she was not. Secretly she almost relished Edmund's absences because, in some strange way, they enhanced everything; he was gone but she knew that he was coming back to her, and each time he came back, being married to him was even better than before. Occupied with Alexa, with her new house, and her new friends, she filled in the empty days and counted the hours until Edmund should return to her. From Hong Kong. From Frankfurt. Once he had taken her with him to New York, and afterwards had indulged in a week's leave. They had spent it at Leesport, and she remembered that time as one of the best in the whole of her life.

And then, Henry.

Henry changed everything, not for the worse, but for the better, if that was possible. After Henry, she didn't want to go away any more. She had never imagined herself capable of such selfless love. It was different from loving Edmund, but all the more precious because it was utterly unexpected. She had never thought of herself as maternal, and never analyzed the true meaning of the word. But this tiny human being, this little life reduced her to wordless wonder.

They all teased her, but she didn't mind. She shared him with Violet and Edie and Alexa, and relished in the sharing because, at the end of the day, Henry belonged to her. She watched him grow and savoured every moment of his progress. He stumbled and walked and spoke words, and she was enchanted. She played with him, drew pictures, watched Alexa push him in her old doll's pram across the lawn. They lay in the grass and watched ants, walked down to the river and threw pebbles into the swift-flowing brown stream. They sat by winter fires and read picture books.

He was two. He was three. He was five years old. She took him to his first day at the Strathcroy Primary School and stood at the gate watching him walk away from her up the path to the school-house door. There were children everywhere but none of them took any notice of him. He seemed, at that moment, especially small and very vulnerable, and she could scarcely bear to see him go.

Three years later, he was still small and vulnerable, and she felt more protective of him than ever. And this was the cause of the cloud that had gathered and now lay on the edge of her own personal horizon. She was afraid of it.

From time to time the subject of Henry's future had come up, but she had shied from discussing it through with Edmund. He knew, however, her opinion. Lately, nothing had been said. She was happy to leave it this way, on the principle that it was best to leave a sleeping tiger to lie. She did not want to have to fight Edmund. She had never stood up to him before because she had always been happy to leave important decisions to him. He was, after all, older, wiser, and infinitely more competent. But this was different. This was Henry.

Perhaps, if she did not look, if she paid no attention, the problem would go away.

When Archie and Violet had left, trundling away down the drive in the battered old

Land Rover, Virginia stayed where she was, in front of the house, feeling unsatisfactorily aimless and at a loss for something to do. The church meeting had broken the day in half, and yet it was too early to go indoors and start thinking about dinner. The weather was improving by the moment, and the sun was about to appear. Perhaps she should attempt a little gardening. She considered this idea and then rejected it. In the end she went into the house, gathered up the tea-mugs from the dining-room table and carried them through to the kitchen. Edmund's spaniels were dozing in their baskets under the table. As soon as they heard her footsteps, however, they were awake, on their feet and anxious for exercise.

"I'll just put these in the dishwasher," she told them, "and then we'll go out for a bit." She always talked aloud to the dogs, and sometimes, like right now, it was comforting to hear the sound of her own voice. Mad old people talked to themselves. At times it was not difficult to understand why.

In the back kitchen, with the dogs milling around her, she took an old jacket off a hook and pushed her feet into rubber boots. Then they set off, the dogs racing ahead, down the wooded lane that ran along the south bank of the river. Two miles upstream another bridge crossed the water, leading back to the main road, and so to the village. But she left this behind her and walked on to where the trees stopped and the moor began, untrammelled miles of heather and grass and bracken, leaning up into the hills. Far away, the sheep grazed. There was only the sound of flowing water.

She came to the dam, the river sliding over its rim, the deep pool beyond. This was Henry's favourite swimming place. She sat on the bank where, in summer, they brought picnics. The dogs loved the river. They stood now knee-deep, and drank as though they had not seen water for months. When they had done this, they came out and shook themselves lustily all over her. The afternoon sun felt warm. She pulled off her jacket and would have sat on, revelling in the sun's warmth, but inevitably the midges appeared in droves and started biting, so she got to her feet, whistled the dogs, and went home.

She was in the kitchen preparing dinner when Edmund returned. They were having

roast chicken and she was grating breadcrumbs for bread sauce. She heard the car,
looked with surprise at the clock, and saw
that it was only half past five. He was very
early. Driving from Edinburgh, he did not
usually arrive back at Balnaid until seven or
even later. What could have happened?

Speculating, hoping there was nothing
wrong, she finished the breadcrumbs and
dumped them into the saucepan with the
milk and the onion and the cloves. She
stirred. She heard his footsteps coming down
the long passage from the hall. The door
opened and she turned, smiling but faintly
anxious.

"I'm back," he announced unnecessarily.

Her husband's masculine appearance, as
always, filled Virginia with satisfaction. He
wore a navy-blue chalk-striped suit, a light-
blue shirt with a white collar, and a Christian
Dior silk tie that she had given him for
Christmas. He carried his brief-case and
looked a bit creased, as well he might after a
day's work and a long drive, but not in the
least weary. He never looked weary and he
never complained of feeling tired. His mother
swore he had never been tired in his life.

He was tall, his figure youthful as it had ever been, and his handsome face, with the quiet, hooded eyes, hardly lined. Only his hair had changed. Once so black, it was now silvery-white but thick and smooth as ever. For some reason the ageless face, in juxtaposition to that white hair, rendered him more distinguished and attractive than ever.

She said, "Why so early?"

"Reasons. I'll explain." He came to kiss her; looked at the saucepan. "Good smells. Bread sauce. Roast chicken?"

"Of course."

He dumped his brief-case on the kitchen table. "Where's Henry?"

"With Edie. He won't be back till after six. She's given him his tea."

"Good."

She frowned. "Why good?"

"I want to talk to you. Let's go into the library. Leave the sauce, you can cook it later. . . ."

He was already on his way out of the kitchen. Puzzled and apprehensive, Virginia put the saucepan aside and replaced the big lid on the hob. Then she followed him. She found him in the library, crouched by the fireplace, setting a match to the newspaper and kindling.

She felt faintly defensive, as though this were some sort of criticism. "Edmund, I was going to light the fire when I'd got the sauce made and the potatoes peeled. But it's a funny sort of day. We spent all afternoon in the dining-room, having the church meeting. We never came in here. . . ."

"Doesn't matter."

The paper had caught, the kindling snapped and crackled. He straightened, dusting his hands, and stood watching the rising flames. His profile gave nothing away.

"We're going to have this sale in July." She sat on the arm of one of the chairs. "I've got the worst job of all, collecting jumble. And Archie wanted some envelope from the Forestry Commission . . . he said you knew about it. We found it in your desk."

"Yes. That's right. I meant to give it to you."

". . . oh, and something frightfully exciting. The Steyntons are going to have a dance, for Katy, in September. . . ."

"I know."

"You know?"

"I had lunch with Angus Steynton in the New Club today. He told me then."

"They're going the whole hog. Marquees and bands and caterers and everything. I'm going to get a really sensational dress. . . ."

He turned his head and looked at her, and her chatter died. She wondered if he had even been listening. After a little, she asked, "What is it?"

He said, "I'm home early because I haven't been in the office this afternoon. I drove down to Templehall. I've been with Colin Henderson."

Templehall. Colin Henderson. She felt her heart drop into her stomach and her mouth was suddenly dry. "Why, Edmund?"

"I wanted to talk things over. I hadn't made up my mind about Henry, but now I feel sure it's the right thing to do."

"What is the right thing to do?"

"To send him there in September."

"As a boarder?"

"He could scarcely attend as a day-boy."

Apprehension by now had gone, overwhelmed by a slow, consuming anger. She had never experienced anger like this against Edmund. As well, she was shocked. She had

known him to be overbearing, even dictato-
rial, but never underhanded. Now, behind
her back, it seemed that he had betrayed her.
She felt betrayed, without defences, de-
stroyed before she had even time to fire a
single gun.

"You had no right." Her own voice, but it
did not sound like Virginia. "Edmund. You
had *no* right."

He raised his eyebrows. "No right?"

"No right to go without me. No right to go
without telling me. I should have been there,
to talk things over, as you put it. Henry is my
child just as much as he is yours. How dare
you sneak off and organize everything behind
my back, without saying a single word!"

"I didn't sneak off and I'm telling you
now."

"Yes. As a fait accompli. I don't like being
treated as a person who doesn't matter,
someone who has no say. Why should *you*
always make all the decisions?"

"I suppose because I always have."

"You were underhanded." She rose to her
feet, her arms folded tightly across her
breast, as though the only way to stop them
from actually striking her husband was to

keep them under control. Always so compliant, she was a tigress now, fighting for her cub. "You know, you've always known, that I don't want Henry to go to Templehall. He's too little. He's too young. I know you went when you were eight to boarding-school, and I know that Hamish Blair is there, but why should it have to be a rigid tradition that we all have to follow? It's archaic, Victorian, out of date, to send little children away from home. And what is worse is that it doesn't have to happen. Henry can perfectly well stay at Strathcroy until he's twelve. And then he can go to boarding-school. That's reasonable. But not before, Edmund. *Not now.*"

He gazed at her in genuine perplexity. "Why do you want to make Henry different from other boys? Why should he be marked out as an oddity, staying at home until he's twelve? Perhaps you're confusing him with American children who seem to rule the family household until they're practically adult. . . ."

Virginia was incensed. "It's nothing to do with America. How can you say such a thing? It's to do with what any sensible, normal mother feels about her children. It's you who are on the wrong tack, Edmund. But you won't ever consider the possibility that you might be wrong. You're behaving like a Victorian. Old-fashioned and pigheaded and chauvinistic."

She got no reaction from this outburst. Edmund's expression did not change. On such occasions, his was a poker-face, with sleepy eyes and an unsmiling mouth. She found herself longing for him to behave naturally, let himself go, lose his temper, raise his voice. But that was not Edmund Aird's way. In business, he was known as a cold fish. He stayed unmoved, controlled, unprovoked.

He said, "You are thinking only of yourself."

"I'm thinking of *Henry*."

"No. You want to keep him. And you want your own way. Life has been kind to you. You've always had your own way; spoiled and indulged by your parents. And perhaps I continued where they left off. But there comes a time when we all have to grow up. I suggest that you grow up now. Henry is not your possession and you must let him go."

She could scarcely believe that he was saying these things to her.

"I *don't* think of Henry as a possession. That is the most insulting accusation. He's a person in his own right, and I've made him that person. But he's eight years old. Scarcely out of the nursery. He needs his home. He needs *us*. He needs the security of surroundings he's known all his life, and he needs his Moo under the pillow. He *can't* be just sent away. I don't want him to be sent away."

"I know."

"He's too little."

"So he needs to grow."

"He'll grow away from me."

Edmund made no comment on this. Her bracing anger had dissolved and she was left hurt and defeated, and near to tears. To hide these, she turned away from her husband and walked to the window, and stood there with her forehead against the cool glass. She stared, hot-eyed, unseeing, at the garden.

There was a long silence. And then, reasonable as ever, Edmund began to speak again. "Templehall's a good school, Virginia, and Colin Henderson's a good headmaster.

The boys are never pushed, but they're taught to work. Life is going to be hard for Henry. It's going to be hard for all these youngsters. Competitive and tough. The sooner they face up to this, and learn to take the rough with the smooth, the better. Accept the situation. For my sake. See it my way. Henry is too dependent on you."

"I'm his mother."

"You smother him." With that, he walked calmly from the room.

7

IN THE GOLDEN EVENING, Henry walked home. There were few people about because it was nearly six o'clock and they were all indoors eating their tea. He imagined this comforting meal. Soup perhaps, and then haddock or chops and then cakes and biscuits, all washed down with strong and scalding tea. He himself felt pleasantly full of sausages. But perhaps before he went to bed there would be space for a mug of cocoa.

He crossed the curving bridge that spanned the Croy between the two churches. At the top of the curve he stopped and leaned over the ancient stone parapet to gaze down at the river. There had been much rain, too much for the farmers, and it was running deeply, carrying on its spate stray scraps of flotsam gathered on its journey. Branches of trees and bits of straw. Once he had seen a

poor little dead lamb swept away beneath the
bridge. Farther down the glen the land flat-
tened out and there the Croy changed character, to widen and wind through pasture
land, between fields where the peaceful cattle
came down at evening time to drink at the
water's edge. But here it flowed steeply
downhill, leaping and sliding over the rocks
in a series of miniature waterfalls and deep
pools.

The sound of the Croy was one of Henry's
earliest memories. At night he could hear it
from the open window of his bedroom, and
he awoke to its voice every morning. Upstream was the pool where Alexa had taught
him to swim. With his friends from school he
played many wet, muddy games on its banks,
building dams and making camps.

Behind him, the big clock on the Presbyterian church tower struck the hour with six
solemn, donging tolls. Reluctantly he drew
back from the parapet and went on his way,
down the lane that bordered the south bank
of the river. Tall elms towered overhead,
their topmost branches noisy with a colony
of cawing rooks.

Reaching the open gates of Balnaid and

anxious all at once to be home, he began to run, his satchel bumping at his side. As he came around the house he saw his father's dark-blue BMW parked on the gravel. Which was splendid, and an unexpected treat. His father did not usually get home until after Henry was in bed. But now he would find them in the kitchen, comfortably chatting and exchanging news of the day, while his mother prepared dinner and his father had a cup of tea.

But they were not in the kitchen. He knew this the moment he went through the front door because he could hear voices from behind the closed library door. Just voices and the closed door, so why did he have this feeling that it was wrong; that nothing was as it should be?

His mouth had gone dry. He tiptoed down the wide passage and stood outside the door. He had truly meant to go in and surprise them, but instead he found himself listening.

". . . Scarcely out of the nursery. He needs his home. He needs *us.*" His mother, speaking in a voice he had never heard before, high-pitched and sounding as though she was about to burst into tears. ". . . He *can't* be just sent away. I don't want him to be sent away."

"I know." That was his father.

"He's too little."

"So he needs to grow."

"He'll grow away from me."

They were quarrelling. They were having a row. The unbelievable had happened: his mother and father were fighting. Cold with horror, Henry waited for what was going to happen next. After a bit, his father spoke again.

"Templehall's a good school, Virginia, and Colin Henderson's a good headmaster. The boys are never pushed, but they're taught to work. Life is going to be hard for Henry. . . ."

So that was what the row was about. They were going to send him to Templehall. To boarding-school.

". . . and learn to take the rough with the smooth, the better."

Away from his friends, from Strathcroy, from Balnaid, from Edie and Vi. He thought of Hamish Blair, so much older, so superior, so cruel. *Only babies have teddies.*

". . . Henry is too dependent on you."

He could not bear to listen any more. Every fear that he had ever known crowded in on Henry. He backed away from the library door and then, reaching the safety of the hall, turned and ran. Across the floor, up the stairs and down the passage to his bedroom. Slamming the door shut behind him, he tore off his satchel and threw himself onto his bed, bundling the duvet around him. He reached under his pillow for Moo.

Henry is too dependent on you.

And so he was going to be sent away.

Plugging his mouth with his thumb, pressing Moo to his cheek, he was, for the moment, safe. Comforted, he would not cry. He closed his eyes.

⁌ 8 ⁍

THE DRAWING-ROOM AT CROY, used only for formal occasions, was of enormous size. The high ceiling and scrolled cornices were white, the walls lined with faded red damask, the carpet a vast Turkey rug, threadbare in places but still warm with colour. There were sofas and chairs, some loose-covered, some in their original velvet upholstery. None of them matched. Small tables stood about, littered with Battersea boxes, silver-framed photographs, stacks of back numbers of *Country Life*. There were a great many dark oil-paintings, portraits and flower arrangements, and on the table behind the sofa stood a Chinese porcelain jar containing a flowering and scented rhododendron.

Behind the leather-seated club fender, a log fire burned brightly. The hearthrug was shaggy and white, and if wet dogs sat about

upon it, smelled strongly of sheep. The fireplace was marble with an impressive mantelpiece, and on this stood a pair of gilt-and-
enamel candelabra, two Dresden figures, and
a florid Victorian clock.

This clock, chiming sweetly, now struck
eleven o'clock.

It surprised everybody. Mrs. Franco, sleek
in black silk trousers and creamy crêpe
blouse, announced that she could not believe
it was so late. They had all been talking so
much that the evening had just flown by. She
must get to bed, and her husband as well, if
he was to be fit and ready for his golf game at
Gleneagles. With that, the Francos gathered
themselves and rose to their feet. So did Mrs.
Hardwicke.

"It's been perfect, and such an elegant dinner. . . . Thank you both for your hospitality. . . ."

Good-nights were said. Isobel, in the two-
year-old green silk dress that was her best,
led them from the drawing-room to see them
safely on their way upstairs. She closed the
door behind her and did not return. Archie
was left with Joe Hardwicke, apparently dis-
inclined to retire so early. He had settled

back in his chair again and looked good for at least another couple of hours.

Archie did not mind, and was content to be left in his company. Joe Hardwicke was one of their better guests, an intelligent man with liberal views and a dry sense of humour. Over dinner . . . often a sticky session . . . he had done his bit to keep the easy conversation going; he told, against himself, one or two extremely funny stories, and proved to be unexpectedly knowledgeable about wine. Discussing Archie's inherited cellar had taken up most of the second course.

Now Archie poured him a nightcap, which the American gratefully accepted. He then filled a tumbler for himself, threw a log or two on the fire, and sank deep into his own chair, his feet on the sheepskin rug. Joe Hardwicke began to question him about Croy. He found these old places fascinating. How long had his family lived here? From where had the title come? What was the history of the house?

He was not curious but interested, and Archie happily answered his questions. His grandfather, the first Lord Balmerino, had been an industrialist of some renown, who had made his fortune in heavy textiles. His elevation to the peerage had followed on from this, and he had bought Croy and its lands at the end of the nineteenth century.

"There wasn't a dwelling house here then. Just a fortified tower dating back to the sixteenth century. My grandfather built the house, incorporating the original tower. So, although bits at the back are ancient, it's basically Victorian."

"It seems large."

"Yes. They lived on a grand scale in those days. . . ."

"And the estate . . . ?"

"Mostly let out. The moor's gone to a syndicate for the grouse shooting. I have a friend, Edmund Aird, and he runs it, but I have a half-gun in the syndicate and I join them on days when they're driving. I've kept some stalking, but that's just for my friends. The farm is tenanted." He smiled. "So you see, I have no responsibilities."

"So what do you do?"

"I help Isobel. I feed the dogs and exercise them when I can. Deal with all the fallen timber, keep the house supplied with logs. We've got a circular saw in one of the outbuildings and an old villain comes up from the village every now and then and gives me a hand. I cut the grass." He stopped. It wasn't much of an answer but he couldn't think of anything more to tell.

"Do you fish?"

"Yes. I have a beat on the Croy, about two miles upstream from the village, and there's a loch up in the hills. It's good to go up there for the evening rise. Take the boat out. It's very peaceful. And when it's winter and dark at four, I have a workshop down in the basement. There's always something that needs repairing. I mend gates, renew skirtings, build cupboards for Isobel, put up shelves. And other things. I like to work with wood. It's basic, very therapeutic. Perhaps instead of joining the Army I should have been a joiner."

"Were you with a Scottish Regiment?"

"I was a Queen's Loyal Highlander for fifteen years. We spent two of those in Berlin with the American forces. . . ."

The conversation moved on, from Berlin to the Eastern Bloc, and so to politics and international affairs. They had another night cap, lost track of time. When they finally decided to call it a day, it was past one o'clock in the morning.

"I've kept you up." Joe Hardwicke was apologetic.

"Not at all." Archie took the empty glasses and went to place them on the tray that stood on the grand piano. "I'm not much of a sleeper. The shorter the night, the better."

"I . . ." Joe hesitated. "I hope you don't think I'm being impertinent, but I see that you're lame. Did you have an accident?"

"No. My leg was shot off in Northern Ireland."

"You have an artificial leg?"

"Yes. Aluminium. Marvellous piece of engineering. Now, what time do you want breakfast? Would eight-fifteen do you? That should give you time before the car comes to collect you and take you to Gleneagles. And shall I call you in the morning?"

"If you would. About eight o'clock. I sleep like the dead in this mountain air."

Archie moved to open the door. But Joe Hardwicke was offering to dispose of the tray of drinks. Could he perhaps carry it to the kitchen for Archie? Archie was grateful but firm. "Not at all. House rule. You're guests. Not allowed to lift a finger."

They went out into the hall. "Thank you," said Joe Hardwicke, standing at the foot of the staircase.

"Thank you. Good night. And sleep well."

He stayed at the foot of the stairs until the American had disappeared and Archie had heard the opening and the shutting of his bedroom door. Then he returned to the drawing-room, settled the fire, put on the fire-guard, drew back the heavy curtains. Outside, the garden lay washed in moonlight. He heard an owl. He went out of the room, leaving the drink tray where it was, switched off lights. He crossed the hall to the dining-room. The table had been cleared of all traces of dinner, and was now set for breakfast. He felt guilty, for this was, by tradition, his job, and Isobel had accomplished it all alone, while he had sat talking.

He went on to the kitchen. Here again, all was neat and orderly. His two black Labrador bitches slumbered by the Aga in their round baskets. Disturbed, they woke and raised their heads. Thump, thump, went their tails.

"Have you been out?" he asked them. "Did Isobel take you out before she went to bed?"

Thump, thump. They were content and comfortable. There was nothing left for him to do.

Bed. He found himself, all at once, very tired. He climbed the staircase, switching off lights as he went. In his dressing-room, he took off his clothes. His dinner jacket, his bow-tie, his studded white shirt. Shoes and socks. Trousers were the most complicated, but he had perfected a routine for their removal. The tall mirror in his wardrobe reflected his image, but he made a point of not looking at it, because he so hated to see himself unclothed; the livid stump of his thigh, the shining metal of the leg, the screws and hinges, the belts and strappings that kept it in place—all revealed, shameless and somehow obscene.

Quickly he reached for and pulled on his night-shirt, easier to deal with than pyjamas. He went to the adjoining bathroom, peed, and cleaned his teeth. In their vast bedroom, no lights burnt but moonlight flowed through the uncurtained window. On her side of the wide double bed, Isobel slept. But as he moved across the room, she stirred and woke.

"Archie?"

He sat down on his side of the bed.

"Yes."

"What time is it?"

"About twenty past one."

She thought about this. "Were you talking?"

"Yes. I'm sorry. I should have been helping you."

"It doesn't matter. They were nice."

He was unstrapping the harness, gently easing the padded leather cup away from his stump. When it was free, he bent to lay the hateful contraption on the floor beside the bed, the webbing arranged neatly, so that in the morning he could put it on again with the least possible inconvenience. Without it, he felt lopsided and strangely weightless, and his stump burnt and ached. It had been a long day.

He lay beside Isobel and pulled the cool sheets up to his shoulders.

"Are you all right?" Her voice was drowsy.

"Yes."

"Did you know that Verena Steynton's going to throw a dance for Katy? In September."

"Yes. Violet told me."

"I shall have to get a new dress."

"Yes."

"I haven't got anything to wear."

She drifted back to sleep.

As soon as it started, he knew what was going to happen. It was always the same. Forsaken, bleak streets, plastered with graffiti. Dark skies and rain. He wore a flak jacket and drove one of the armoured Land Rovers, but there was something amiss because he should have a companion and he was on his own.

All he had to do was to get to the safety of the barracks. The barracks was a requisitioned Ulster Constabulary police station, fortified to the hilt and bristling with armoury. If he could get there, without them coming, he would be safe. But they were there. They always came. Four figures, spread out across the road ahead, shrouded by the rain. They had no faces, only black hoods, and their weapons were trained upon him. He reached for his rifle, but it had gone. The Land Rover had stopped. He could not remember stopping it. The door was open and they were upon him, dragging him out. Perhaps this time they were going to beat him to death. But it was the same. It was the bomb. It looked like a brown paper parcel but it was a bomb, and they loaded it into the back of the Land Rover, and he stood and watched them. And then he was back behind the wheel and the nightmare had truly begun. Because he was going to drive it in through the open gates of the barracks, and it would explode and kill every man in the place.

He was driving like a lunatic and it was still raining, and he could see nothing, but would soon be there. All he had to do was to get through the gates, drive the explosive vehicle into the bomb pit, and somehow get out and run like Jesus before the bomb went off.

Panic was destroying him, and his ears roared with the sound of his own breathing.

The gates swung up, he was through them, down the ramp, into the bomb pit. Its concrete walls rose on either side of him, shutting out the light. Escape. He tugged at the door handle but it was stuck. The door wouldn't open, he was trapped, the bomb was ticking like a clock, lethal and murderous, and he was trapped. He screamed. Nobody knew he was there. He went on screaming. . . .

He awoke, screaming like a woman, his mouth open, sweat streaming down his face . . . arms caught him. . . .

"Archie."

She was there, holding him. After a little, she drew him gently down onto the pillows. She comforted him like a child, with small sounds. She kissed his eyes. "It's all right. It was a dream. You're here. I'm here. It's all over. You're awake."

His heart banged like a hammer and he streamed with sweat. He lay still in her embrace and gradually his breathing calmed. He reached for a glass of water, but she was there before him, holding it for him to drink, setting the glass back on the table when he had had enough.

When he was quiet, she said, with a ghost
of a smile in her voice, "I hope you haven't
woken anybody up. They'll think I'm murdering you."

"I know. I'm sorry."

"Was it . . . the same?"

"Yes. Always the same. The rain, and the
hoods and the bomb and that fucking pit.
Why do I have nightmares about something
that never happened to me?"

"I don't know, Archie."

"I want them to stop."

"I know."

He turned his head, burying his face in her
soft shoulder. "If only they would stop, perhaps then I could make love to you again."

AUGUST

1

Monday the Fifteenth

THE ARRIVAL OF THE MORNING POST at Croy was a movable feast. Tom Drystone, the postman, driving his scarlet van, covered, during the day, an enormous area. Long, winding single-track roads led up into the glens, to remote sheep farms and distant crofts. Young wives, isolated with small children, would watch for his coming while hanging out lines of washing in the cold, fresh wind. Old people, living on their own, depended on him to deliver their prescriptions, pause for a chat, even sit down and drink a cup of tea with them. In winter-time, he swapped his van for a Land Rover, and only the worst of blizzards prevented him from somehow getting through and delivering the long-awaited letter from Australia, or a new blouse ordered from the Littlewoods catalogue, and when the howling north-west gales damaged telephone lines and power cables, he was very often the only source of communication with the outside world.

Because of this, even if he had been a dour-faced man with no small talk and a sharp tongue on him, Tom's daily appearance would always be welcome. But he was a cheerful fellow, born and bred in Tullochard, and so unfazed by anything that the wild country or the elements could throw at him. As well, when he was not being a postman, he was greatly admired for his ability to play the accordion, and was a kenspeckle figure at local ceilidhs, up on the platform with a glass of beer on the floor beside him, and leading the bank in an endless round of jigs and reels. This catchy music went with him every-where, because, as he delivered the mail, he whistled.

It was now the middle of August. A Mon-day. A blowy day with a good deal of cloud. Not hot but, at least, not raining. Isobel Balmerino, tied up in an apron, sat at one end of the kitchen table at Croy and plucked three brace of grouse. They had been shot on Friday and hung in the game larder for three days. They should, perhaps, hang a little longer, but she wanted to be shed of the messy job and have the grouse safely in the deep-freeze before the next lot of Americans arrived.

The kitchen was vast and Victorian, filled with every evidence of her busy life. A dresser was stacked with a set of chipped ironstone dinner-ware, a notice-board was pinned with postcards, addresses, scribbled reminders to ring the plumber. The dogs' baskets lay near the great four-oven Aga, and large bunches of drying flowers hung from hooks in the ceiling, once employed for curing hams. Over the Aga was a drying rack, on a pulley, where sodden tweeds were hoisted after a day on the hill, or ironed linen, still not quite dry, put to air. This was not a wholly satisfactory arrangement because if there were kippers for breakfast, then pillowcases smelt faintly of fish, but as Isobel had no airing cupboard, there was nothing to be done about it.

Once, a long time ago in old Lady Balmerino's day, this pulley had been the source of a long-standing family joke. Mrs. Harris was then resident cook, and a splendid cook but not one troubled by any silly prejudices concerning hygiene. Her habit had been to keep, on the Aga, an enormous black iron stock-pot simmering with bones and the remains of any vegetable she thought fit to scrape off a plate. With this, she made her famous soups. One year a house party stayed for the shooting. The weather was appalling, so the rack above the Aga constantly drooped with soaked jackets, knickerbockers, sweaters, and hairy stockings. The soup that fortnight got better and better, more and more tasty. Guests begged for recipes. "How do you do it, Mrs. Harris? The flavour! Quite delicious." But Mrs. Harris simply bridled and smugly said that it was just a wee knack she'd picked up from her mother. The week ended and the house party left, tucking large tips into Mrs. Harris's boiled red hand as they left. When they had gone, the stock-pot was finally emptied for scouring. At the bottom was found a felted and none-too-clean shooting stocking.

Four birds plucked and two to go. Feathers

floated everywhere. Isobel gathered them cautiously, bundling them into newspaper, stowing the bundles into a black plastic dustbin bag. Spreading fresh newspaper and starting in on number five, she heard whistling.

The back door flew open, and Tom Drystone burst cheerfully in on her. The draught caused a cloud of feathers. Isobel let out a wail, and he hastily shut it behind him.

"I see the laird's keeping you busy." The feathers settled. Isobel sneezed. Tom slapped a pile of mail down on the dresser. "Can you not get young Hamish to give you a hand?"

"He's away. Gone to Argyll for a week with a school friend."

"What kind of day did they have at Croy on Friday?"

"Disappointing, I'm afraid."

"They got forty-three brace over at Glenshandra."

"They were probably all ours, flown over the march fence to call on their friends. Do you want a cup of coffee?"

"No, not today, thanks. I've a full load on board. Council circulars. Well, I'll be off. . . ."

And he was away, whistling before he had even banged the door shut behind him.

Isobel went on tearing feathers out of the grouse. She longed to go and inspect the letters, see if there was anything exciting, but was firm with herself. She would finish the plucking first. Then she would clear away all the feathers. Then she would wash her hands and look at the mail. And then she would embark upon the bloody job of cleaning the birds.

The post-van sped away. She heard footsteps approaching down the passage from the hall. Painful and uneven. Down the few stone steps, one at a time. The door opened and her husband appeared.

"Was that Tom?"

"Didn't you hear the whistle?"

"I'm waiting for that letter from the Forestry Commission."

"I haven't looked yet."

"Why didn't you tell me you were doing those grouse?" Archie sounded more accusing than guilty. "I'd have come to help."

"Perhaps you'd like to clean them for me?"

He made a distasteful face. He could shoot

birds, and wring the neck of an injured runner. He could, if pressed, pluck them. But he was squeamish about cutting them open and pulling out their innards. This had always been a small cause of friction between himself and Isobel, and so he swiftly changed the subject. As she had known he would.

"Where is the mail?"

"He put it on the dresser."

He limped over to collect it, brought it back to the other end of the table, well out of reach of the general mess. He sat down and leafed through the envelopes.

"Hell. It's not here. I wish they'd put their skates on. But there's one from Lucilla . . ."

"Oh, good, I hoped there would be. . . ."

". . . and something very large and stiff and thick, which might be a summons from the Queen."

"Verena's writing?"

"Could be."

"That's our invitation."

"And two more, similar, to be forwarded on. One for Lucilla, and another for"—he hesitated—"Pandora."

Isobel's hands were still. Down the long,

feather-strewn table, their eyes met. "Pandora? They've asked Pandora?".

"Apparently."

"How extraordinary. Verena never told me she was going to ask Pandora."

"No reason why she should."

"We'll have to send it on to her. Open ours and let's see what it looks like."

Mrs. Angus Steynton

At Home

For Katy

Friday, 16th September 1988

R S V P
Corriehill
Tullochard
Relkirkshire

Dancing 10 P.M.

Archie did so. "Very impressive." He raised his eyebrows. "Embossed, copperplate, and gold edges. The sixteenth of September. Verena's left it pretty late, hasn't she? I mean, that's scarcely a month away."

"There was a disaster. The printers made a mistake. They printed the first batch of invitations on the wrong side of the paper, and so she sent them all back and they had to be done again."

"How did she know they were printed on the wrong side of the paper?"

"Verena knows about things like that. She's a perfectionist. What does it say?"

"It says, 'Lord and Lady Balmerino. Mrs. Angus Steynton. At Home. For Katy. Blah Blah. Dancing at ten. R.S.V.P.' " He held it up. "Impressed?"

Without her glasses, Isobel screwed up her eyes and peered. "Very impressed. It'll look splendid on the mantelpiece. The Americans will think we've been invited to something Royal. Now, read me Lucilla's letter. That's much more important."

Archie slit the flimsy envelope with the French stamp and postmark and unfolded two sheets of cheap, lined, and very thin paper.

"Looks as though she's written it on lavatory paper."

"Read it."

" 'Paris. August sixth. Darling Mum and Dad. Sorry I've been such ages in writing. No time for news. This is just a short note to let you know my movements. Am leaving here in a couple of days and going down to the south. I am travelling by bus, so no need to anguish about hitch-hiking. Going with an Australian boy I've met called Jeff Howland. Not an art student but a sheep-farmer from Queensland, with a year off to bum round Europe. He has friends in Ibiza, so we might possibly go there. I don't know what we'll do when we get to Ibiza, but if there is the chance of getting over to Majorca, would you like me to go and see Pandora? And if you would, will you send me her address because I've lost it. And I'm a bit short of cash, so could you possibly float me a loan till my next allowance comes through? Send all c/o Hans Bergdorf, PO Box 73, Ibiza. Paris has been heaven but only tourists here just now. Everybody else has disappeared to beaches or mountains. Saw a blissful Matisse exhibition the other day. Lots of love, darlings, and DON'T WORRY. Lucilla. PS. Don't forget the money.' "

He folded the letter and put it back into the envelope.

Isobel said, "An Australian."

"A sheep-farmer."

"Bumming round Europe."

"At least they're travelling by bus."

"Oh well, I suppose it could be worse. But thinking that she might go and see Pandora . . . isn't that extraordinary? We don't mention Pandora's name for months and all at once it keeps popping up everywhere we turn. Is Ibiza very far from Majorca?"

"Not very."

"I wish Lucilla would come home."

"Isobel, she's having the time of her life."

"I hate her being short of money."

"I'll send her a cheque."

"I miss her so."

"I know."

She was done with plucking, the feathers all painfully collected and stowed in the black rubbish bag. The six small corpses lay in a pathetic row, their heads askew, their clawed feet pointed like dancers. Isobel reached for her lethally sharpened knife and without ado sliced into the first little flaccid body. Then she laid down the knife and plunged her hand into the bird. She withdrew it, red with blood, drawing out a long string of pearly, greyish entrails. These piled in surprising profusion onto the newspaper. The smell was overwhelming.

Archie sprang to his feet. "I'll go and write that cheque." He gathered the mail. "Before I forget." And he headed for his study, firmly closing the kitchen door behind him, shutting away the small scene of domestic carnage.

At his desk, he held Pandora's envelope for a moment or two. He thought about writing to her. Tucking a letter from himself in with Verena's invitation. It's a party, he would say. It'll be fun. Why not come home for it, and stay with us at Croy? We would so love to see you. Please, Pandora. Please.

But he had written thus before and she had scarcely bothered to reply. It was no good. He sighed and carefully readdressed the envelope. He added a few stamps for good measure and an airmail sticker, then laid it aside.

He wrote a cheque payable to Lucilla Blair, for a hundred and fifty pounds. He then began a letter to his daughter.

Croy, August 15th.

My darling Lucilla.

Thank you very much for your note which we received this morning. I hope you will have a good journey to the south of France, and are able to raise enough cash to get you to Ibiza, as I am sending this cheque there as you asked me to. As for Pandora, I am sure she would be delighted to see you but suggest that you telephone before you make any plans, and let her know that you propose to visit her.

Her address is Casa Rosa, Puerto del Fuego, Majorca. I haven't got her telephone number but I am sure you will be able to find it in the phone book in Palma.

As well, I am forwarding on an invitation to a party that the Steyntons are throwing for Katy. It's only a month off and you may have other and better things to do, but I know that your mother would be so happy if you could be there.

A good day on the twelfth. They were driving, and so I joined the guns for the morning only. Everybody was kind and I was allowed the bottom butt. Hamish came with me to carry my gun and my game bag, and help his old father up the hill. Edmund Aird shot exceptionally well, but at the end of the day the bag was only twenty-one and half brace, and two hares. Hamish went off yesterday for a week in Argyll with a school friend. He took his trout rod, but hopes for some deep-sea fishing. My love, my darling child. Dad.

He read this missive through, then folded it neatly. He found a large brown envelope and into this put the letter, the cheque, and Verena's invitation. He sealed and stamped it and addressed it to Lucilla at the Ibiza address that she had given them. He took both letters out into the hall and laid them on the chest that stood by the door. The next time that anyone went to the village they would be posted.

꞉ 2 ꞉

Wednesday the Seventeenth

THE STEYNTONS' INVITATION was delivered to Ovington Street on the Wednesday of that week. It was early morning. Alexa, barefoot and wrapped in her bathrobe, stood in the kitchen, waiting for the kettle to boil. The door to the garden was open, and Larry was out there, having his routine sniff-around. Sometimes he found traces of cat and became very excited. It was a grey morning. Perhaps later the sun would come out and burn the mist away. She heard the rattle of the letter-box and, looking up through the window, saw the postman's legs as he strode on down the pavement.

She laid a tray, put tea-bags into the teapot. The kettle boiled and she made the tea, and then, leaving her little dog to his own devices, carried the tray up the basement stairs. The letters lay on the doormat. Juggling with the tray, she stooped to gather them up and push them into the capacious pocket of her robe. Up again, the thick carpet soft beneath her bare feet. Her bedroom door stood open, the curtains already drawn back. It was not a very large room, and almostly completely filled by the bed that Alexa had inherited from her grandmother. It was an impressive bed, wide and downy, with tall brass bedsteads at either end. She put the tray down and climbed back between the sheets.

She said, "Are you awake, because I've brought you a cup of tea?"

The hump on the other side of the bed did not instantly respond to this summons. Then it groaned and heaved. A bare brown arm appeared from the covers, and Noel turned to face her.

"What's the time?" His hair, so dark on the white linen pillow, was tousled, his chin rough with stubble.

"A quarter to eight."

He groaned again, ran his fingers through his hair. She said "Good morning," and bent to kiss his unshaven cheek. He put his hand

on the back of her head and held her close.
He said, mumbling, "You smell delicious."

"Lemon shampoo."

"No. Not lemon shampoo. Just you."

He took his hand away. Released, she
kissed him again, and then turned to the domestic business of pouring his tea. He pum-
melled pillows, heaved himself up to lean
against them. He was naked, brown-chested
as though he had just returned from some
tropical holiday. She handed him the steaming Wedgwood mug.

He drank slowly, in silence. He took a long
time to come to in the mornings, and
scarcely said a word before breakfast. It was
something she had found out about him, one
of his small routines of existence. Like the
way he made coffee, or cleaned his shoes, or
mixed a dry martini. At night he emptied his
pockets, laying their contents in a neat row
on the dressing-table, always in the same order. Wallet, credit cards, penknife, small
change, the coins tidily stacked. The best of
all was lying in bed and watching him do
this; then watching him undress, waiting for
him to be ready, to come to her.

Each day brought new knowledge; each

night fresh, sweet discovery. All the good things piled up so that every moment, every hour was better than the moment and the hour before. Living with Noel, sharing this blissful blend of domesticity and passion, made her understand for the first time why people ever wanted to get married. It was so that it would go on for ever.

And once . . . only three months ago . . . she had thought herself perfectly satisfied. Alone in the house, with only Larry for company, occupied with her work, her little routine, occasional evenings out, or visits to friends. No more than half a life. How had she endured it?

You never miss what you've never had. Edie's voice, loud and clear. Thinking of Edie, Alexa smiled. She poured her own mug of tea, stood it beside her, and then reached into her pocket for the letters. She spread them on the eiderdown. A bill from Peter Jones, a circular for double glazing, a postcard from a woman who lived in Barnes and wanted some goodies concocted for her deepfreeze, and finally the huge, stiff, white envelope.

She looked at it. A Scottish postmark. An invitation? To a wedding, perhaps . . .

She ripped the envelope with her thumb and took out the card.

She said, "Goodness me."

"What is it?"

"An invitation to the ball. 'You *shall* go to the ball,' said the Fairy Godmother to Cinderella."

Noel reached out and took it from her.

"Who's Mrs. Angus Steynton?"

"They live near us in Scotland. About ten miles away."

"And who's Katy?"

"Their daughter, of course. She works in London. You've maybe met her. . . ." Alexa thought about this and then changed her mind. "No. I don't think you would have. She's inclined to go round with young men in the Guards . . . lots of race meetings."

"Sixteenth of September. Are you going to go?"

"I shouldn't think so."

"Why not?"

"Because I wouldn't want to go without you."

"I haven't been invited."

"I know."

"Will you say, 'I shall come if I can bring my lover with me'?"

"Nobody knows I've got a lover."

"You still haven't told your family that I've moved in with you?"

"Not yet."

"Any particular reason?"

"Oh, Noel . . . I don't know." But she did know. She wanted to keep it all to herself. With Noel, she inhabited a secret magic world of love and discovery, and she was afraid that if she let anybody in from the outside, then it would all dissolve and somehow be spoilt.

As well . . . and this was a pathetic admission . . . she lacked any form of moral courage. She was twenty-one but that didn't help, because she still felt, inside, about fifteen, and as anxious to please as she had ever been. The thought of possible family reactions filled her with agonized distress. She imagined her father's disapproval, Vi's horrified astonishment, and Virginia's concern. Then, the questions.

But who is he? Where did you meet him? You've been living together? At Ovington

Street? But why is this the first we've heard of it? What does he do? What is his name?

And Edie. *Lady Cheriton must be turning in her grave.*

It wasn't that they wouldn't understand. It wasn't that they were strait-laced or hypocritical in any way. Nor was it that they didn't all love Alexa—she couldn't bear any of them to be upset.

She drank some tea.

Noel said, "You're not a little girl any longer."

"I know I'm not. I'm adult. I just wish I wasn't such a wet adult."

"Are you ashamed of our sinful cohabitation?"

"I'm not ashamed of anything. It's just . . . the family. I don't like hurting them."

"My sweet, they'll be much more hurt if they hear about us before you've got around to telling them."

Alexa knew that this was true. "But how could they find out?" she asked him.

"This is London. Everybody talks. I'm astonished your father hasn't got the buzz already. Take my advice and be a brave girl."

He gave her his empty mug and a swift kiss

on the cheek. Reaching for his bathrobe, he swung his legs over the side of the bed. "And then you can write to Mrs. Stiffden, or whatever her name is, and say yes, please, you'd love to come to the ball, and you're bringing Prince Charming with you."

Despite herself, Alexa smiled. "Would you come?"

"Probably not. Tribal dances are scarcely my scene." And with that he took himself off to the bathroom. Almost at once Alexa heard the gushing of the shower.

So what was all the fuss about? Alexa picked up the invitation again, and frowned at it. I wish you'd never come, she told it. You've just stirred up a lot of trouble.

⚜ 3 ⚜

Monday the Twenty-second

THAT AUGUST, THE ENTIRE ISLAND simmered in an unprecedented heat wave. The mornings started hot, and by midday the temperatures had risen to unbearable heights, driving any person with sense indoors for the afternoon, to loll breathless upon a bed, or sleep on some shady terrace. The old town, up in the hills, quiet and shuttered, slumbered through the hours of siesta. The streets were empty and the shops closed.

But, down in the port, it was a different story. There were too many people about, and too much money being spent, to respect this time-honoured custom. The tourists did not want to know about siestas. They did not want to waste a moment of their costly holiday in sleeping. And the day visitors had nowhere to go. So, instead, they sat about in droves, red and perspiring, in the pavement cafés; or wandered aimlessly in air-conditioned gift arcades. The beach was littered with palm-thatch umbrellas and half-naked, kippering bodies, and the Marina packed with seagoing craft of every description. Only the boat people seemed to know what was good for them. Usually bustling with activity, the yachts and launches dipped lazily in the swell of the oily water, and in the shade of canvas awnings supine bodies, brown as mahogany, lay about on the decks, as though already dead.

Pandora awoke late. She had tossed and turned her way through the night and finally, at four in the morning, taken a sleeping pill and fallen at last into a heavy, dream-troubled sleep. She would have slept on but the sound of Seraphina clattering away in the kitchen disturbed her. The clatter shattered the dream, and after a little, reluctantly, she opened her eyes.

The dream had been of rain, and brown

rivers, and cold wet scents, and the sound of wind. Of deep lochs and dark hills with boggy paths leading to their snow-capped summits. But most important was the rain. Not falling straight, not thunderous and tropical as it was when it fell here, but gentle and misty. Rolling in on clouds, insidious as smoke . . .

She stirred. The images dissolved, were gone. Why should she dream of Scotland? Why, after all these years, did those old chilly memories come back to tug at her sleeve? Perhaps it was the heat of this cruel August, the endless days of relentless sunshine, the dust and the dryness, the hard-edged black shadows of noon. One yearned for that gentle, scented mist.

She turned her head on the pillow and saw, beyond the sliding glass doors that had stood open all night, the balustrade of the terrace, the glaring brilliance of geraniums, the sky. Blue, cloudless, already brazen with heat.

She propped herself up on an elbow and reached across the wide empty bed to the bedside table and her watch. Nine o'clock. More racket from the kitchen. The sound of the dishwasher churning. Seraphina was making her presence heard. And if she was here, that meant that Mario—her husband and Pandora's gardener—was already scratching away with his archaic hoe in the garden. Which precluded all possibilities of an early skinny-dip. Mario and Seraphina lived in the old town and came to work each morning on Mario's moped, roaring full throttle up the hill. Mario drove this noisy brute of a contraption with Seraphina perched behind him, riding, modestly, side-saddle, and with her strong brown arms wrapped around his waist. It was a wonder that the daily assault of din that proclaimed their arrival had not woken Pandora before this, but then the sleeping pills were very strong.

It was too hot to go on lying in this rumpled, messy bed. She had been here long enough. Pandora threw aside the thin sheet and, barefoot and naked, crossed the wide expanse of marbled floor and went into her bathroom. She collected her bikini—no more than two scraps of knotted handkerchief—climbed into it, and then walked back through her bedroom, out onto the terrace, and down the steps that led to the swimming pool.

She dived. It was cool, but not cool enough for true refreshment. She swam. She thought of diving into the loch at Croy and coming up screaming with agony because the cold bit into every painful pore of one's body; it was a numbing cold that took all breath away. How could she have swum in what was virtually snow-water? How could she and Archie and all the rest of them have indulged in such masochistic pleasures? But what fun it had been. And then coming out, and struggling damply into warm sweaters, and lighting a fire on the pebbly shore of the loch, and cooking the best trout in the world over the smoky embers. Trout, ever since, had never tasted so good as at those impromptu campfire meals.

She swam on. To and fro, up and down the long pool. Scotland again. Not dreams now but conscious memories. So what? She let them have their way. Let them lead her away from the loch, down the rough turfy track that followed the course of the burn, tumbling and spilling its way down the hill, finally to join the Croy. Peaty water brown and frothy as beer, spilling over rocks and splashing into deep pools where the trout lurked in the shadows. Over the centuries this stream had cut for itself a little valley, and the banks of this were green and verdant, sheltered from the north winds and bright with wild flowers. Foxgloves grew, and starwort, sweet green bracken and tall purple thistles. One particular spot was special. They called it the Corrie and it was the venue for many spring and winter picnics when the winds from the north were too cold to light camp-fires by the loch.

The Corrie. She did not let her memories linger there but hurried them on. The track steepened, winding between great rock formations, cliffs of granite older than time. A final turn and the glen lay spread far below, sunlit, rolling with cloud shadows, revealed in all its pastoral beauty. The Croy a glittering thread, its two arched bridges just visible through the trees; the village reduced by distance to a child's plaything, set out on some nursery carpet.

A pause for contemplation and then on again. The track levelled off. The deer-fence lay ahead and the tall gate. Now visible, the first of the trees. Scots pines, and beyond them the green of the beeches. Then Gordon Gillock's house, with Mrs. Gillock's washing line flying a bunting of laundry, and the gun dogs, disturbed, exploding into a cacophony of frenzied barking from their kennels.

Nearly home. The track a proper road now, Tarmacked, leading between farm buildings, stone steadings, and barns and byres. The smell was of cattle and dung. Another gate and past the farmhouse with its bright cottage garden and drystone wall smothered in honeysuckle. The cattle-grid. The drive lined with rhododendrons . . .

Croy.

Enough. Pandora jerked her wayward memories back into line as though they were over-eager children. She had no wish to go farther. Enough of self-indulgence. Enough of Scotland. She swam a final length and then climbed the shallow steps up and out of the pool. The stones beneath her bare feet were already hot. Dripping, she made her way back into the house. In her bathroom, she showered, washed her hair, put on a fresh dress, loose and sleeveless, the coolest garment she owned. She left her bedroom, crossed the hall, went into the kitchen.

"Seraphina."

Seraphina swung around from the sink where she was busily engaged in scrubbing a bucket of mussels. She was a small, squat, brown woman with sturdy bare legs thrust into espadrilles, and dark hair drawn back into a knot at the nape of her neck. She always wore black because she was perpetually in mourning. No sooner was she out of mourning for one old grandparent or distant relation than another of her clan passed on and she was back in mourning again. The black dresses all looked exactly the same, but as if to make up for their gloom, her pinafores and aprons were invariably brightly coloured and hectically patterned.

Seraphina went with the Casa Rosa. Previously, she had worked for fifteen years for the English couple who had originally built the villa. When, two years ago, due to family pressures and uncertain health, they reluctantly returned to England, Pandora, searching for some place to live, had bought the property from them. Doing this, she discovered that she had inherited Seraphina and

Mario. At first Seraphina was not certain whether she wished to work for Pandora, and Pandora was in two minds about Seraphina. She was not exactly attractive and very often looked quite grumpy. But tentatively they tried out a month together, and then the month stretched to three months, and then to a year, and the arrangement, quite comfortably, settled itself, without anything actually being said.

"*Señora. Buenos días.* You are awake."

After fifteen years with her previous employers, Seraphina spoke reasonable English. Pandora was grateful for this small mercy. Her French was fluent but Spanish a closed book. People said it was easy because of having done Latin at school, but Pandora's education did not include Latin and she was not about to start now.

"Any breakfast?"

"Is on the table. I bring the coffee."

The table was set on the terrace, which faced out over the driveway. Here it was shady and cooled by any breeze that blew from the sea. Crossing the sitting-room, Pandora's eye was caught by a book that lay on the coffee-table. It was a large and lush volume, sent as a present from Archie for her birthday. *Wainwright in Scotland.* She knew why he had sent it. He never stopped, in his simple and transparent way, trying to lure her home. Because of this, she had not even opened it. But now she paused, her attention caught. *Wainwright in Scotland.* Scotland again. Was this a day to be drenched in nostalgia? She smiled at herself, at this weakness that had suddenly come upon her. Why not? She stooped and picked up the book and carried it out onto the terrace. Peeling an orange, she opened it on the table.

It was indeed a coffee-table book, built for browsing. Pen-and-ink drawings, beautifully executed maps, and a simple text. Coloured photographs sprang from every page. The silver sands of Morar. Ben Vorlich. The Falls of Dochart. The old names resounded satisfactorily, like a roll of drums.

She began to eat the orange. Juice dripped on the pages of the book, and she brushed them carelessly away, leaving stains. Seraphina brought her coffee but she never looked up, so engrossed was she.

Here the river, after a long and sedate journey, suddenly erupts into a furious rage, descending in a turbulent cataract of white foam along a wide and rocky channel in a remarkable display of thrashing waters. The flow of the rapids is interrupted by wooded islands, one of which was the burial place of the clan MacNab, and a bower of lovely trees enhances a scene of outstanding beauty. . . .

She poured coffee, turned a page and read on.

Wainwright in Scotland consumed her day. She carried it from the breakfast table to a long chair by the pool and then, after lunch, took it to bed with her. By five o'clock, she had read it from cover to cover. Closed at last, she let it drop to the floor.

It was cooler now, but for once she had scarcely been troubled by the heat. She got off her bed and went out of doors and swam once more, then dressed in white cotton trousers and a blue-and-white shirt. She did her hair, her eyes, found earrings, a gold bracelet. White sandals. She sprayed on scent. Her bottle was nearly finished. She would have to buy more. The prospect of this small luxurious purchase filled her with pleasure.

She said goodbye to Seraphina and went out of the front door and down the steps to where her car was parked in the garage. She got in and drove down the winding hill and so out onto the wide road that led to the port. She parked her car in the courtyard of the post office and went in to collect her mail. She put this in her leather-strapped basket and then left her car and walked slowly through the still-crowded streets, pausing to glance into shop windows, to assess a dress, to price a delectable lacy shawl. At the scent shop, she went in and bought a flagon of Poison, then went on, always walking in the direction of the sea. She came at last to the wide, palm-fringed boulevard that ran parallel to the beach. At the end of the day it seemed as busy as ever, the sands crowded and people still swimming. Far out, windsurfers' sails caught the evening breeze, dipping like birds' wings out across the surface of the water.

She came to a little café where a few tables

stood empty on the pavement. The waiter came and she ordered coffee and cognac. Then, leaning back in the uncomfortable iron chair, pushing her sunglasses up onto the top of her head, she reached into the basket and took out her letters. One from Paris. One from her lawyer in New York. A postcard from Venice. She turned it over. Emily Richter, still staying at the Cipriani. A large stiff white envelope, addressed to Croy and readdressed in Archie's handwriting. She opened it and read, in disbelief and then with some amusement, Verena Steynton's invitation.

At Home

For Katy

Extraordinary. As though she were receiving a summons from another age, another world. And yet a world which, by some strange coincidence, like it or not, she had inhabited for the whole of the day. She knew uncertainty. Was it an omen of some sort? Should she pay heed? And if it was an omen, did she believe in omens in the first place?

At Home For Katy. She remembered

other invitations, "stiffies" she and Archie
had called them, propped on the mantelpiece
of the library at Croy. Invitations to garden
parties, cricket matches, dances. Dances ga-
lore. There had been a week in September
when one scarcely slept, somehow surviving
with the stolen naps in the backs of cars, or a
doze in the sun while others played tennis.
She remembered a wardrobe filled with ball
dresses, and she herself perpetually complaining to her mother that she had nothing
to wear. Everybody had seen the ice-blue
satin because she'd worn it at the Northern
Meetings, and anyway, some man had spilt
champagne all down the front and the stain
wouldn't come out. And the rose-pink? The
hem was torn and one of the straps had come
loose. Whereupon her mother, the most in-
dulgent and patient of women, instead of
suggesting that Pandora find a needle and
thread and mend the rose-pink, would put
her daughter into the car and drive to
Relkirk or Edinburgh and there suffer the
traumas of Pandora's capricious whims,
trudging from shop to shop until the most
beautiful—and inevitably most costly—dress
was finally run to earth.

How spoilt Pandora had been, how adored, how cherished. And in return . . .

She laid down the card and looked up at the sea. The waiter came with her coffee and brandy on a little tray. She thanked him and paid. As she drank the bitter, black, scalding coffee, Pandora watched the windsurfers and the slow ambling flow of passers-by. The evening sun slipped down out of the sky and the sea became like molten gold.

She had never gone back. Her own decision. Nobody else's. They had not come chasing after her but they had never lost touch. Always letters, still filled with love. After her parents died, she thought the letters would stop but they didn't, because then Archie took over. Detailed descriptions of shoots, news of his children, scraps of village gossip. Always they ended in the same way. "We miss you. Why don't you come and stay for a few days? It is too long since we have seen you."

A yacht was moving out of the Marina, motoring gently until it was clear of the beach and able to fill its sails with wind. Idly, she watched its passage. She saw it, but her inner eye was filled with images of Croy. Her thoughts, once more, ran ahead and this time she did not pull them back, but let them go. To the house. Up the steps to the front door. The door stood open. Nothing to stop her. She could go. . . .

She set down her coffee-cup with some force. What was the point? The past was always golden because one recalled only the good times. But what about the darker side of memory? Happenings better left where they were, shut away, like sad mementoes stuffed in a trunk, the lid closed down, the key turned in the lock. Besides, the past was people, not places. Places without people were like railway stations where no trains ran. I am thirty-nine. Nostalgia drains all energy from the present, and I am too old for nostalgia.

She reached for her brandy. As she did this, a shadow came between herself and the sun, to lie across her table. Startled, she looked up and into the face of the man who stood beside her. He gave a little bow.

"Pandora."

"Oh, Carlos! What are you doing creeping up on me?"

"I have been to the Casa Rosa but found

nobody there. You see, if you don't come to
me, then I have to come to you."

"I *am* sorry."

"So I tried the port. I thought that I
should find you somewhere here."

"I was shopping."

"May I join you?"

"Of course."

He drew out a chair and sat facing her. He
was a tall man in his mid-forties, formally
attired in collar and tie and a light jacket. His
hair was dark, as were his eyes, and even on
this sultry evening his appearance was cool
and crisp. He spoke impeccable English and
looked, Pandora always thought, like a
Frenchman. But he was, in fact, a Spaniard.

As well, extremely attractive. She smiled.
She said, "Let me order you a brandy."

⚘ 4 ⚘

Wednesday the Twenty-fourth

VIRGINIA AIRD SHOULDERED HER WAY through the swing-doors of Harrods and stepped out into the street. In the store, the heat and the hassle had become oppressive. Outside, it was scarcely better. The day was humid, the air heavy with petrol fumes and the claustrophobia of surging humanity. Brompton Road stood solid with traffic, and the pavements were choked with a slow-moving river of people. She had forgotten that city streets could contain so many people. Some had to be Londoners, one supposed, going about their daily business, but the general impression was of some global immigration from all points of the compass. Tourists and visitors. More visitors than one could have believed possible. Great blond students with backpacks passed by. Entire families of

Italians or possibly Spaniards; two Indian ladies in brilliant saris. And, of course, Americans. My fellow countrymen, thought Virginia wryly. They were instantly recognizable
by their clothes and the plethora of camera
equipment slung about their necks. One huge
man was even wearing his ten-gallon hat.

It was four-thirty in the afternoon. She
had been shopping all day and was now
laden with loot, carrier bags, and parcels.
Her feet hurt. But still she stood there, because she had not yet made up her mind
what she was going to do next.

There were two alternatives.

She could return forthwith, by any means
of transport that made itself available, to
Cadgewith Mews, where she was staying in
great comfort with her friend Felicity Crowe.
She had been given a latchkey, so even if the
house was empty—Felicity out shopping, or
taking her dachshund for a turn around the
gardens—Virginia could let herself in, kick
off her shoes, make a cup of tea, and fall, in a
stupor of exhaustion, onto her bed. The prospect of such a course of action was immensely tempting.

Or she could go to Ovington Street and

risk finding Alexa out. This was what she *ought* to do. Alexa was not exactly on her conscience, but there could be no question of returning to Scotland without having made contact with her stepdaughter. She had already tried to do this, telephoning last night from Felicity's, but there had been no answer to the call and she had finally replaced the receiver, deciding that, for once, Alexa was out on some spree. Then she had tried again this morning, and at lunch-time, and again from the hairdresser's, boiled with heat from the blow drier. Still no reply. Was Alexa perhaps out of London?

At that moment a small Japanese, gazing in the opposite direction, barged into her and knocked one of her parcels to the ground. He apologized profusely in his polite Japanese way, picked up the parcel, dusted it off, returned it to her, bowed, smiled, raised his hat, and went on his way. Enough. A taxi drew up to unload its cargo and, before anyone else could claim it, Virginia did so.

"Where to, love?"

She had made up her mind. "Ovington Street." If Alexa was not at home, she would keep the taxi and go on to Felicity's. With the small decision taken, she felt better. She opened the window, sat back, thought about taking off her shoes.

It was a short journey. As the taxi turned into Ovington Street, Virginia sat forward to search for Alexa's car. If her car was there, then, in all probability, Alexa would be at home. It was—a white minivan with a red stripe was parked at the pavement outside the blue front door. Relief. She directed the cab driver and he drew up in the middle of the street.

"Can you wait a moment? I just want to make sure somebody's in."

"Okay, love."

She gathered up her shopping and bundled out, climbed the steps and pressed the bell. She heard Larry barking, Alexa's voice telling him to be quiet. She dumped her parcels on the doorstep and, opening her bag, went back to pay off the taxi.

Alexa was in her kitchen, dealing bravely with the detritus of her day's work, all of which she had brought back from Chiswick in the back of her van. Saucepans, plastic containers, wooden salad bowls, knives, egg-whisk, and a cardboard wine crate filled with dirty glasses. When all was clean, dried, and put away, she planned to go upstairs, strip off her crumpled cotton skirt and shirt, take a shower, and then put on an entirely fresh set of clothes. After that, she would make a cup of tea . . . Lapsang souchong with a slice of lemon . . . and then she would take Larry for a little stroll, and later start thinking about dinner. On the way back from Chis-wick, she had stopped off at the fishmonger and bought rainbow trout, Noel's favourite. Grilled, with almonds. And perhaps . . .

She heard the taxi approaching slowly down the street. Standing at the sink, visibility was limited. The taxi stopped. A woman's voice. High-heeled footsteps tapped across the pavement. Alexa, rinsing a wineglass under the tap, waited, listening. Then her doorbell rang.

Larry hated the doorbell and burst into an aria of barking. And Alexa, so occupied and busy, resented the interruption and was equally unenthusiastic. Who on earth could

this be? "Oh, be quiet, you stupid creature."
She set down the glass, untied her apron and
went upstairs to find out. Hopefully, it would
be no one of importance. She opened the
door to a pile of expensive-looking parcels.
The taxi made a U-turn and trundled away.
And . . .

She gaped. Her stepmother. Dressed for
London but still instantly recognizable. She
wore a black dress and a scarlet jacket and
patent pumps, and her hair, fresh from the
hands of some exclusive expert, had been
dressed in a new style, drawn back from her
face and clasped in a huge black velvet bow.

Her stepmother. Looking fantastic but
unannounced and entirely unexpected. The
implications of this caused every thought but
one to fly from Alexa's head.

Noel.

"Virginia."

"Don't die of shock. I kept the taxi waiting
because I thought you might be out." She
kissed Alexa. "I've been shopping," she explained unnecessarily, and stooped to gather
up the parcels. Alexa, with an effort, pulled
herself together and helped.

"But I didn't even know you were in London."

"Just for a day or two." They dumped it all on the hall table. "And don't say why didn't you ring me up, because I've been calling non-stop. I thought you must be away."

"No." Alexa shut the door. "We . . . I went out for dinner last night, though, and I've been out on a job all day. I was just washing up. That's why I'm looking such a mess. . . . "

"You look great." Virginia eyed her. "Have you lost weight?"

"I don't know. I never weigh myself."

"What was the job?"

"Oh, a lunch for an old man's ninetieth birthday. In Chiswick. A lovely house, right on the river. Twenty guests, and all relations. Two great-grandchildren."

"What did you give them?"

"Cold salmon and champagne. That's what he wanted. And a birthday cake. But why didn't you tell me you were coming . . . ?"

"Oh, I don't know. It was all done on the spur of the moment. I just felt I wanted to get away for a day or two. I've been shopping all day."

"It looks like it. And I love your hair. You must be exhausted. Go on in and take the weight off your feet. . . . "

"That's all I want. . . ." Pulling off her jacket, Virginia went through the open door, tossed her jacket aside, headed for the largest armchair, collapsed into it, kicked off her shoes and placed her feet on a stool. "Heaven."

Alexa stood and looked at her. How long did she plan to stay? Why . . . ? "Why aren't you staying here with me?" Thank heavens she wasn't, but it was the obvious question to ask.

"I would have invited myself, of course, but I promised Felicity Crowe next time I came to London I'd stay with her. You know, she's my childhood friend. She'd have been my bridesmaid if I'd had bridesmaids. And we never see much of each other, and when we do we talk and giggle non-stop."

So that was all right. "Where does she live?"

"A dear little house in Cadgewith Mews. But I must say, it's not as pretty as this."

"Would you . . . would you like a cup of tea?"

"No, don't bother. A cold drink would do."

"I've got a can of Coke in the fridge."

"Perfect."

"I . . . I'll just get it."

She left Virginia and went down to the kitchen. She opened the fridge and took out the can of cola. Virginia was here and it was necessary to be cool and objective. Being cool and objective was not Alexa's strong point. Downstairs, evidences of Noel were scarce. His Barbour jacket and a tweed cap hung in the downstairs loo. A *Financial Times* lay in the drawing-room. That was all. But upstairs was different. His personal belongings were everywhere, and the bed, very obviously, made up for the occupancy of two people. There could be no question of trying to hide it all away. If Virginia went upstairs . . .

She found herself overwhelmed with indecision. On the one hand, perhaps this was the best way to do it. She hadn't planned anything but it had happened; and Virginia was here. As well, Virginia was young and not even, strictly speaking, family. She would hopefully understand, and perhaps even approve. She, after all, had had strings of men in her life before she married Fa. Virginia could be Alexa's advocate, the best person of all to break the news gently that the shy and puddingy Alexa had not only found a man of her own at last but had taken him into her heart and her home, and was openly living with him.

On the other hand, if she did this, then the secret was out and Alexa would be expected to share Noel. Speak about him and allow them all to meet him. She imagined her father coming to London, ringing up. "I'll take you both to Claridges for dinner." The prospect caused her knees to shake, but in the end, she knew that she would be able to cope with such a situation. The unanswered question was how Noel would react. Would he, perhaps, feel that he was being pressurized in some way? Which would be disastrous because, after three months of living with him and learning all the capricious twists of another person's character, Alexa knew that this was the one thing in life that Noel could not stand.

At a loss, totally out of her depth, she

made a huge effort to be rational. There is nothing you can do about it, she told herself in Edie's voice. You'll just need to take things the way they come. Thinking of Edie made her feel a bit stronger. She closed the door of the fridge, found a glass, and went back upstairs.

"Sorry I've been so long." Virginia was smoking. "I thought you'd given up cigarettes."

"I did but I started again. Don't tell your father."

Alexa opened the Coke and poured it, and handed Virginia the glass.

"Oh, marvellous. Delicious. I thought I was going to die of thirst. Why are all the shops so hot? Why are there so many people everywhere?"

Alexa curled up in the corner of the sofa.

"Visitors. It took me hours to get back from Chiswick. And you've got on the wrong sort of shoes for shopping. You should be wearing trainers."

"I know. It's crazy, isn't it? Dressing up to come to London. Habit, I suppose."

"What have you been buying?"

"Clothes. Basically something for the

Steyntons' party. I see you've got your invitation."

"I haven't answered it yet."

"You're coming, of course."

"I . . . I don't know . . . I'm pretty busy round then."

"But of course you must come. We're counting on you. . . ."

Alexa diverted her. "What sort of a dress did you get?"

"It's dreamy. Sort of voile, white, in layers, with black spots everywhere. Tiny shoestring straps. I'll have to try to step up my suntan."

"Where did you find it?"

"Caroline Charles. I'll show it to you before I go. But, Alexa, do try to come. It's September, so everybody will be there and it'll be a great do."

"I'll see. How's Fa?"

"He's fine." Virginia turned away to stub out her cigarette in the ashtray. Alexa waited for her to enlarge on this flat statement, but she didn't say any more.

"And Henry?"

"Henry's great too."

"Are they both at home?"

"No. Edmund's spending this week in the flat in Edinburgh, and Henry's taken his sleeping-bag and gone to stay at Pennyburn with Vi. I took him to Devon for his summer holidays. We had three weeks, and it was a success. I took him riding for the first time in his life, and he liked all the farm animals and going fishing with my father." Another pause, not entirely comfortable, or was that Alexa's imagination? Then Virginia went on. "I really wanted to take him out to the States. I suddenly got this yen for Leesport and Long Island. But Gramps and Grandma had taken themselves off for a long cruise, so there wasn't much point our going."

"No, I suppose not." A car started up and sped away down the street. "So what's happening at home?"

"Oh, not a lot. The usual. We had the church sale in July, to try to raise money for the electrics. It was more work than you can possibly imagine, and we ended up with around four hundred pounds. I thought it was scarcely worth the effort, but Archie and the rector seemed quite satisfied. Henry won a bottle of rhubarb wine in the raffle. He's going to give it to Vi for her birthday."

"Lucky Vi. How is she? And how's Edie?"

"Oh, *Edie.* That's a real problem. Haven't you heard?"

It sounded disastrous. "Heard what?"

"She's got this dreadful cousin come to stay with her. She arrived last week and Edie's already looking demented."

The idea of Edie looking demented was enough to fill Alexa's heart with chill. "*What* dreadful cousin?"

Virginia told her, in some detail, the saga of Lottie Carstairs. Alexa was horrified. "I remember the Carstairses. They were very old, and they lived in a croft up the hill from Tullochard. And sometimes on Sundays they used to come to Strathcroy to have their dinner with Edie."

"That's right."

"They used to drive a tiny, rattly car. The two little old people sitting in the front and the great gawky daughter in the back."

"Well, the two little old people are now dead and the gawky daughter has gone witless. Which is putting it mildly."

Alexa was indignant. "But why should Edie have to look after her? Edie's got enough to do without such a responsibility."

"That's what we all told her, but she wouldn't listen. She says there's nowhere else for the poor soul to go. Anyway, last week she arrived in an ambulance and she's been with Edie ever since."

"But not for ever? She'll surely go back to her own house?"

"Let's hope so."

"Have you seen her?"

"Have I? She wanders round the village and talks to everybody. And not just the village. I took the dogs up to the dam the other day, and I was just sitting there on the bank when, all of a sudden, I had this queer feeling and I turned around, and there was Lottie sneaking up behind me."

"How spooky."

"Spooky's the word. Edie can't keep track of her. And that's not the worst of it. She goes out at night too, and drifts around the place. I suppose she's quite harmless, but the thought of her peering through windows is enough to put the fear of God into anybody."

"What does she look like?"

"She doesn't *look* mad. Just a bit strange. With very pale skin and eyes like boot buttons. And she's always smiling, which makes

her spookier than ever. Ingratiating. I think
that's the word. Edmund and Archie Balmerino say she was always like that. She
worked at Croy one year as a housemaid. I
don't think Lady Balmerino could find anybody else. Vi said it was the year Archie and
Isobel were married. Archie swears every
time you opened a door, Lottie was always
lurking behind it. And then she smashed so
much china that Lady Balmerino sacked her.
So all in all, as you can gather, it's something
of a problem."

The telephone rang.

"Oh, bother." Alexa, engrossed in the
drama of Strathcroy, resented the interruption. Reluctantly she got to her feet and went
to her desk to answer the call.

"Hello?"

"Alexa Aird?"

"Speaking."

"You won't remember me—Moira Bradford—but I was a guest at the Thomsons'
dinner party last week . . . and I wondered . . ."

Business. Alexa sat down, reached for her
note pad, her Biro, her engagement diary.

". . . not until October, but thought it better to fix things right away . . ."

Four courses, for twelve people. Perhaps, Mrs. Bradford suggested delicately, Alexa could give her some idea of cost?

Alexa listened, answered questions, made notes. Behind her, she was aware that Virginia had got out of her chair and was making for the door. She looked up. Virginia made gestures, mouthed "Just going to the john . . ." and before Alexa had the opportunity to tell her to use the cloakroom and not go upstairs, was gone.

". . . of course, my husband will see to the wine . . ."

"I beg your pardon?"

"I said my *husband* will see to the *wine*."

". . . oh, yes, of course . . . look, shall I get back to you?"

"But can't we decide everything now? I'd rather do it that way. And another thing is serving. Do you have a colleague, or do you do the serving yourself?"

Virginia had gone upstairs. She would see everything, draw the obvious conclusions, guess the truth. In a strange way, Alexa felt a sort of resigned relief. There wasn't much point in feeling anything else because it was too late to do anything about it.

She took a deep breath. She said, in her most capable voice, "No. I don't have a colleague. But you don't have to worry, because I can manage it all very easily on my own."

Virginia, in stockinged feet, climbed the staircase, reflecting, as she always did, that this was one of the prettiest of small London houses. So fresh, with its wallpaper and shining white paint. And so comfortable, with thick carpets and extravagantly generous curtains. On the landing, the doors to the bedroom and the bathroom both stood open. She went into the bathroom and saw that Alexa had new curtains here, a quilted chintz patterned with leaves and birds. Admiring them, she looked around for other signs of refurbishment.

There were none, but other unexpected objects caught her eye and the implication of these drove all other thoughts from her head. Two tooth-brushes in the tooth-mug. Shaving-tackle on the glass shelf, a wooden bowl of soap and a shaving-brush. A bottle of aftershave—Antaeus by Chanel—the same that Edmund used. By the side of the bath was a huge Turkish sponge, and hanging from the tap a ball of soap on a cord. From hooks behind the door hung two towelling robes, one large, blue-and-white-striped, the other smaller and white.

By now she had totally forgotten her reason for coming upstairs. She went out of the bathroom, back onto the landing. Downstairs was silent. The telephone call apparently was finished, and Alexa's voice stilled. She looked at the bedroom door, then put out her hand, pushed it completely open and went in. Saw the bed, piled with double pillows; Alexa's night-gown neatly folded on one set, a man's sky-blue pyjamas on the other. On the bedside table a pigskin travelling clock softly ticked. That clock did not belong to Alexa. Her eyes moved around the room. Silver brushes on the dressing-table, silk ties slung on the mirror. A row of masculine shoes. A wardrobe door, perhaps faulty, hung open. She saw rows of suits on hangers, and on the chest of drawers a pile of immaculately ironed shirts.

A step on the stair behind her. She turned. Alexa stood there, in her crumpled cotton clothes looking much as she had always looked. Yet different. "Have you lost weight?" Virginia had asked, but she knew now no diet was responsible for that indefinable radiance about Alexa that she had noticed the moment she saw her.

Their eyes met, and Alexa's were steady. She did not look away. There was no guilt there, no shame, and Virginia was glad for her. Alexa was twenty-one. It had taken long enough, but now it seemed that, at last, she had grown up.

Standing there, she remembered Alexa as a child, as she had first known her, so shy, so unsure, so eager to please. Then, the newly married Virginia had trod with the greatest of care, chosen her words, always painfully aware of the pitfalls of impetuously saying or doing the wrong thing.

It was the same now.

In the end it was Alexa who spoke first. She said, "I was going to tell you to use the downstairs loo."

"I'm sorry. I didn't mean to pry."

"You didn't have to. It's pretty obvious."

"Do you mind me knowing?"

"No. You would have found out some-time."

"Want to talk about it?"

"If you like."

Virginia came out of the bedroom and closed the door behind her. Alexa said, "Let's go back downstairs and I'll tell you there."

"I haven't been to the john yet." And all at once they were both laughing.

"He's called Noel Keeling. I met him in the street. He'd come to dinner with some people called Pennington—they live a couple of doors down—but he'd got the wrong night, so he was at a loose end."

"Was that the first time you'd ever seen him?"

"Oh, no, we'd met before that, but not very memorably. At some cocktail party, and then I did a directors' lunch for his firm."

"What does he do?"

"He's in advertising. Wenborn and Wein-burg."

"How old is he?"

"Thirty-four." Alexa's face became dreamy, the very picture of a girl able to talk at last about the man she loves. "He's . . . oh, I can't describe him. I was never any good at describing people."

A pause fell. Virginia waited. And then, in an effort to get Alexa back to the point of the story, said, "So, he'd come to dine in Ovington Street on the wrong night."

"Yes. And he was tired out. You could see how tired he was. He'd just flown in from New York and he hadn't had any sleep, and he looked so down in the mouth, I asked him in. And we had a drink, and then something to eat. Chops. And then he went to sleep on the sofa."

"You can't have been very entertaining."

"Oh, Virginia, I *told* you. He was tired."

"Sorry. Go on."

"And then the next evening was the night he was meant to have dinner with the Penningtons, so he dropped in for a moment first, and brought me a great bunch of roses.

A sort of thank-you. And then a couple of nights later, we went out for dinner. And . . . well, it sort of snowballed from there."

Virginia wondered if 'snowballed' was, under the circumstances, an appropriate word. But she said, "I see."

"And then a weekend came along and we drove out into the country for a day. And it was very warm and blue-skyed, and we took Larry and walked for miles over the downs, and we had dinner on the way back to London, and then we went to his flat for coffee. And then . . . well . . . it was dreadfully late . . . and . . ."

"You spent the night with him."

"Yes."

Virginia reached for another cigarette and lit it. Snapping out her lighter, she said, "And the following morning, you had no regrets?"

"No. No regrets."

"Was it . . . the first time? For you?"

"Yes. But you didn't have to ask that, did you?"

"Oh, honey, I know you very well."

"It made everything a bit embarrassing to begin with. Because I couldn't just let him find out. I couldn't pretend. It would have been like pretending you can swim frightfully well, and then jumping into the deep end and drowning. I didn't want to drown. So I told him. I was sure he would think I was dreadfully schoolgirlish or prissy. But do you know what he said? He said it was like being given a really splendid and unexpected present. And the next morning he woke me up by opening a bottle of champagne with a tremendous pop and a flying cork. And we sat in bed and drank it together. And after that . . ."

She paused, having apparently run out of both breath and words.

"More snowballing . . . ?"

"Well, you know. We were always together, I mean when we weren't working. And after a bit, it seemed ludicrous, at the end of the evening, driving off in different directions or having to borrow the other person's tooth-brush. So we talked about it. He's got a very nice flat in Pembroke Gardens and I would happily have gone there, but I couldn't leave this house empty when it's so full of Granny Cheriton's precious things. And for the same reason I didn't feel very keen to let it. It was a bit of a dilemma but then Noel met up with these friends who'd just got married and wanted a place to rent until they'd found somewhere of their own. So he let them have his flat and moved in with me."

"How long has he been here?"

"About two months."

"And you never let on."

"It wasn't that I was ashamed or secretive. It was just that it was all so incredibly marvellous, I wanted to keep it to ourselves. Somehow that was part of the magic."

"Does he have family?"

"His parents are both dead but he's got two sisters. One's married and lives somewhere in Gloucestershire. The other's in London."

"Have you met her?"

"No, and I don't really want to. She's much older than Noel and she sounds rather frightening. She's Editor-in-Chief of *Venus,* and terribly high-powered."

"So when I get home, do you want me to say anything?"

"It's up to you."

Virginia thought about it. "It would surely

be better to tell Edmund before he hears about it from some other person. He's in London a lot and you know how people talk. Especially men."

"That's what Noel says. Would you mind telling Fa? And Vi? Would it be very difficult to tell them?"

"Not difficult at all. Vi's amazing. She takes everything in her stride. And as for your father, at the moment I don't really care what I have to say to him."

Alexa frowned. "What *do* you mean?"

Virginia shrugged. She was frowning. When she frowned, all the fine lines on her face sprang into relief and she no longer looked so young. "I suppose you might as well know. We're not on the best of terms at the moment. We have a running row going on, no harsh words, but a certain frigid politeness."

"But . . ." Noel was forgotten and Alexa filled with apprehension. She had never heard Virginia speak about Fa in that cold tone of voice, could not remember them ever having quarrelled. Virginia adored him, fell in with all his plans, agreed with everything he suggested. There had never been anything but loving accord, every evidence of physical affection, and always—even from behind closed doors—much laughter and chat when they were together. They never seemed to run out of things to talk about, and the stability of their marriage was one of the reasons Alexa returned home to Balnaid whenever she could grab a holiday. She liked to be with them. The very thought of their falling out, not speaking, not loving, was unendurable. Perhaps they would never love again. Perhaps they would divorce. . . . "I can't *bear* it. What's happened?"

Virginia, seeing all the joy flow from Alexa's face, felt guilty and knew she had said too much. It was just that, talking about Noel, she had forgotten that Alexa was her stepdaughter and had allowed herself to speak bluntly and coldly about her problems, as though confiding in some old and intimate friend. A contemporary. But Alexa was not a contemporary.

She said quickly, "Don't look so horrified. It's not as bad as that. It's just that Edmund is insisting on sending Henry to boarding-school and I don't want him to go. He's only eight, and I think he's too young. Edmund has always known how I feel, but he settled it all without consulting me and I was very hurt. It's got to a pitch when we can't even talk about it. The subject is never mentioned. We've both dug our toes in and that seems to be it. Which is one of the reasons I took Henry away to Devon. He knows he's got to go away to school, and he knows that we're angry with each other. For his sake, I try to have fun with him, and do things with him the way I always have. And I would never dream of saying a word to him against Edmund. You know how he adores his father. But it's not easy."

"Oh, poor little Henry."

"I know. I thought maybe a day or two with Vi would make things better for him. You know what buddies they are. So I made the excuse of a new dress and seeing you, and came to London for a few days. I don't really need a new dress, but I've seen you, and the way things have turned out, that's made it worthwhile."

"But you've still got to go home to Balnaid."

"Yes. But perhaps things will be better."

"I am sorry. But I do understand. I know

how Fa can be once he's made up his mind about something. Like a brick wall. It's the way he works. I suppose it's one of the reasons that he's been so successful. But it's not easy if you're on the other side of the fence and you've got a point of view of your own."

"That's right. I sometimes think he would be a little more human if, just once in his life, he'd made a real cock-up of something. Then he could admit to the possibility of being mistaken. But he never has and he never does."

In total agreement, they gazed at each other glumly. Then Alexa said, without much conviction, "Perhaps Henry will love school, once he gets there."

"Oh, I hope so much that he will. For all our sakes. For Henry's sake in particular, I'd be grateful to be proved wrong. But I'm terribly afraid that he'll hate it."

"And you . . . ? Oh, Virginia. I can't imagine you without Henry."

"That's the trouble. Neither can I."

She reached for another cigarette and Alexa decided that the time had come to take some positive action.

She said, "Let's have a drink. After all

this, I think we could both do with one.
What for you? A Scotch?"

Virginia looked at her watch. "I should go.
Felicity's expecting me for dinner."

"There's heaps of time. And you must stay
and meet Noel. He won't be long now. Now
that you know about him, please don't go.
And it'll make it much easier for you, telling
Fa, if you've met Noel and can say how
much you like him."

Virginia smiled. Alexa was twenty-one and
now a woman of some experience but still
wondrously naïve.

"All right. But don't make it too strong."

Noel had bought the flowers from a street
vendor near the office. Carnations and sweet
peas and a misting of gypsophila. He had not
intended to buy flowers but had seen them as
he passed, thought about Alexa, and then
gone back to take a second look. The flower-
lady was anxious to be home and let him
have two bunches for the price of one. Two
bunches made a good show.

Nowadays, living in Ovington Street, he walked home from the office each evening. It gave him the chance to stretch his legs and yet was not too great a distance to be tiring at the end of a day's work. It was pleasant to turn in at the end of the street and know that this was where he now belonged.

Domesticity with Alexa, he had discovered, had many advantages, for she had proved to be not only a charming, compliant lover but the most undemanding of companions. At first Noel had harboured fears that she might become possessive, and jealous of any time that he spent away from her. He had suffered such resentments before, and had ended up feeling as though he had a millstone hanging round his neck. But Alexa was different, generous and understanding about evenings when he was committed to giving dinner to some overseas client, or the regular twice-weekly games of squash at his club.

Now, he knew that when he opened the blue front door she would be there, waiting for the sound of his key in the door, running up the stairs from the basement to greet him. He would relax with a drink, take a shower, eat an excellent dinner; later, watch the news, perhaps, or listen to some music. And, finally, bear Alexa off to bed.

His pace quickened. He took the steps in a single stride, juggling with the flowers in order to reach into his trouser pocket for his latchkey. The door, well-oiled, swung silently inwards, and he heard at once the voices from beyond the open drawing-room door. Alexa apparently had a caller. Which was unusual because ever since Noel had moved into Ovington Street, she had firmly kept all visitors at bay.

". . . I wish you'd stay for dinner," she was saying. He closed the door, being careful to make no sound. "Can't you ring Felicity and make some excuse?"

The hall table was piled with some person's expensive-looking shopping. He put his brief-case down on the floor.

"No, it would be too rude." A female visitor. He paused for a second to check on his appearance, sagging at the knees in front of the oval mirror, smoothing back his hair with his hand.

"It's grilled trout and almonds. . . ."

He went through the open door. Alexa was on the sofa with her back to him, but her visitor saw him at once, and their eyes met across the room. She had the most astonishingly blue eyes that he had ever seen, and their bright glitter was cool as a challenge.

She said, "Hi!"

Alexa, alerted, sprang up. "Noel. I never heard you come in." She looked rosy and faintly grubby but very sweet. He gave her the flowers and stooped to kiss the top of her head.

"You were talking too hard," he told her, and turned to the guest, who was now on her feet; a tall and stunning blonde, wearing a slender black dress and a huge black velvet bow at the back of her head. "How do you do. I'm Noel Keeling."

"Virginia Aird." Her handshake was firm and friendly and, it occurred to him, at variance with the light in those brilliant eyes. He knew then that Alexa had been confiding, and that this glamorous creature was totally *au fait* with their situation. It was up to him to carry it off.

"And you're . . . ?"

"My stepmother, Noel." Alexa spoke quickly, which meant that she was a little agitated and somewhat out of her social depth. "She's just down from Scotland to do some shopping. She dropped in out of the blue. It was the most lovely surprise. Oh, what gorgeous flowers. You are dear." She buried her nose in them and sniffed luxuriously. "Why do carnations always make me think of bread sauce?"

Noel smiled at Virginia. "She's got a one-track mind. Food."

"I'll go quickly and put them in water. We're having a drink, Noel."

"So I see."

"Do you want one?"

"Yes, of course, but don't worry, I'll help myself."

She left them bearing her bouquet, headed for the kitchen. Alone with Virginia, Noel turned to her. "Do sit down again. I didn't mean to disturb you." She did so, arranging her long limbs with some grace. "Tell me, when did you come to London? And how long are you staying?"

She explained. A spur-of-the-moment decision, an invitation from an old friend. Her voice was deep, with the attractive trace of an American accent. She had tried to get in touch with Alexa by telephone but had not been successful. Finally, she had just come around and taken Alexa by surprise.

As she told him all this, Noel fixed his drink. Now he brought it back to where she sat, and settled himself in the chair facing her. She had, he noticed, exceptional legs.

"And when are you going back to Scotland?"

"Oh, tomorrow, maybe. Or the day after."

"I heard Alexa inviting you to dinner. I wish you'd stay."

"That's kind of you, but I'm already committed. I shall have to go very soon, but Alexa wanted me to be here when you got home." Her eyes were bright as sapphires, unblinking. "She wanted me to meet you." She was splendidly direct, with no beating about the bush. He decided to meet her challenge head-on.

"I imagine that she's explained the situation to you."

"Yes, she has. I am entirely in the picture."

"I'm glad. It will make things much easier for all of us."

"Have they been difficult?"

"Not at all. But I think her conscience was troubling her."

"Her conscience has always troubled her."

"She's been a little worried about her family."

"Her family means a lot to her. She's had a strange upbringing. It's left her in some ways quite mature, and in others still childlike."

Noel wondered at her saying this. She must realize, surely, that he had already found that out for himself. He said, "She didn't want anybody hurt."

"She's asked me to tell her father."

"I think that's a splendid idea. I have been urging her to do so." He smiled. "Do you imagine that he will appear at our door with a horsewhip?"

"I shouldn't think so." Virginia reached for her handbag, took a cigarette and lit it with a gold lighter. "He's not a man who gives way to his emotions. But I think that, as soon as possible, you should make his acquaintance."

"It was never I who balked at the idea."

She eyed him through the drifting smoke of her cigarette. "I think it would be best if you were to come to Balnaid. Then we would all be around you, and Alexa would have a little moral support."

He realized that he was being invited to stay. In that solid old Edwardian house with the dogs and the conservatory and the country all around. Alexa had spoken to him, with great enthusiasm and at some length, of the joys of Balnaid. The garden, the picnics, the small brother, the grandmother, the old Nanny. He had shown polite interest but not much more. It did not sound like a place where amusing things might happen, and Noel's greatest horror was to be trapped, a guest in another person's house, and bored.

But now, faced by Virginia Aird, he found his preconceptions of Balnaid doing a swift about turn. For this elegant and sophisticated woman, with her mesmerizing eyes and her charming suggestion of a transatlantic drawl, could never be dull. Perceptive enough to leave you alone with *The Times*, if that was what you wanted, but still the sort of hostess who could, on the spur of the moment, think up some new and amusing ploy or ask a party of entertaining friends around for an impromptu drink. His imagination moved on to other delights. There would probably be some fishing. And shooting, too. Although that wouldn't be much use to Noel because he had never shot. Nevertheless . . .

He said, "How very kind of you to invite me."

"It would be best if we kept it very casual . . . as though, for some reason, you were coming anyway." She thought about this, and then her face lit up with bright inspiration. "Of course. The Steyntons' dance. What could be more natural than that? I know Alexa is in two minds about coming, but . . ."

"She said she wouldn't go without me and of course I haven't had an invitation."

"That's no problem. I'll have a word with Verena Steynton. There are never enough men at these affairs. She'll be delighted."

"You may have to persuade Alexa."

As he said this, Alexa came back into the room, bearing a pink-and-white jug in which she had loosely arranged Noel's offering. "Are you talking about me behind my back?" She put the jug on the table behind the sofa. "Don't those look lovely? You are kind, Noel. It makes me feel special, being brought flowers." She fiddled with a stray carnation, and then abandoned the arrangement and returned to her seat in the corner of the sofa. "Persuade Alexa to do what?"

"Come to the Steyntons' dance," said Virginia, "and bring Noel with you. I'll fix an invitation for him. And stay with us at Balnaid."

"But perhaps Noel doesn't want to go."

"I never said I didn't want to go."

"You did so!" Alexa was indignant. "The morning the invitation came you said tribal dances were scarcely your scene. I thought that was the end of the matter."

"We never really discussed it."

"You mean you *would* come?"

"If you want me to, of course."

Alexa shook her head in disbelief. "But Noel, it *will* be tribal dances. Reels and things. Could you bear that? It's no fun if you can't do them."

"I'm not totally inexperienced. That year I fished in Sutherland, there was a hooley in the hotel one evening and we all leaped around like savages, and as far as I remember, I leaped with the best of them. A couple of whiskies are all I need to lose my inhibitions."

Virginia laughed. "Well, if it all becomes too much for the poor man, I'm sure there'll be a night-club or a disco, so he can go and smooch in there." She stubbed out her cigarette. "What do you say, Alexa?"

"There doesn't seem to be much for me to say. Between the two of you, you've fixed the whole thing up."

"In that case, that's our little dilemma solved."

"What little dilemma?"

"Noel casually meeting Edmund."

"Oh. I see."

"Don't look so miserable. It's the perfect plan." She glanced at the clock, laid down her glass. "I must go."

Noel got to his feet. "Can I drive you somewhere?"

"No. You're sweet, but if you could find me a taxi, that would be great. . . ."

While he was gone on this errand, Virginia put her shoes back on, checked on her beautiful hairdo, reached for her scarlet jacket. Fastening the buttons, she caught Alexa's anxious gaze and smiled encouragingly.

"Don't worry about a thing. I'll make it

okay for you before you've even set foot in the house."

"But you and Fa. You won't still be having a row, will you? I couldn't bear it if there was a hateful atmosphere with the two of you being angry with each other."

"No, of course not. Forget that. I shouldn't have told you in the first place. We'll have a great time. And your being there will cheer me up after poor Henry's gone to school."

"Poor little boy. I can't bear to think about it."

"Like I said, neither can I. However, there doesn't seem to be much either of us can do about it." They kissed. "Thank you for the drink."

"Thank you for coming. And for being so marvellous. You . . . you do like him, don't you, Virginia?"

"I think he's dishy. You'll answer the invitation now?"

"Of course."

"And, Alexa, buy yourself a peachy new dress."

❦ 5 ❧

Thursday the Twenty-fifth

EDMUND AIRD DROVE HIS BMW into the
car-park of Edinburgh Airport just as the
seven-o'clock shuttle from London drifted
down out of the clouds and lined up for landing. Unhurriedly, he found a slot for himself,
got out of the car and locked the door,
watching, as he did so, the approach of the
plane. He had timed things exactly, and this
gave him much satisfaction. Standing around
and waiting, for any thing or anybody, filled
him with impatience. Every moment of time
was precious, and to fill in so much as five
minutes kicking his heels and doing nothing
caused him considerable frustration and anguish.

He walked through the car-park, crossed
the road, entered the terminal. The aircraft,
with Virginia on board, had landed. A num-

ber of people stood around, come to meet friends or relations. They were a mixed bunch and appeared to be either in a state of wild excitement or total unconcern. A young mother with three small children milling noisily around her knees lost her patience and slapped one of them. The child roared in indignation. The carousel began to move. Edmund stood jingling the loose change in his trouser pocket.

"Edmund."

He turned to see a man he met most days lunching at the New Club. "Hello, there."

"Who are you meeting?"

"Virginia."

"I've come to pick up my daughter and her two children. They're coming to stay for a week. There's some wedding on and the wee girl's going to be a bridesmaid. At least the plane's on time. I caught the three-o'clock shuttle from Heathrow last week and we didn't take off until half past five."

"I know. It's hell, isn't it?"

The doors at the top of the stairway had opened, the first trickle of passengers started to descend. Some searched for the one who had come to meet them; some looked lost and anxious, laden by too much hand-lug-gage. There was the usual proportion of businessmen returning from London conferences and meetings, complete with brief-cases, umbrellas, folded newspapers. One, quite unselfconsciously, bore a sheaf of red roses.

Edmund watched them, waiting for Virginia. His appearance, tall and elegantly suited, his demeanour, the heavily lidded eyes and expressionless features gave nothing away, and a stranger observing him would glean no clue as to his inner uncertainties. For the truth was that Edmund could not be sure either of his welcome from Virginia, nor what her reactions would be when she saw him standing there.

Relations between them, ever since the evening he had broken the news of his plans for sending Henry away to school, had been painfully strained. They had never had a row before, never quarrelled, and although he was a man who could exist very well without other people's approval, he was bored by the whole business, longed for a truce, and for this chill politeness that lay between them to come to an end and be finally finished.

He was not hopeful. As soon as the Strathcroy Primary had broken up for the summer, Virginia had packed Henry up and taken him to Devon to stay there with her parents for three long weeks. Edmund had hoped that this extended separation would somehow heal the wounds and bring Virginia's sulks to an end, but the holiday, spent in the company of her beloved child, appeared only to have hardened her attitude, and she returned home to Balnaid as cool as ever.

For a limited time, Edmund could deal with this, but he knew that the chill atmosphere that existed between them did not go unnoticed by Henry. He had become uncommunicative, prone to easy tears, and more dependent than ever on his precious Moo. Edmund hated Moo. He found it offensive that his son was still unable to sleep without that disgusting old scrap of baby blanket. He had been suggesting for some months that Virginia should wean Henry from Moo, but Virginia, as far as he could see, had ignored his advice. Now, with only weeks to go before Henry left for Templehall, she was going to have her work cut out.

After the debacle of the Devon holiday, and becoming frustrated with Virginia's resolute non-communication, Edmund had considered precipitating another row with his young wife, so bringing matters to a head. But then he decided that this could do nothing but worsen the situation. In her present state of mind, she was quite capable of packing her bags and hightailing it off to Leesport, Long Island, to stay with her devoted grandparents, now returned from their cruise. There she would be petted and spoiled as she had always been, and vociferously reassured that she was in the right and Edmund a hard-hearted monster even to contemplate sending small Henry away from her.

And so Edmund had kept his counsel and decided to ride out the emotional storm. He was, after all, not about to change his mind nor make any compromises. It was, at the end of the day, up to Virginia.

When she announced that she was going to London by herself for a few days, Edmund greeted the news with nothing but relief. If a few days of fun and shopping did not put her in a more sensible frame of mind, then nothing would. Henry, she told him, was going to stay with Vi. He could do what he pleased.

And so he put the dogs into kennels with Gordon Gillock, closed Balnaid, and spent the week in his flat in Moray Place.

The time alone had come as no hardship to him. He simply cleared his mind of all domestic problems, allowed himself to become absorbed in his work, and enjoyed being able to put in long and productive days at his office. As well, the word went swiftly around that Edmund Aird was in town and on his own. Extra attractive men were always at a premium, and the invitations to dinner had poured in. During Virginia's absence he had not once spent an evening at home.

But the hard truth was that he loved his wife and deeply resented this constraint that had lain for so long, like a fetid bog, between them. Standing waiting for her to appear, he hoped devoutly that the time spent enjoying herself in London had brought her to her senses.

For Virginia's sake. Because he had no intention of living under the cloud of her disapproval and umbrage for so much as one more day, and had already made the decision to stay in Edinburgh, and not return to Balnaid, if she had not relented.

Virginia was one of the last to appear. Through the door and down the stairs. He saw her at once. Her hair was different and she was dressed in unfamiliar and obviously brand-new clothes. Black trousers and a sapphire-blue shirt, and an immensely long raincoat that reached almost to her ankles. She was carrying, along with her flight bag, a number of shiny and extravagant-looking boxes and carriers, the very picture of an elegant woman fresh from a mammoth shopping spree. As well, she looked sensationally glamorous and about ten years younger.

And she was *his* wife. Despite everything, he realized all at once how dreadfully he had missed her. He did not move from where he stood, but he could feel the drum-beat of his own heart.

She saw him and paused. Their eyes met. Those blue and brilliant eyes of hers. For a long moment they simply looked at each other. Then she smiled, and came on down towards him.

Edmund took a long, deep breath in which relief, joy, and a surge of youthful well-being were all inextricably mingled. London, it appeared, had done the trick. Everything was going to be all right. He felt his face break into an answering, unstoppable smile, and went forward to greet her.

Ten minutes later, they were back in the car, Virginia's luggage stowed in the boot, doors closed, seat-belts fastened. Alone and together.

Edmund reached for the car keys, tossed them in his hand. "What do you want to do?" he asked.

"What suggestions do you have?"

"We can head straight back to Balnaid. Or we can go to the flat. Or we can go and have dinner in Edinburgh and then drive back to Balnaid. Henry is spending another night with Vi, so we are completely free."

"I should like to go out for dinner and then go home."

"Then that is what we shall do." He inserted the car key, switched on the ignition. "I have a table booked at Rafaelli's." He manoeuvred the crowded car-park, drove to the toll-gate, paid his dues. They moved out onto the road.

"How was London?"

"Hot and crowded. But *fun.* I saw masses of people, and went to about four parties, and Felicity had got tickets for *Phantom of the Opera.* I spent so much money, you're going to pass out when the bills come in."

"Did you get a dress for the Steyntons' dance?"

"Yes. At Caroline Charles. A really dreamy creation. And I got my hair done."

"I noticed."

"Do you like it?"

"Very elegant. And that coat is new."

"I felt such a country frump when I got to London, I went slightly mad. It's Italian. Not much use in Strathcroy, I admit, but I couldn't resist it."

She laughed. His own sweet-tempered Virginia. He was filled with grateful satisfaction, and swore to himself that he would remember this when the inevitable American Express account came in. She said, "I can see I shall have to go to London more often."

"Did you see Alexa?"

"Yes, and I've lots to tell you, but I'll save

that up till we're having dinner. How's Henry?"

"I rang up a couple of evenings ago. He's having, as usual, the time of his life. Vi asked Kedejah Ishak to tea at Pennyburn, and she and Henry made a dam in the burn and sailed paper boats. He was quite happy to spend an extra night with Vi."

"And you? What have you been doing?"

"Working. Going out to dinner. I've had a social week."

She glanced at him wryly. "I'll bet," she said without rancour.

He drove into Edinburgh by the old Glasgow road, and as they approached, the Old City looked its most impressive, etched like a romantic engraving beneath the immense and steely sky. The wide streets were verdant with leafy trees, the skyline pierced by spires and towers, and the Castle on its rock brooded over all, with flag snapping at the mast-head. Coming to the New Town, they entered the gracefully proportioned purlieus of Georgian terraces and spacious crescents. All had been newly sandstoned, and the buildings, with their classic windows and porticoes and airy fanlights, stood honey-coloured in the evening light.

Circling the one-way system, Edmund made his way through a labyrinth of hidden lanes and turned at last into a narrow cobbled street to draw up at the pavement's edge outside the little Italian restaurant. On the opposite side of this street stood one of Edinburgh's many beautiful churches. High up on the tower, above the massive arched doorway, the hands of a golden clock moved to nine o'clock, and as they got out of the car, its chimes pealed out across the rooftops, striking the hours. Flocks of pigeons, disturbed from their airy roosts, exploded upwards in a flurry of flight. When the last chime had struck, they settled again, on sill and parapet, cooing to themselves, folding their wings, pretending nothing had happened, as though ashamed of their silly agitation.

"You'd think," said Virginia, "that they'd get used to the din. Become blasé."

"I never met a blasé pigeon. Did you?"

"Come to think of it, no."

He took her arm and led her across the pavement and through the door. Inside the restaurant was small, dimly lighted, smelling of fresh coffee and garlic and delicious Mediterranean food. The place was pleasantly busy and most of the tables were occupied, but the head waiter spied them at once and made his way across the floor to welcome them.

"Good evening, Mr. Aird. And Madame."

"Good evening, Luigi."

"I have your table ready."

The table Edmund had particularly asked for, in the corner, tucked under the window. A starched pink damask cloth, pink damask napkins, a single rose in a slender vase. Charming, intimate, seductive. The ultimate ambience for the ending of a feud.

"Perfect, Luigi. Thank you. And the Moët et Chandon?"

"No problem, Mr. Aird. I have it on ice."

They drank the chilled champagne. Virginia filled in the details of her social activities, the art exhibitions she had been to, the concert at the Wigmore Hall.

They ordered in a leisurely fashion. Eschewed the ravioli and tagliatelli, and went instead for duck pâté, and cold Tay salmon.

"Why do I bring you to Italian restaurants, when you can eat Tay salmon at home?"

"Because there is nothing in the world so delicious, and after my whirl in London I seem to have had my fill of ethnic food."

"I shall not ask with whom you have been dining."

She smiled. "Nor I you."

Without haste, they ate their way through the perfect meal, ending with fresh raspberries coated in thick cream, and a Brie of exactly the right consistency. She told him of the exhibition at Burlington House, Felicity Crowe's plans to buy a country cottage in Dorset, and tried to explain, with a certain amount of confusing detail, the plot of *Phantom of the Opera*. Edmund, who knew the plot anyway, listened with absorbed interest, simply because it was so marvellous to have her back, to listen to her voice, to have her sharing her pleasures with him.

Finally, their plates were cleared, and coffee brought, black and fragrant, steaming in the tiny cups. As well as a dish of chocolate peppermints thin as wafers.

By now most of the other tables had emptied, the diners gone home. Only one other couple sat, as they sat, but drinking brandy. The man smoked a cigar.

The Moët et Chandon was finished, up-ended in the ice-bucket. "Would you like a brandy?" Edmund asked.

"No. Not a thing more."

"I'd have one, but I have to drive."

"I could drive."

He shook his head. "I don't need a brandy." He leaned back in his chair. "You've told me everything, but you still haven't told me about Alexa."

"I was keeping it to the end."

"Does that mean it's good?"

"I think it's good. I'm not sure what you'll think."

"Try me."

"You won't become Victorian, will you?"

"I don't think I ever am."

"Because Alexa's got a man. He's moved in with her. He's living with her in the house in Ovington Street."

Edmund did not at once reply to this. Then he said, quite calmly, "When did this happen?"

"In June, I think. She didn't tell us because she was afraid we would all be upset or disapproving."

"Does she think we wouldn't like him?"

"No. I think she thinks you'd like him very much. It's just that she wasn't sure how you'd take it. So she gave me the job of telling you."

"Have you met him?"

"Yes. Just for a little while. We had a drink together. There wasn't time for more."

"Did you like him?"

"Yes, I did. He's very good-looking, very charming. He's called Noel Keeling."

Edmund's coffee-cup was empty. He caught Luigi's eye and asked for it to be refilled. When this was done, he stirred it thoughtfully, his eyes downcast, his handsome features giving nothing away.

"What do you think?" Virginia asked.

He looked up at her and smiled. "I think I'm thinking that I thought it would never happen."

"But you're pleased that it has?"

"I'm pleased that Alexa has found someone who is sufficiently fond of her to want to spend much time with her. It would be easier for everybody if it could have taken a less dramatic course, but I suppose nowadays it's inevitable that they should shack up together and give it a try before making any momentous decision." He took a mouthful of the scalding coffee, set down the cup. "It's just that she's such an extraordinarily unsophisticated child."

"She isn't a child any more, Edmund."

"It's hard to think of Alexa as anything else."

"We have to."

"I realize that."

"She was in rather a state about my telling you all. She *asked* me to tell you, but I know, in a funny way, she was dreading the secret coming out."

"What do you think I should do?"

"You don't have to do anything. She's going to bring him up to Balnaid in September for the weekend of the Steyntons' dance. And we'll all behave as casually as all-get-out . . . just as though he were an old childhood chum or a school friend. I don't think we can do more. After that, it's up to them."

"Was that your idea or Alexa's?"

"Mine," Virginia told him, not without pride.

"What a clever girl you are."

"I told her other things as well, Edmund. I told her that, over the last few weeks, we haven't exactly been the best of friends."

"That must be the understatement of the year."

She fixed him with her brilliant gaze. She said, "I haven't changed my mind. I haven't changed my attitude. I don't want Henry to go and I think he's too young, and I think you're making a dreadful mistake; but I know that Henry's been upset by all this ill feeling, and I've decided we've got to stop thinking about ourselves and think about the children instead. Think about Henry and Alexa. Because Alexa said that if we were still glowering at each other, then she wasn't going to come up with Noel because she couldn't stand the idea of any sort of bad atmosphere between us." She paused, waiting for Edmund to make some sort of comment. But he said nothing and so she continued. "I've been thinking about that. I tried to imagine going back to Leesport and finding my grandparents snapping each other's heads off, but it was unimaginable, and that's the way we've got to make it for Henry and

Alexa. I'm not giving in, Edmund. I'll never come round to your way of thinking. But what can't be cured must be endured. Besides, I've missed you. I don't really like being on my own. In London I kept wishing you were there." She put her elbows on the table, her chin in her hands. "You see, I love you."

After a little, Edmund said, "I'm sorry."

"Sorry I love you?"

He shook his head. "No. Sorry I went to Templehall and settled the whole affair with Colin Henderson without consulting you. I should have had more consideration. It was overbearing."

"I've never heard you admit to being in the wrong before."

"I hope you never have to again. It's painful." He reached out and took her hand in his. "It's a truce then?"

"With one proviso?"

"What would that be?"

"That when the terrible day comes and poor Henry has to go to Templehall, I am not asked nor expected to take him. Because I don't think that I could physically bear to do that. Later on maybe, when I've got used to being without him. But not the first time."

"I'll be there," said Edmund. "I shall take him."

It was growing late. The other couple had departed, and the waiters were standing around trying not to look as though they were longing for Edmund and Virginia, too, to go home and let them close up for the night. Edmund called for the bill and, while this was coming, leaned back in his chair, put his hand in the pocket of his jacket and brought out a small package wrapped in thick white paper and sealed with red wax.

"It's for you." He put it on the table between them. "It's a welcome-home present."

✿ 6 ✿

IF HENRY COULD NOT BE AT HOME, at
Balnaid, then the next best thing was staying
with Vi. At Pennyburn, he had his own bedroom, a tiny room over what had once been
the front door, with a narrow window looking out over the garden and the glen and the
hills beyond. From this window, if he
screwed his neck around a bit, he could even
see Balnaid, half-hidden in trees beyond the
river and the village. And in the mornings
when he awoke and sat up, he could watch
the rising sun stretching long fingers of early
light across the fields, and listen to the song
of the blackbird that had its nest in the top
branches of the old elder tree by the burn. Vi
did not like elder trees, but she had let this
one stand, because it was a good tree for
Henry to climb. That was how he had found
out about the blackbird's nest.

The room was so small, it was a little like sleeping in a Wendy house, or even a cupboard, but that was part of its charm. There was space for his bed and a chest of drawers with a mirror hanging over it, but no more. A couple of hooks on the back of the door did duty as a wardrobe, and there was a neat little light over his bedhead, so that he could read in bed if he wanted to. The carpet was blue and the walls were white. There was a nice picture of a bluebell wood, and the curtains were white with bunches of field flowers spattered all over them.

This was his last night with Vi. Tomorrow, his mother was going to come and fetch him, and take him home. It had been a funny sort of few days, because the Strathcroy Primary had already opened for the winter term, and all his friends were back at their lessons. And so Henry, destined for Templehall, had nobody to play with. But somehow it hadn't mattered. Edie was there most mornings, and Vi was always full of bright ideas for a small boy's amusement and entertainment. They had gardened together, and she had taught him how to make fairy cakes, and for the evenings she had produced a mammoth jig-

saw puzzle with which they had struggled together. One afternoon Kedejah Ishak had
come for tea after school, and she and Henry
had built a dam in the stream and become
extremely wet. Another day he and Vi had
taken a picnic lunch up to the loch and made
a collection of twenty-four different wild
flowers. She had shown him how to press
them dry between leaves of blotting paper
and thick books, and when they were ready
he was going to stick them into an old exercise book with bits of Sellotape.

He had had his supper and his bath, and
was now in bed in his sleeping-bag, and reading his library book, which was by Enid
Blyton and called *The Famous Five*. He
heard the clock in the hall strike eight
o'clock, and then Vi's footsteps treading
heavily up the staircase, which meant that
she was coming to say good night to him.

His door was open. He laid down his book
and waited for her to come through it. She
appeared, tall and large and solid, and settled
herself comfortably on the foot of his bed.
The springs creaked. He was cosy in his own
sleeping-bag, but she had tucked a blanket
over the top of it, and he thought that it was

one of the best feelings, having someone sit on your bed, with the blanket pulled tight over your legs. It made him feel very safe.

Vi wore a silk blouse with a cameo brooch at the collar, and a soft, heathery-blue cardigan, and she had brought her spectacles with her, which meant that she was quite prepared, if he wished, to read aloud a chapter or two from *The Famous Five*.

She said, "This time tomorrow, you'll be back in your own bed. We've had a good time, though, haven't we?"

"Yes." He thought of all the fun they had had. Perhaps it was wrong to want to go home and leave her, but at least he knew that she was safe and happy alone in her little house. He wished that he could feel the same about Edie.

Lately, Henry had stopped dropping in on Edie, because he was frightened of Lottie. There was something witchy about her, with her strange dark eyes that never blinked, and her ungainly, unaccountable movements, and her endless flood of chat that was too disjointed to be called conversation. Most of the time Henry hadn't the least idea what she was talking about, and he knew that it exhausted Edie. Edie had told him to be nice to Lottie, and he had done his best, but the truth was that he hated her, and could not bear to think of Edie closeted up with her scary cousin, and having to deal with her, day in and day out.

From time to time he had seen headlines in the newspapers about poor people being murdered with axes or carving knives, and felt certain that Lottie, if roused or thwarted, was perfectly capable of attacking darling Edie—perhaps late at night, in the dark— and leaving her, dead and blood-stained, on the kitchen floor.

He shivered at the thought. Vi noticed the shiver. "Is something worrying you? A ghost just went over your grave."

This observation was too close for comfort. "I was thinking about Edie's cousin. I don't like her."

"Oh, Henry."

"I don't think Edie is safe with her."

Vi made a little face. "To be honest, Henry, I'm not very happy either. But I think that it's just a great trial for Edie. We talk about her cousin in the mornings, over coffee. Lottie's certainly a very tiresome lady, but apart from driving Edie to distraction with her ways, I don't think Edie's in any real danger. Not the kind you're imagining."

He hadn't told her what he imagined, but she knew. Vi always knew things like that.

"You will take care of her, won't you, Vi? You won't let anything happen?"

"No, of course I won't. And I shall make a point of seeing Edie every day, and keeping an eye on the situation. And I'll ask Lottie for tea one day, and that'll give Edie a bit of a breather."

"When do you think Lottie will go away?"

"I don't know. When she's better. These things take time."

"Edie was so happy, on her own. And now she's not happy a bit. And she has to sleep on the Put-U-Up. It must be horrid not being in her own room."

"Edie is a very kind person. More kind than most of us. She is making a sacrifice for her cousin."

Henry thought of Abraham and Isaac. "I hope Lottie doesn't make a sacrifice of her."

Vi laughed. "You're letting your imagination run away with you. Don't go to sleep worrying about Edie. Think about seeing your mother again tomorrow."

"Yes." That was much better. "What time do you think she'll come?"

"Well, you've got a busy day tomorrow, out with Willy Snoddy and his ferrets. I should think about tea-time. When you get back, she'll be here."

"Do you think she'll bring me a present from London?"

"Sure to."

"Perhaps she'll bring you a present, too."

"Oh, I don't expect a present. Besides, it's my birthday soon, so I'll get one then. She always gives me something quite special, something that I never realized how much I wanted."

"What day is your birthday?" He had forgotten.

"The fifteenth of September. The day before the Steyntons' party."

"Are you going to have the picnic?"

Vi always arranged a picnic for her birthday. Everybody came, and they all met up at the loch and lit a fire and cooked sausages, and Vi brought her birthday cake in a big box, and when she cut it, the assembled party stood around and sang "Happy Birthday to You." Sometimes it was a chocolate cake, and sometimes it was an orange cake. Last year it had been an orange cake.

He remembered last year. Remembered the inclement day, the racing wind and the scattered showers that had dampened nobody's enthusiasm. Last year he had given Vi a picture that he had drawn with his felt pens, and which his mother had had framed and mounted, just like a proper picture. Vi had it hanging in her bedroom. This year he was giving her the bottle of rhubarb wine that he had won in the raffle at the church sale.

This year . . . He said, "This year, I shan't be there."

"No. This year, you'll be at boarding-school."

"Couldn't you have your birthday earlier, so that I could be there?"

"Oh, Henry, birthdays don't work that way. But it won't be the same without you."

"Will you write me a letter, and tell me all about it?"

"Of course I will. And you shall write to

me. There'll be such a lot that I will want to hear."

He said, "I don't want to go."

"No. I don't suppose you do. But your father thinks that you should go, and he nearly always knows best."

"Mummy doesn't want me to go, either."

"That's because she loves you so. She knows that she'll miss you."

He realized then that this was the first time he and Vi had talked about his going away. This was because Henry did not even want to think about it, let alone discuss it, and Vi had never brought the subject up. But now they had started speaking about it, he discovered that he felt easier. He knew that he could say anything to Vi, and knew, too, that she would never repeat it.

He said, "They've been quarrelling. They've been cross with each other."

"Yes," said Vi. "I know."

"How do you know, Vi?"

"I may be old, but I'm not stupid. And your father is my son. Mothers know lots about their sons. The good bits and the not-so-good bits. It doesn't stop them loving

them, but it makes them a little bit more understanding."

"It's been so horrid, with them so unkind
to each other."

"It must have been."

"I don't want to go away to school, but I
hate them being cross with each other. I simply *hate* it. It makes the house feel all head-
achy and ill."

Vi sighed. "If you want to know what I
think, Henry, I think they've both been very
short-sighted and selfish. But I haven't been
able to say anything, because it's none of my
business. That's another thing a mother
mustn't do. She must never interfere."

"I really want to go home tomorrow,
but . . ." He gazed at her, his sentence left
unfinished, because he didn't really know
what he was trying to say.

Vi smiled. When she smiled her face
creased into a thousand wrinkles. She laid
her hand on his. It felt warm and dry, and
rough from all the gardening she did.

She said, "There's an old saying, that parting makes the heart grow fonder. Your
mother and father have had a few days apart,
on their own, with time to think things over.

I'm sure they'll both have realized how wrong they both have been. You see, they love each other very much, and if you love someone, you need to be with them, close to them. You need to be able to confide, to laugh together. It's just about as important as breathing. By now, I'm certain that they will have found this out. And I'm just as certain that everything will be just as it was before."

"Really certain, Vi?"

"Really certain."

She sounded so certain that Henry felt that way too. Such a relief. It was as though a huge weight had dropped from his shoulders. And this made everything much better. Even the prospect of leaving home and parents and being sent to board at Templehall had lost some of its fearfulness. Nothing could be as bad as thinking that his home would never be the same again. Reassured, and filled with grateful love for his grandmother, he held out his arms, and she leaned forward, and he embraced her, hugging her tight around her neck and pressing kisses on her cheek. When he drew back, he saw that her eyes were very shiny and bright.

She said, "It's time to sleep."

He was ready for it, now suddenly drowsy. He lay back on the pillow and felt beneath it for Moo.

Vi laughed at him, but gently, teasing him. "You don't need that old bit of baby blanket. You're a grown-up boy now. You can make fairy cakes, and do jigsaw puzzles, and remember the names of all those wild flowers. I think you can do without Moo."

Henry screwed up his nose. "But not tonight, Vi."

"All right. Not tonight. But tomorrow, maybe."

"Yes." He yawned. "Maybe."

She stooped to kiss him, and then got up off the bed. The springs creaked once more. "Good night, my lamb."

"Good night, Vi."

She turned out his light and went out of the room, but she left the door open. The darkness was soft and blowy and smelt of the hills. Henry turned on his side, curled up in a ball, and closed his eyes.

❦ 7 ❧

Friday the Twenty-sixth

WHEN, TEN YEARS AGO, VIOLET AIRD bought Pennyburn from Archie Balmerino, she had become owner of a sad and drab little house with little to commend it save its view and the small stream that tumbled down the hill on the western march of its land. It was from this stream that the house took its name.

It stood in the heart of Archie's estate, on the face of the hill that sloped up from the village, and access was by the Croy back drive and then a rutted track overgrown by thistles and fenced by sagging posts and broken barbed wire.

The garden, such as it was, lay on the slope to the south of the house. This too was surrounded by rotting posts and straggling wire, and consisted of a small drying-green, a weedy vegetable patch, and dismal evidences of hen-keeping—leaning wooden sheds, much wire netting, and nettles grown waist-high.

The house was built of dull coloured stone, with a grey-tiled roof and maroon paintwork in a sad state of repair. Concrete stairs led up from the garden to the door, and inside were small and lightless rooms, hideous peeling wallpaper, the smell of damp, and the persistent drip of some faulty tap.

In fact, so unattractive was the entire property that Edmund Aird, viewing it for the first time, strongly recommended that his mother abandon the idea of ever living there and start to look for somewhere else.

But Violet, for reasons of her own, liked the house. It had stood empty for some years, which accounted for its dereliction, but despite the mould and the gloom, it had a pleasant feel to it. And it had that little burn within its lands, tumbling away down the hill. And, as well, the view. Inspecting the house, Violet would pause from time to time to glance out, rubbing a clear space on the dusty glass of the windows, seeing the village below, the river, the glen, the distant hills.

She would never find another house with such a view. The view and the burn seduced her, and she disregarded her son's advice.

Doing it all up had been tremendous fun. It had taken six months to complete the work, and during that time Violet—politely spurning Edmund's invitation to remain at Balnaid until such time as she could move into her new abode—camped in a caravan that she had rented from a tourist park a few miles up the glen. She had never lived in a caravan before, but the idea had always appealed to her gypsy instincts and she leaped at the chance. The caravan was parked at the back of the house, along with the concrete mixers and barrows and shovels and daunting piles of rubble, and from the open door she could keep an eye on the workmen, and dash out to have a word with the long-suffering architect the moment she spied his car come bumping up the road. For the first month or two of this cheerfully vagabond existence, it was summer, and the only hazards were the midges and a leaky roof whenever it rained. But when the winter gales blew, the caravan trembled beneath their blast and rocked unsteadily at its temporary mooring, not unlike a small boat in a storm. Violet found this quite exciting and relished the dark and gusty nights. She could lie in her bunk, which was far too short and too narrow for such a sizy lady, listening to the keening wind and watching the clouds racing across the cold, moonlit skies.

But she did not spend all her time alternately bullying and cajoling the builders. To Violet, a garden was even more important than a house. Before the workmen had started in on their labours, she had already engaged a man with a tractor, who tore up all the old fence posts and broken wire. In their place she planted a beech hedge on either side of her driveway and all around her small plot of land. After ten years, this was still not high, but thick and firm, always leafy, and so providing good shelter for birds.

Within this hedge, on either side, she planted trees. To the east, conifers. Not her favourites, but quick-growing and good for keeping the worst of the coldest wind at bay. On the west, overhanging the stream, grew gnarled elder, willows, and double white cherries. At the foot of the garden she had kept her planting low, in order to conserve the view. Azaleas grew there, and potentillas, with drifts of spring bulbs in the rough grass.

There were two curving flower-beds, one herbaceous and one filled with roses, and between them a good-sized lawn. This was on the slope and tricky to cut. Violet had bought an electric lawn-mower, but Edmund—interfering again—decided that she was likely to sever the flex and electrocute herself, and so engaged the services of Willy Snoddy to come once a week and do the job for her. Violet knew perfectly well that Willy was a great deal less competent than she herself at handling complicated equipment, but she went along with the arrangement as being the line of least resistance. Every now and then Willy, being laid low with a killing hangover, did not turn up, and then Violet, quite happily and efficiently, cut the grass herself.

But she did not tell Edmund that she had done so.

As for the house, that she had transformed, turning it back to front and opening out all the poky and ill-proportioned rooms. Now the main entrance stood to the north and the old front door had become a glassed garden door, opening straight out of her sitting-room. The concrete stairs she had demolished, and in their place stood a semi-circular flight of steps built of old stone salvaged from a fallen dyke. Aubrietia and scented thyme grew from crannies between these rocks and smelt delicious when one trod upon them.

After some consideration, Violet decided that she could not bear the dull colour of the stone walls of Pennyburn, and so had them all harled and painted white. Windows and doorways were outlined in black, which gave the face of the house a crisp and down-to-earth appearance. To embellish it, she had planted a wistaria, but, after ten years, it had scarcely grown as high as her shoulder. By the time it reached the roof, she would probably be dead.

At seventy-seven one was perhaps better off sticking to hardy annuals.

All that was missing was a conservatory. The one at Balnaid had been built at the same time as the house. Its erection was due to the insistence of Violet's mother, Lady Primrose Akenside, a woman not addicted to the great outdoors. It was Lady Primrose's opinion that, if forced to live in the wilds of Scotland, a conservatory was absolutely essential. Quite apart from the fact that it was useful for keeping the house supplied with pot plants and grapes, it was somewhere to sit when the sun shone and yet the wind blew with an edge like ice to it. Such days, everybody knew, occurred with amazing frequency during the winter and spring and autumn months. But Lady Primrose spent a good deal of the summers in her conservatory as well, entertaining her friends and playing bridge.

Violet had loved the Balnaid conservatory for less social reasons, relishing the warmth, the peace, the smell of damp earth and ferns and freesias. When the weather was too inclement to garden, you could always potter about in the conservatory, and what better place to sit down after lunch and try to do *The Times* crossword?

Yes, she missed it, but after deliberation had decided that Pennyburn was too small and modest for such an extravagant addition. It would make the house look pretentious and foolish, and she was not about to inflict such an indignity upon her new home. And it was scarcely a hardship to sit in her sheltered and sunny garden and try to do the crossword there.

She was in her garden now, and had been out working all afternoon, staking clumps of Michaelmas daisies before the autumn winds arrived to fell them flat. It was a day to start thinking about autumn. Not cold but fresh, with a certain smell about the air, a briskness. The farmers were harvesting, and the distant rumble of combine harvesters working in tall fields of barley was seasonal and strangely reassuring. The sky was blue but sailing with clouds blown in from the west. A blinking day, the old country people called it, as the sun went in and out.

Unlike many people, Violet did not mourn the passing of the summer and the prospect of a long dark winter ahead. "How can you bear to live in Scotland?' she was sometimes asked. "The weather so unpredictable, so much rain, so cold." But Violet knew that she could not bear to live anywhere else, and never yearned to move away. When Geordie was alive they had travelled together extensively. They had explored Venice and Istanbul, paced the art galleries of Florence and Madrid. One year they had taken an archaeological cruise to Greece; another time had sailed the fjords of Norway, as far north as the Arctic Circle and the midnight sun. But without him, she knew no urge to journey abroad. She preferred to stay right here, where her roots were deep, surrounded by a countryside that she had known since she was a child. As for the weather, she disregarded it, caring not if it froze or snowed or blew or rained or scorched, provided she could be out of doors and part of it all.

Which was proved by her complexion, weather-beaten and lined as an old farm worker's. But again, at seventy-seven, what did a few wrinkles matter? A small price to pay for an energetic and active old age.

She drove in the last stake, twisted the last length of wire. Finished. She stepped back onto the grass to survey her work. The canes showed, but once the Michaelmas daisies had thickened out a bit, they would be concealed. She looked at her watch. Nearly half past three. She sighed, always reluctant to stop gardening and go indoors. But she stripped off her gloves and dropped them into her wheelbarrow, then collected her tools, the last of the canes, the drum of wire, and barrowed the lot around the house to her garage, where all was stowed neatly away until the next day's labour.

Then she went into the house by the kitchen door, toeing off her rubber boots and hanging her jacket on a hook. In the kitchen, she filled the kettle and switched it on to boil. She laid a tray with two cups and saucers, a milk jug, a sugar bowl, and a plate of chocolate digestive biscuits. (Virginia would not eat anything at teatime but Violet was never averse to a small snack.)

She went upstairs to her bedroom, washed her hands, found a pair of shoes, tidied her hair, slapped a bit of face powder onto her shining nose. As she did this, she heard the car come up the hill and turn into the lane. A moment later came the slam of its door, her own front door opening, and Virginia's voice.

"Vi!"

"Just coming."

She settled her pearls, fixed a stray wisp of

hair, and went downstairs. Her daughter-in-law stood in the hall waiting for her; her long legs were in corduroys and a leather jacket was slung around her shoulders. She had a new hair-do, Violet noticed, drawn back from her brow and fastened at the nape of her neck with a ribbon bow. She looked, as always, casually elegant, and happier than Violet had seen her for a long time.

"Virginia. How lovely to have you home again. And how chic you look. I love the hair." They kissed. "Did you have it done in London?"

"Yes. I thought perhaps it was time I changed my image." She looked about her. "Where's Henry?"

"He's out ferreting with Willy Snoddy."

"Oh, *Vi.*"

"It's all right. He'll be home in half an hour."

"I didn't mean that. I meant what's he doing spending his time with that old reprobate?"

"Well, there are no children to play with because they're all in school. And he got talking to Willy when he came to cut the grass this week, and Willy invited him to go ferreting. He seemed very keen to go, so I said he could. You don't disapprove, do you?"

Virginia laughed and shook her head. "No, of course not. It's just rather unexpected. Do you think Henry realizes what ferreting entails? It's quite a bloodthirsty business."

"I've no idea. We'll doubtless hear all about it when he gets back. Willy will see that he's on time, I know."

"I always thought you thought the old drunk was quite undependable."

"He wouldn't dare break his promise to me, and he never gets drunk in the afternoons. Now, how are you? Did you have a good time?"

"A great time. Here . . ." She thrust a flat package, impressively wrapped, into Violet's hands. "I brought you a present from the big city."

"My dear, you didn't need to."

"It's a thank-you for having Henry."

"I've loved having him. But he's longing to see you and go home to Balnaid. He was all packed up and ready long before breakfast this morning. Now, I want to hear all about everything. Come and watch me open my present."

She led the way into her sitting-room and settled herself in comfort in her own fireside chair. It was a relief to get the weight off her feet. Virginia perched herself on the arm of the sofa and watched. Violet undid the ribbon bow and unwrapped the paper. A flat box, orange and brown, was revealed. She removed the lid. Inside, folded and silken beneath the layers of tissue paper, was a Hermès scarf.

"Oh, Virginia. This is far too much."

"No more than you deserve."

"But having Henry was a *treat.*"

"I've brought him a present, too. It's in the car. I thought he could open it here, before I take him home."

The scarf was all pinks and blues and greens. Just the thing for brightening up that grey woollen dress. "I can't thank you enough—I'm really delighted with it. And now . . ." She folded the scarf, returned it to its box, and set it aside. "Let's have a cup of tea, and you can tell me everything that's happened in London. I want to hear all the details. . . ."

"When did you get back?"

"Yesterday evening, on the shuttle. Edmund met me at Turnhouse and we went into Edinburgh and had dinner at Rafaelli's, and after that we drove home to Balnaid."

"I hope"—Violet fixed Virginia with a firm stare—"that you used the time together to sort out your differences."

Virginia had the grace to look abashed. "Oh, Vi. Did it show so much?"

"It was obvious to anyone but a blind man. I didn't say anything, but you must realize that it's very worrying for Henry if you and his father are not on good terms."

"Did Henry talk to you about it?"

"Yes, he did. He's much upset. I think he feels that going to Templehall is bad enough, but having you and Edmund at each other's throats is more than he can bear."

"We weren't exactly at each other's throats."

"Icy politeness is almost worse."

"I know. And I'm sorry. And Edmund

and I have made it up. By that I don't mean
anything's changed. Edmund won't budge
from his decision, and I still think it's a
dreadful mistake. But at least we've called a
truce." She smiled and held out a slender
wrist circled by a wide bracelet of gold.
"Over dinner, he gave me this. It's a welcome-home present. So I'd be churlish to
carry on sulking."

"That is a great relief to me. I managed to
persuade Henry that you would both have
come to your senses and would be friends
again. And I'm grateful to you both, because
now I don't feel that I am letting him down.
He needs a lot of reassurance, Virginia. A lot
of security."

"Oh, Vi, don't I know it?"

"And there's another thing. He's very
bothered about Edie. He's frightened of Lottie. He thinks that Lottie might harm Edie in
some way."

Virginia frowned. "Did he say so?"

"We talked about it."

"Do you think he's right?"

"Children are perceptive. Like dogs. They
recognize evil where, perhaps, we adults
don't see it."

"Evil is a strong word, Vi. I know she gives me the shivers, but I've always told myself she's just harmlessly dotty."

"I really don't know," said Violet. "But I've promised Henry that we will all keep a weather eye on the situation. And if he talks to you about it, you must listen to him, and try to set his mind at rest."

"Of course."

"Now." With that necessary exchange safely disposed of, Violet steered the conversation into a more cheerful direction. "Tell me about London. Did you get a dress? And what else did you do? And did you see Alexa?"

"Yes." Virginia leaned forward to refill her cup from the teapot. "Yes, I did get a dress, and yes, I did see Alexa. That's what I want to talk to you about. I've already told Edmund."

Violet's heart sank. What on earth was happening now?

"She's all right?"

"Never better." Virginia leaned back in her chair. "There is a man in her life."

"Alexa has a young man? But that's splendid news! I was beginning to think that nothing exciting was ever going to happen to the dear child."

"They're living together, Vi."

For an instant, Violet was silenced. Then: "*Living* together?"

"Yes. And I'm not telling tales out of school. She particularly asked me to let you know."

"And *where* are they living together?"

"At Ovington Street."

"But . . ." Violet, flustered, sought for words. "But . . . how long has this been going on?"

"About two months."

"Who is he?"

"He's called Noel Keeling."

"What does he do?"

"He's in advertising."

"How old is he?"

"About my age. Good-looking. Very charming."

About Virginia's age. A dreadful thought occurred to Violet. "I hope he's not already married."

"No. A very eligible bachelor."

"And Alexa . . . ?"

"Alexa is radiantly happy."

"Do you think they will marry?"

"I have no idea."

"Is he kind to her?"

"I think so. I only saw him for a little while. He came home from the office and we all had a drink together. He brought Alexa flowers. And he didn't know I was going to be there, so he didn't buy them to impress me."

Violet fell silent, trying to come to terms with this astonishing revelation. They were living together. Alexa was living with a man. Sharing a bed, sharing a life. Unmarried. She did not approve but her own opinions were best kept to herself. All that mattered was that Alexa should know that they all would support her, whatever might happen.

"What did Edmund say when you told him?"

Virginia shrugged. "Not a lot. He's certainly not about to fly to London with a loaded shotgun. But I think he is concerned, if only for the fact that Alexa is a girl of some wealth . . . she has that house and she has the money she inherited from Lady Cheriton. Which, as Edmund pointed out, is considerable."

"He's afraid this young man is after her money?"

"It's a possibility, Vi."

"You've met him. What do you think of him?"

"I liked him. . . ."

"But you have reservations?"

"He's so personable. Cool. Like I said, charming. I'm not *certain* if I trust him. . . ."

"Oh dear."

"But that's just me talking. I may be making a total misjudgement."

"What can we do?"

"We can't do anything. Alexa is twenty-one, she must make her own decisions."

Violet knew that this was true. But Alexa . . . so far away. In London.

"If only we could *meet* him. That would put everything on a much more normal footing."

"I entirely agree with you, and you will meet him." Violet glanced at her daughter-in-law and saw that she was smiling, looking as pleased with herself as the cat that got the cream. "I'm afraid I stuck my oar in and made noises like a mother. I talked to the two of them and they've agreed to come north together for the weekend of the Steyntons' dance. They're going to stay at Balnaid."

"Oh, what a clever idea!" Violet could have kissed Virginia, so delighted was she. "What a brilliant girl you are. Quite the best way of doing things, without making too much of an occasion of it."

"That's what I thought. And even Edmund approves. But we'll have to be very casual and tactful and matter-of-fact. No suggestive glances or meaningful remarks."

"You mean I'm not to say anything about their getting married?" Virginia nodded. Violet thought about this. "I wouldn't, you know. I'm sufficiently modern to know when to hold my tongue. But, by living together, young people create for themselves such difficult situations. They make it so difficult for *us.* If we make too much of the young man, then he will think he is being pressurized and he'll back off and break Alexa's heart. And if we don't make enough of him, Alexa will think we disapprove and *that* will break her heart."

"I wouldn't be too sure about that. She's

grown up a lot. She has much more confidence. She's changed."

"I couldn't bear her to be hurt. Not Alexa."

"I'm afraid we can't protect her any longer. The affair has already gone too far."

"Yes," said Violet, feeling in some way admonished. This was no time for apprehensive sentiment. If she was to be of any use to anybody, then she must remain sensible. "You are absolutely right. We must all—"

But there was no time for more. They heard the front door open and slam shut. *"Mummy!"*

Henry was back. Virginia laid down her teacup and sprang to her feet, Alexa forgotten. She made for the door but Henry was there first, bursting in on them, red-cheeked with excitement and the effort of running up the hill.

"Mummy!"

She held out her arms, and he flung himself, bodily, into them.

❦ 8 ❧

Saturday the Twenty-seventh

EDMUND WAS FREQUENTLY ASKED, by well-meaning fellow-guests at dinner parties, if he did not find the long commute between Edinburgh and Strathcroy an almost unbearable strain, every morning and evening each day of the week that he was working in Edinburgh. But the truth was that Edmund thought nothing of the miles that he covered. Getting home to Balnaid and his family was more important than the considerable effort that it involved, and only a late business dinner in Edinburgh, an early plane to catch, or impassable winter roads persuaded him to stay in town and spend the night in the flat in Moray Place.

As well, he enjoyed driving. His car was both powerful and safe, and the motorway, slicing over the Forth and through Fife to

Relkirk, had become as familiar as the back of his hand. Once through Relkirk, he was onto country roads that necessitated slowing down to a more prudent speed, but even so the journey rarely took him more than an hour.

He used this time to switch off at the end of a day of stress and decision-making, and to let his mind concentrate instead upon the many other, but equally absorbing, facets of his busy life. In winter-time, he listened to the radio. Not the news nor political discussions . . . he had had enough of both by the time he finally cleared his desk and locked away all confidential documents . . . but Radio Three, classical concerts and erudite plays. For the rest of the year, as the hours of daylight lengthened and he no longer made the journey in the dark, he found much pleasure and solace in simply watching the unfolding seasons of the countryside. The ploughing, the sowing, the greening of the trees; the first young lambs in the fields, the crops turning gold, the raspberry pickers out in the long drills of canes, the harvest, the autumn leaves, the first of the snows.

They were harvesting now, on this fine,

blowy evening. The scenery was both peaceful and spectacular. Fields and farmlands
were washed in fitful sunlight, but the air was
so clear that every crag and corrie on the
distant hills presented itself with startling visibility. The light flowed over these hills,
touching their summits with reflected radiance; the river running alongside the road
glittered and sparkled; and the sky, skim-
ming with clouds, was infinite.

He felt more content than he had for a
long time. Virginia was back, restored to
him. His gift to her was the nearest he could
get to an apology for the things that he had
said on the day of the original explosion: accusing her of smothering Henry; wanting to
keep him by her side for selfish reasons;
never thinking of any person but herself. She
had accepted the bracelet with gratitude and
love, and her unqualified pleasure was as
good as forgiveness.

Last night, after their dinner at Rafaelli's,
he had driven her home to Balnaid through a
twilit countryside and beneath the banner of
a spectacular skyscape, rose-pink to the west,
and streaked as though by some gargantuan
paintbrush with dark charcoal clouds.

They had returned to an empty house. He could not remember when this had last happened, and it made their homecoming even more special. No dogs, no children; just the two of them. He had dealt with the luggage, then taken two malt whiskies up to their bedroom and sat on the bed and watched her unpack. There was no sense of urgency, because the whole of the house, the night, the sweet darkness belonged to them. Later, he showered; Virginia took a bath. She came to him, scented and cool, and they made the most satisfying and blissful love.

He knew that the bone of contention still lay between them. Virginia did not want to lose Henry, and Edmund was determined that he should go. But for the time being they had ceased snarling over this particular bone and, with a bit of luck, it would stay buried and forgotten.

As well, there were other good things to look forward to. This evening, he would see his small son again after a week of separation. There would be much to tell and much to hear. And then, next month, in September, Alexa was bringing her young man to stay.

Virginia's bombshell about Alexa had

caught Edmund unawares, rendering him confounded but not shocked nor disapproving. He was extremely fond of his daughter, and recognized her many sterling qualities; but during the last year or two he had privately wished, more than once, that she would take her finger out and start to grow up. At twenty-one, her lack of sophistication, her shyness, her dumpy shape had become an embarrassment to him. He was used to being surrounded by elegant and worldly women (even his secretary was a stunner) and disliked himself for his own impatience and irritation with Alexa. But now, all by herself, she had found a man, and a personable one, if Virginia was to be believed.

Possibly he should be taking a tougher line. But he had never relished the image of himself as a paterfamilias, and was more concerned with the human side of the situation rather than the moral.

As always, when faced with a dilemma, he planned to go by his own set of rules. Act positively, plan negatively, expect nothing. The worst that could happen would be Alexa's getting hurt. For her, it would be a frightening new experience, but at least she would come out of it more adult and, hopefully, stronger.

He drove into Strathcroy as the church clock was striking seven. He thought, in pleasant anticipation, of getting home. The dogs would be there, rescued from the kennels by Virginia; and Henry, in his bath or eating his tea in the kitchen. He would sit with Henry while he consumed his fish fingers or beefburgers or whatever horror he had chosen to eat, listening to all that Henry had been up to during the week, and drinking, meanwhile, a very long and strong gin and tonic.

Which reminded him that they were out of tonic. The drink cupboard had been allowed to run dry of this precious commodity, and Edmund had meant to stop off and buy a crate before he left Edinburgh, but had forgotten to do this. And so he passed the bridge that led to Balnaid and drove on into the village, drawing up outside the Pakistani supermarket.

All the other shops had long since shut their doors and closed their shutters, but the Pakistanis never seemed to close. Long after nine o'clock in the evening they were still selling cartons of milk and bread and pizzas and frozen curries to anybody who wanted to buy them.

He got out of the car and went into the shop. There were other customers but they were filling their own wire baskets from the shelves or being assisted by Mr. Ishak, and it was Mrs. Ishak who dimpled at Edmund from behind the counter. She was a comely lady, with huge dark eyes ringed in kohl, and this evening dressed in butter-yellow silk, with a paler yellow silk scarf draped around her head and shoulders.

"Good evening, Mr. Aird."

"Good evening, Mrs. Ishak. How are you?"

"I am very well, thank you for asking."

"How's Kedejah?"

"She is watching television."

"I hear she had an afternoon at Pennyburn with Henry."

"That is true, and my God, she came home soaking wet."

Edmund laughed. "They were building dams. I hope you weren't annoyed."

"Not at all. She has had a most lovely time."

"I want some tonic water, Mrs. Ishak. Have you got some?"

"But of course. How many bottles do you need?"

"Two dozen?"

"If you wait, I will fetch them for you from the store."

"Thank you."

She went. Edmund, unimpatient, stood waiting for her to return. A voice spoke from behind him.

"Mr. Aird."

It was so close, just behind his shoulder, that he was much startled. He swung around and found himself faced by Edie's cousin, Lottie Carstairs. Since she had come to stay with Edie, he had glimpsed her once or twice, pottering about the village, but had taken some pains and avoiding action, not wishing to be confronted by her. Now it seemed she had him cornered and there was no escape.

"Good evening."

"Remember me?" She spoke almost coyly. Edmund did not relish finding himself so close to her with her pallid, bloodless skin and the strong suggestion of a moustache upon her upper lip. Her hair was the colour —and roughly the texture—of steel wool, and under wildly arched eyebrows her eyes were brown as currants, and round and quite unwinking. Apart from all this, her appearance was reasonably normal. She wore a blouse and skirt, a long green cardigan perkily embellished with a sparkling brooch, and shoes with high heels upon which she tottered slightly as she engaged Edmund in conversation. "I used to be with Lady Balmerino, staying with Edie Findhorn right now I am. Seen you around the village, never had the chance of an old chin-wag . . ."

Lottie Carstairs. She must be nearly sixty now, and yet she had not changed so much since those days when she had worked at Croy and caused every person in the house untold annoyance and aggravation, with her stealthy tread and her habit of always appearing just when least wanted or expected. Archie always swore that she listened at keyholes, and he had been perpetually throwing doors open in the expectation of catching Lottie there, crouched and eavesdropping. In the afternoons, Edmund remembered, she had always worn a brown woollen dress with a muslin apron tied over it. The muslin apron was not Lady Balmerino's idea but Lottie's. Archie said it was because she wanted to appear servile. The brown dress had stains under the armpits, and one of the worst things about Lottie was her smell.

The family complained vociferously and Archie demanded that his mother take some step to rectify the situation. Either sack the bloody woman or do something to ensure a little personal daintiness. But poor Lady Balmerino, with Archie's wedding on her mind, every bed filled with guests and a party planned at Croy on the evening of the great day, did not feel strong enough to sack her housemaid. And she was far too kind-hearted actually to send for Lottie, face her fair and square, and tell her that she smelt.

Under attack, she fell back on feeble excuses.

"I must have someone to clean the rooms and make the beds."

"We'll make our own beds."

"Poor thing, she's only got one dress."

"Well, buy her another."

"Perhaps she's nervous."

"Not too nervous to wash. Give her a bar of Lifebuoy."

"I'm not certain that that would make much difference. Perhaps . . . for Christmas . . . I could give her some talcum powder . . . ?"

But even this timid notion came to nothing, for, soon after the wedding, Lottie dropped the tray and broke the Rockingham china, and Lady Balmerino was finally driven to firing her. By Christmas Lottie was gone from Croy. Now, trapped in Mr. Ishak's shop, Edmund wondered if she still smelt. He was not about to risk finding out. Trying not to make it too obvious, he moved a pace or two away from her.

"Yes," he said, sounding as pleasant and friendly as he could. "Of course, I remember you . . ."

"Those days at Croy! The year Archie was wed to Isobel. Oh my, what times those were. I remember you coming up from London for the wedding and around the place all that week, helping Lady Balmerino with one thing and another."

"It seems a long time ago."

"Yes."

"And all of you so young. And old Lord and Lady Balmerino so good and kind. Croy's changed now, I hear, and not for the better. But then, hard times come to everybody. It was a sad day when Lady Balmerino died. She was always so good to me. She was good to my parents too. My mother and my father died. You knew that, didn't you? I've been wanting to talk to you, but somehow I missed you in the village. And all of you so young. And Archie with his two good legs . . . fancy getting his leg shot off! Never heard of anything so ridiculous . . ."

Oh, Mrs. Ishak, come back quickly. Please, Mrs. Ishak, come back to me.

". . . hear all your news from Edie, of course; very worried about Edie, she's grown so fat, can't be good for her heart. And all of you so young. And that Pandora! Flying around the place like a spinning top. Dreadful way she went, wasn't it? Funny she never came home. Always thought she might come back for Christmas, but no. And not to be

there for Lady Balmerino's funeral, well, I'm
sorry and I don't like to say such things, but
in my view, it was downright un-Christian.
But then, she always was a wee fly-by-night
. . . in more ways than one . . . you and I
know that, don't we?"

At this point she burst into a peal of manic
laughter and actually struck Edmund a play-
ful, but quite painful, blow on his arm. His
immediate and instinctive reaction was to hit
her right back, a good punch, bang, square
on the end of her long, inquisitive nose. He
imagined it crumpling, concertinaed, into her
face. He imagined the headlines in the local
newspapers: "Relkirkshire Landowner As-
saults Strathcroy Lady In Village Supermarket." He thrust his hands, the fists balled,
into his trouser pockets.

". . . and your wife's been in London?
Nice. And the wee boy with his gran. Seen
him sometimes around the place. He is
peaky, isn't he?" Edmund could feel the
blood rising to his cheeks. He wondered how
long he could continue to control himself. He
could not remember when any person had
cast him into such a confusion of impotent

rage. ". . . small for his age, I'd say . . . not strong . . ."

"I am sorry, Mr. Aird, to keep you so long." It was Mrs. Ishak's soft voice that finally stilled the flood of Lottie's mindless malice. Mrs. Ishak, bless her darling heart, come to his rescue with the cardboard crate of tonic water borne before her like a votive offering.

"Oh, thank you, Mrs. Ishak." And not a moment too soon. "Here, let me take that." He went to relieve her of the heavy load. "I wonder, can you put that down to my account?" He could easily pay in cash but did not wish to linger a moment longer than he had to.

"Of course, Mr. Aird."

"Thank you." The crate was transferred. With its weight safely in his arms, he turned to take his leave of Lottie and make his escape.

But Lottie had jumped the gun and was gone. Abruptly and disconcertingly, she had simply disappeared.

9

Tuesday the Thirtieth

"HAS SHE ALWAYS LIVED IN MAJORCA, this aunt of yours?"

"No. She's only been here for about two years. She lived in Paris before that, and New York before that, and then California before that," Lucilla said.

"A rolling stone."

"Yes, I suppose you could call her that, except that she's gathered lots of lovely moss."

Jeff laughed. "What's she like?"

"I don't know because I've never seen her. By the time I was born, she was gone, married to an immensely wealthy American and living in Palm Springs. It seemed to me that she must be the most glamorous woman in the world. So wicked and sophisticated like someone out of those old 1930 plays, with men falling for her like ninepins, and always unashamedly outrageous. She eloped when she was eighteen. Such a frightfully brave thing to do. I'd never have had the nerve. *And* she was beautiful."

"Will she still be beautiful?"

"I don't see why not. After all, she's only about forty, not over the hill yet. There's a portrait of her at Croy in the dining-room. It was painted when she was about fourteen and even then she was a stunner. And photographs too, all over the place, in frames or the old albums that my grandfather used to fill with snapshots. I used to welcome wet afternoons because then I could spend them poring over those old albums. And when people talked about her, even if they started by being disapproving because she'd been so thoughtless and uncaring to her parents, they always ended up by remembering some funny anecdote about Pandora, and then of course there could be nothing but laughter."

"Was she surprised when you spoke to her on the telephone?"

"Of course she was. But pleased surprised, not horrified surprised. You can always tell. At first she could hardly believe it was me.

But then she just said 'Of course you can come. As soon as possible. And stay for as long as you like.' And she gave me directions and hung up." Lucilla smiled. "So you see, we're good for at least a week."

They had hired a car, a little Seat, the cheapest they could get, and were now well on their way across the island, driving over flat, intensely cultivated countryside, dotted here and there with slow-moving windmills. It was afternoon and the road ahead of them shimmered in the heat. On their left, far-distant and hazy, marched a range of impassable-looking mountains. On the other side, somewhere out of sight, lay the sea. For air, they had opened all the windows of the car, but the wind was scorching and dusty and very dry. Jeff was driving and Lucilla sat beside him, holding the scrap of paper on which she had scribbled the directions that Pandora had given her over the telephone.

She had rung Pandora from Palma, having arrived with Jeff that morning in a boat from Ibiza. They had spent a week in Ibiza, staying with Jeff's friend, Hans Bergdorf. Hans was a painter and *his* house had taken some finding, being at the very top of the old town, within the ancient walls of the fortified city. Finally discovered, it had proved very picturesque. It was thick-walled and whitewashed, but primitive beyond belief. The views from its jutting stone balcony took in the whole panorama of the old town, the new town, the harbour, and the sea, but even this delight scarcely made up for the fact that any cooking had to be done on a miniature Calor gas stove and the only running water came from a single cold tap. Consequently, both Jeff and Lucilla were extremely dirty, if not to say smelly, and the bulging backpacks piled onto the back seat of the car were stuffed with unsavoury, soiled and sweaty clothes. Lucilla, never a girl to spend time worrying about her appearance, had started to have fantasies about washing her hair, and Jeff in desperation had allowed his beard to grow. It was blonde like his hair, but uneven and straggly and made him look more like a down-and-out than a Viking. In fact, the pair of them presented such a disreputable picture that it was a wonder that the hire-car man had agreed to rent them the Seat. Lucilla had noticed a certain suspicion on his face, but

Jeff had produced a wad of pesetas and, with cash safely in hand, he could scarcely refuse.

She said, "I hope Pandora's got a washing-machine."

"I'd settle for a pool."

"You can't wash your clothes in a pool."

"Want a bet?"

Lucilla gazed through the open car window. She saw that the mountains had drawn closer and the countryside become more lush. There were pine trees, and the smell of warm resin blew in through the open windows along with the dust. They came to a junction joining another main road. They paused for traffic to pass. The road sign was marked "Puerto del Fuego."

"Well, we're on the right track. What happens now?"

"We take the Puerto del Fuego road, but we have to turn off to the left in another mile or so. It's a little road and it's signposted to 'Cala San Torre.' " The traffic thinned. Taking his chance Jeff cautiously negotiated the junction. "If we find ourselves in the port, then we've gone too far."

"That follows."

Now she could smell the sea. Houses appeared, a new apartment block, a garage. They passed a riding stables with scrubby paddocks where sad, bony horses tried to graze.

"Oh, poor creatures," said the tender-hearted Lucilla, but Jeff had eyes only for the road ahead.

"There's a sign. 'Cala San Torre.'"

"That's it!"

They turned off the sun-baked dual carriageway and found themselves, abruptly, in a green and verdant countryside totally unlike the flat and exposed land through which they had been travelling. Umbrella pines threw shade across the road, speckled by sun splashes, and from ramshackle farms came the contented cackle of hens and the bleat of goats.

"It's suddenly gone pretty," Lucilla observed. "Oh, look at that sweet little donkey."

"Keep your eyes on the map, girl. What happens next?"

Lucilla obediently consulted her notes. "Well, *next* is a very sharp turn to the right, and then we go right up a hill to the last house at the very top."

They came upon the turning around the next corner. Jeff changed down and made the turn. The Seat, sounding as though at any moment it might boil like a kettle, ground painfully up the steep and winding lane. There were other houses, large villas scarcely glimpsed beyond closed gates and burgeoning gardens.

"This," said Lucilla, "is what estate agents call a much-sought-after neighbourhood."

"You mean snob."

"I think I mean expensive."

"I think you do too. Your aunt must be loaded."

"She's got a Californian divorce," Lucilla told him and her voice implied that there was no need to say more.

Another hundred yards or so, another hairpin bend or two, and they had reached their destination. Casa Rosa. The name, embellished on decorated tiles, was set into a high stone wall and clearly visible despite a cloak of pink-blossomed mesembryanthemum. Open gates lay ahead. A driveway, deeply bordered, sloped up to a garage. The garage had a car parked in it, and another car—an enviable silver BMW—was parked in the shade of a gnarled olive tree. Jeff switched off the engine. It was very quiet. Then Lucilla heard water splashing, as though from a fountain, and the distant, gentle clangour of sheep bells. The mountains now were close by, their summits bleached and barren, their lower slopes silvery with groves of olive.

They got slowly and gratefully out of the car, stretching their sweaty limbs. Up here, so high, there was a breeze blowing off the sea, cool and refreshing. Lucilla, looking about her, saw that the Casa Rosa stood on a rocky bluff above them, the main entrance reached by a flight of steps. The risers of these steps were set with blue-and-white tiles, and pots of geraniums stood sentry all the way to the top. As well, all was entwined by a torrent of purple bougainvillaea; and hibiscus grew, and plumbago, and a tangle of azure-blue morning glory. The air was sweet with flowery scents mingled with the damp smell of newly watered earth.

So amazing was it all, so unlike anything they had previously experienced, that for a moment neither of them could think of anything to say. Then Lucilla whispered, "I'd no *idea* it would be as grand as this!"

"Well, one thing's for sure, we can't stand here all day."

"No." He was right. Lucilla turned towards the first step, leading the way. But before she had mounted the first step, the silence was broken by the sound of sharp heeltaps, hurrying along the terrace above them.

"Darlings!" A figure appeared at the head of the stairs, arms outstretched in welcome. "I heard the car. You've come. And you've not lost the way. How clever you are and how perfect to see you."

Lucilla's first impression of Pandora was one of insubstantial thinness. She looked ethereal, as though at any moment she might blow away. Embracing her was like holding a little bird. You didn't want to hug too hard in case she snapped in two. Her hair was chestnut brown, swept back from her forehead and falling, in frondy curls, to her shoulders. Lucilla guessed that Pandora had worn her hair that way when she was eighteen and had never seen any reason to change the style. Her eyes were dark grey, shadowed by sooty black lashes, and her curving mouth full and sweet. On her right cheek, just above the corner of her upper lip, was a round dark beauty spot, too sexy to be called a mole. She was dressed in loose pyjamas of the brilliant pink of the hibiscus flowers, and there were gold chains around her neck and knots of gold in her ears. She smelled . . . Lucilla knew that scent. Poison. She had tried wearing it herself but could never decide whether she loved it or hated it. Smelling it on Pandora, she was still not certain.

"I'd have known you were Lucilla, even if nobody had told me. You look so like Archie. . . ." It seemed that she did not even notice their unsavoury appearance, their soiled cut-off shorts and grubby T-shirts. And if she did, she gave no indication of objecting. "And you must be Jeff. . . ." She held out a pink-tipped hand. "How wonderful that you could come with Lucilla."

He took it in his own enormous paw and, looking a bit overwhelmed by her welcome and her dazzling smile, said, "Pleased to meet you."

She picked up his accent at once. "You're an Australian! How heavenly. I don't think I've ever had an Australian here before. Did you have a hideous drive?"

"No. Not at all. Just hot."

"You must be longing for a drink. . . ."

"Shall we get our stuff out of the car . . . ?"

"You can do that later. A drink first. Come along, I've a friend here for you to meet."

Lucilla's heart sank. It didn't matter about Pandora, but they were certainly in no shape to be introduced to company. "Pandora, we're dreadfully dirty. . . ."

"Oh, heavens, that doesn't matter. He won't mind. . . ." She turned from them and led the way, and there was no alternative but to follow, down a long shaded and airy terrace furnished with white cane and butter-yellow cushions and great blue-and-white porcelain jars planted with palms. "He can't stay for very long and I want you to meet him. . . ."

They turned the corner of the house and,

hard on Pandora's tapping heels, stepped out into blinding sunshine. Lucilla longed for her sunglasses, left in the car. In a dazzle, she saw the wide, open terrace, shaded by striped awnings and paved in marble. Shallow steps led down from this to a spacious garden, massed with flowering trees and shrubs. Grass paths were set with flagged stepping-stones, and these encircled a swimming pool, aquamarine and still as glass. Just seeing it made Lucilla feel cooler. An inflatable sun-bed floated upon the surface of the water, drifting with the undercurrent of the filter.

At the far end of the garden, half hidden by hibiscus, she saw another house, small and single-storied, but with its own little ter-race facing out over the pool. This was shaded by a tall umbrella pine, and beyond the ridge of its roof there was nothing to be seen but the brazen blue sky.

"Here they are, Carlos, safely arrived. My directions can't have been as confusing as we'd feared." At the top of the steps, in the shade of the awning, stood a low table. On this was a tray with glasses and a tall jug. An ashtray, a pair of sunglasses, a paperback. More cane chairs, yellow-cushioned, stood about, and as they approached, a man rose from one of these and stood, smiling, waiting to be introduced. He was tall and dark-eyed and very handsome. "Lucilla, darling, this is my friend Carlos Macaya. Carlos, this is Lucilla Blair, my niece. And Jeff . . . ?"

"Howland," Jeff supplied for her.

"And he's Australian. Isn't that exciting? Now, let's all sit down and have a lovely drink. This is iced tea, but I can get Seraphina to bring something stronger if you'd like. Coke maybe? Or wine?" She began to laugh. "Or champagne? What a good idea. But perhaps a little early in the day. Let's save the champagne till later."

They told her that iced tea would be perfect. Carlos drew forward a chair for Lucilla and then settled himself beside her. But Jeff, who could soak up sun like a lizard, went to lean on the balustrade of the terrace, and Pandora perched herself beside him, legs swinging and one high-heeled sandal dangling from a toe.

Carlos Macaya poured iced tea and handed Lucilla her glass.

"You have come from Ibiza?"

"Yes, this morning, on the boat."

"How long were you there?" His English was perfect.

"A week. Staying with a friend of Jeff's. It was a lovely house but dreadfully primitive. Which is why we look so filthy. Because we are. I'm sorry."

He made no comment on this; simply smiled in an understanding way. "And before Ibiza?"

"I've been in Paris. That's where I met Jeff. I'm meant to be a painter, but there was so much to see and so much to do, I didn't achieve very much."

"Paris is a wonderful city. Was this your first visit?"

"No, I'd been once before. I spent some time as an au pair, to learn the language."

"And how did you get from Paris to Ibiza?"

"We thought of hitch-hiking but in the end we travelled by bus. We did the journey in stops and starts, staying in *gites*, and taking time to do some sightseeing. Cathedrals and wine châteaux—that sort of thing."

"You have not been wasting your time." He glanced at Pandora, chattering away to Jeff, who watched her intently as though she were some strange species of wildlife that he had never before observed. "Pandora tells me that this is the first time you have met each other."

"Yes." Lucilla hesitated. This man was probably Pandora's current lover, which meant that now was neither the time nor the place to enlarge on Pandora's youthful elopement and subsequent life-style. "She was always abroad, you see. I mean, living abroad."

"And your home is in Scotland?"

"Yes. In Relkirkshire. That's where my parents live." A small pause fell. She took a mouthful of iced tea. "Have you ever been to Scotland?"

"No. I studied in Oxford for a couple of years" (that explained his English), "but I never found time to go to Scotland."

"We're always wanting Pandora to come back and see us, but she never will."

"Perhaps she doesn't like the cold and the rain."

"It isn't cold and rainy *all* the time. Only some of the time."

He laughed. "Whatever. It is a splendid thing that you have come to keep her company. And now . . ." He pushed back his silk cuff and glanced at his watch. It was a handsome and unusual watch, the numbers marked by tiny replicas of yachting pennants, and was strapped to his wrist by a heavy gold bracelet. Lucilla wondered if Pandora had given it to him. Perhaps the pennants spelt out "I Love You" in naval code. ". . . it is time for me to take my leave. I hope you will excuse me but I have work to do. . . ."

"Of course. . . ."

He rose once more to his feet. "Pandora, I must go."

"Oh dear, what a shame." She fixed her sandal and hopped down off the balustrade. "Never mind, you've had time to meet my guests. We'll come and see you off."

"Don't disturb everybody."

"They've got to get their luggage anyway. They're dying to unpack and have a swim. Come. . . ." She took his arm.

And so they all made their way back to where his car was waiting in the shade beneath the olive tree. Goodbyes were said, he sketched a kiss over the back of Pandora's hand, and then got in behind the wheel of the BMW.

He started up the engine, and Pandora stood back. But before he drove away, he said, "Pandora."

"Yes, Carlos?"

"You will let me know if you change your mind."

She did not answer immediately, and then shook her head. "I shan't change my mind," she told him.

He smiled, shrugged resignedly, as though good-naturedly accepting her decision. He put the car into gear and, with a final wave, left them, driving away, through the gates, down the hill, out of sight. They stood waiting until the sound of the BMW could be heard no longer. Only the splash of water from that unseen fountain, the tinkle of sheep bells.

You will let me know if you change your mind.

What had Carlos been asking of Pandora? For an instant Lucilla toyed with the idea that he had been proposing marriage, but almost at once put this notion out of her head. It was too prosaic for such a sophisticated and glamorous pair. More likely, he had been trying to persuade her to join him on some romantic trip, to the Seychelles or the palm-fringed beaches of Tahiti. Or perhaps he had simply asked her out for dinner and she didn't feel like going.

Whatever, Pandora was not about to enlighten them. Carlos was gone and now she sprang into practical activity, giving a little clap with her hands. "So. Down to business. Where's your luggage? Is that all? No suitcases or cabin trunks or hat-boxes? I take more than that if I go away for a single night. Now, come along. . . ."

She started up the steps once more, going at a great pace, and yet again they followed her, Lucilla carrying her leather satchel, and Jeff lugging the two bulging backpacks.

"I've put you in the guest-house. You can make yourselves at home, and then be quite independent. And I'm not frightfully good in the mornings, so you'll have to get your own breakfast. The fridge is full of goodies, and there's coffee and stuff in the cupboard." They were now back on the terrace. "You'll be all right?"

"Of course."

"And then I thought we'd have dinner about nine o'clock. Just something cold, because I can't cook to save my life, and Seraphina, my maid, goes home each evening. But she'll leave everything ready for us. Come over at half past eight and we'll have a drink. Now I'm going to have a little nap, so I'll leave you to find your own way and settle yourselves in. Later, I might swim before I change for dinner."

The prospect of Pandora, dressed in an even grander outfit than the pink silk pyjamas, brought up the vexing question of clothes.

"Pandora, we haven't got anything to change into. Nearly everything's dirty. Jeff's got one clean shirt, but it hasn't been ironed."

"Oh, darling, do you want to borrow something?"

"A clean T-shirt?"

"Of course, how stupid of me, I should have offered. Wait a moment."

They waited. She disappeared through wide sliding glass doors into what was presumably her bedroom, and returned almost at once bearing a midnight-blue silk shirt splashed with a rocket-fall of sequins. "Have this, it's frightfully vulgar but rather fun. You can keep it if you want, I never wear it." She tossed it over and Lucilla caught it. "And now, off you go and dig yourselves into your little nest. If you want anything, ring through on the house phone and Seraphina will bring it to you." She blew a kiss. "Half past eight. See you then."

And she was gone, leaving Lucilla and Jeff to their own devices. But still Lucilla hesitated, savouring the anticipation of what was about to happen next.

"Jeff, I can't believe it. We've got a whole house to ourselves."

"So what are we waiting for? If I don't get into that pool in two minutes flat, I'm going to explode."

Lucilla went first, leading the way down the steps and along the length of the garden. The little house awaited them. They crossed the terrace and opened the door into a living-room. Curtains had been drawn, and Lucilla went to pull them back. Light streamed in and she saw the little patio on the far side, the sheltered scrap of garden.

"We've even got our own place to sunbathe!"

There was an open fireplace, stacked with logs. There were a few comfortable chairs, a tray of drinks and glasses, a coffee-table stacked neatly with magazines, and a wall shelved with books. Opening other doors, they found two double bedrooms, and a bathroom of marvellously spacious proportions.

"I think *this* is the nicest bedroom. It's certainly the biggest." Jeff dumped the backpacks onto the tiled floor and Lucilla drew back more curtains. "We can see the sea from here. Just a little scrap, a triangle, but still a view of the sea." She opened cupboard doors, saw rows of padded hangers, smelled lavender. She put the borrowed shirt onto one of the hangers, where it hung in lonely style.

Jeff had toed off his trainers and was stripping off his T-shirt.

"You can play house as much as you like. I'm going to swim. You joining me?"

"I will in a moment."

He departed. An instant later she heard the splash as he took his running dive, and imagined the silken bliss of the cool water. But later. Just now she wanted to explore.

On detailed inspection Pandora's guest-house proved to be quite perfectly complete, and Lucilla was filled with admiration for such meticulous thought and planning. Someone . . . and who else but Pandora? . . . had somehow thought of anything that a visitor might want or need, from fresh flowers and lovely new books right down to spare blankets for chilly nights and hot-water bottles for possibly unsettled tummies. The bathroom was supplied with every sort of soap, scent, shampoo, aftershave, body-lotion, and bath-oil. There were thick white bath towels and bath-mats, and, hanging from the back of the door, a pair of voluminous and snowy-white towelling bathrobes.

Leaving all this luxury, she crossed the sitting-room and went in search of the kitchen, and found it sparkling neat, and lined with dark wooden cupboards filled with Spanish pottery, shining saucepans, casseroles, and a complete *batterie de cuisine*. If one wanted— which Lucilla didn't—it would be quite possible to concoct a dinner party for ten. There were an electric cooker and a gas cooker and a dishwasher and a fridge. She opened the fridge and discovered there, along with all the fixings for a robust breakfast, two bottles of Perrier water and a bottle of champagne. A second door led out of the kitchen. She opened this and found . . . joy of joys . . . a compact laundry with clothes washer, dry-ing-lines, an ironing-board, and an iron. The sight of these homely items gave her more satisfaction than all the other luxuries put to-gether. Because now, at last, they could be clean.

She set to work, losing no time. Went back to the bathroom, stripped off her clothes, put on one of the towelling robes and then started in on the unpacking. Which consisted of emptying the contents of the backpacks onto the bedroom floor. At the bottom of her own backpack were her wash-bag, her brush and comb, her sketch-pad, a book or two, and the envelope from her father, which had contained his cheque, his letter, and the invi-tation to a dance from Verena Steynton. She took this out of the envelope and propped it on the empty dressing-table. By now it was a bit dog-eared but bestowed, she decided, a personal note to the room, as though Lucilla had put her name to it and claimed it as her own.

Lucilla Blair

Mrs. Angus Steynton

At Home

For Katy

Why did it seem so ludicrous? She laughed. Another life, another world away. She gathered up armfuls of dirty socks, shorts, jeans, pants, and T-shirts and headed back to the laundry. Without bothering to sort any of these garments (her mother would have a fit if she could see red socks going in with white shirts, but her mother was not here to remonstrate so what did it matter?) Lucilla stuffed the open face of the washing-machine, poured in detergent, slammed the door, and switched it on. Water gushed and the drum revolved, and she stood back and observed this with as much delight as if it had been a longed-for programme on television.

Then she kicked aside the remainder of the

dirty clothes, went to find her bikini, and joined Jeff in the pool.

She swam for a long time. After a bit Jeff got out and lay in the sun to dry off. Another two lengths and she saw he was gone, had taken himself indoors. She came out of the pool and wrung the water from her long dark hair. She went indoors. She found him in the bedroom, flat out on one of the beds. He looked as though he might be going to sleep. She did not want him to go to sleep. She said his name and took a running jump, and landed flat on top of him.

"Jeff."

"Yeah?"

"I told you she was beautiful."

"Who?"

"Pandora, of course." Jeff did not immediately reply to this. He was drowsy and on the edge of sleep, and not inclined to conversation. His arm, out-flung, pillowed Lucilla's head. His skin smelled of chlorine and swimming pool. "Don't you think she's beautiful?"

"She's certainly one sexy sheila."

"You think she's sexy?"

"But too old for me."

"She doesn't *look* old."

"And a bit too skinny as well."

"Don't you like skinny ladies?"

"No. I like my women with big tits and fat bums."

Lucilla, who had inherited her shape from her father and was tall and thin and almost breastless, gave Jeff a thump with her fist. "You do *not*."

He laughed. "Well, what do you want me to say?"

"You know what I want you to say."

He pulled her face towards his own and kissed her soundly. "Will that do?"

"I think you'll have to shave that beard off."

"Now why should I do that?"

"Because my face is going to start looking as though it's been cleaned off by sandpaper."

"I'll have to stop kissing you then. Or start

kissing you someplace where it doesn't show."

They fell silent. The sun was dropping in the sky, and soon, quite suddenly, it would be dark. Lucilla thought of Scottish summer twilights that went on until midnight. She said, "Do you think they're lovers? Do you think they're having a raging affair?"

"Who?"

"Pandora and Carlos Macaya."

"I wouldn't know."

"He's terribly handsome."

"Yeah. A real smoothie."

"I thought he was nice. Rather cosy. Easy to talk to."

"I liked his car."

"You have a one-track mind. What do you think it was he asked her?"

"Come again?"

"He said, 'Let me know if you change your mind.' And she said, 'I won't change my mind.' He must have asked her something. He must have wanted her to do something with him."

"Well, whatever it was, she didn't look too bothered."

But Lucilla was not satisfied. "I'm certain

it was something terribly significant. A turning-point in both their lives."

"You have a runaway imagination. More likely he was trying to fix a tennis game."

"Yes." But somehow, Lucilla did not feel that this was so. She sighed, and the sigh turned into a yawn. "Perhaps."

At half past eight they were ready to join Pandora, and Lucilla decided that, after all her anxiety, they didn't look too bad. Both of them had showered and scrubbed and now smelled sweetly of the gratuitous shampoo. Jeff had neatened up his beard with a pair of nail scissors, and Lucilla had ironed his one clean shirt and salvaged from the pile of clothes on the laundry floor his tidiest pair of jeans.

As for herself, she had washed her long dark hair and brushed it dry, pulled on a pair of black leggings, and now buttoned up the borrowed shirt. The heavy silk felt deliciously cool against her bare skin, and the sequined embroidery, viewed in the mirror through half-closed eyes, was not nearly as outrageous as she had first imagined. Perhaps it had something to do with these unaccustomed surroundings. Perhaps the ambience of enormous luxury helped absorb such small vulgarities. It was an interesting notion and one that she would have liked to discuss at length, but right now there was no time.

"Come on," Jeff told her. "Time to be off. I need a drink."

He made for the door and she followed him, first making sure that all the lights in the guest-house were switched off. She was fairly certain that Pandora would not give a damn if every light was left burning, but, brought up by a thrifty Scottish mother, such small housewifely economies were engrained in Lucilla, as though her subconscious were a programmed computer. She found this strange, because later strictures had left as little impression as water on a duck's back. Another interesting thought worth chewing over at a later date.

Out of doors, they stepped into a blue night, star-bright and soft and warm as velvet. The garden was headily fragrant, the swimming pool floodlit, and lamps lit the way along the stepping-stones of the path. Lucilla heard the incessant chirp of the cicadas, and there was music coming from Pandora's house.

Rachmaninoff. The Second Piano Concerto. Banal, maybe, but perfect for just such a Mediterranean night. Pandora had set the scene and now she was waiting for them on the terrace, lying in a long chair with a wineglass on the table beside her.

"There you are!" she called as they approached. "I've already opened the champagne. I couldn't wait any longer."

They went up the steps and into the pool of light that illuminated their hostess. She had changed into something black and cobwebby and wore gold sandals on her bare feet. The smell of Poison was even stronger than the scents of the garden.

"Don't you both look sleek! I can't think why you were so worried about yourselves. And Lucilla, the shirt is divine on you, you must keep it. Now, find chairs and settle down. Oh, blast, I've forgotten the glasses. Lucilla, darling, go and get some, will you? The little bar's just behind the door, you'll find everything there. There's a second bottle of bubbly in the fridge, but we'll leave it there till we've finished this one. Now, Jeff, you come and sit *here,* beside me. I want to hear all about what you and Lucilla have been up to. . . ."

Lucilla left them and obediently went in search of the wineglasses, stepping indoors through wide, curtained doors. The bar was immediately at hand, no more than a large closet fitted with everything that any human being could need to fix a drink. She took two wineglasses from the shelf but did not at once return to the terrace. This was the first time she had actually been inside Pandora's house, and she found herself in a room so spacious and spectacular that she was momentarily diverted from her errand. All was cool and creamy, sparked here and there with touches of brilliant colour. Sky-blue and turquoise cushions, and coral-pink lilies massed in a square glass vase. Alcoves, cunningly lit, displayed a collection of Dresden figures and Battersea enamel. A plate-glass coffee-table was stacked with books and magazines, more flowers, a silver cigarette box. There was an open fireplace faced with blue-and-white tiles, and above this hung a mirror-framed flower painting. At the other end of the room the dining-table—glass again—was set for dinner with candles and crystal and yet more flowers, and to Lucilla's bemused eyes it all seemed more like a stage set than a room designed for living in. And yet, she realized, there were homely touches too. An open paperback tossed onto a sofa; a half-finished tapestry lying close at hand for an empty moment. And there were photographs. Archie and Isobel on their wedding day. Lucilla's grandparents, sweet old things in their tweeds, standing in front of Croy with their dogs beside them.

Lucilla found these evidences of nostalgia immensely touching. For some reason, she had not expected them, perhaps not imagining Pandora capable of such sentiment. Now she pictured Pandora taking them everywhere with her, all through her wayward love affairs and her turbulent nomad's life. Saw her unpacking them from her suitcase in houses in California, hotel bedrooms, apartments in New York and Paris. And now, Majorca. Setting the seal of her past and her identity upon yet another temporary home.

(There did not seem to be any pictures of

the men who had owned these apartments and occupied so much of Pandora's life, but perhaps she kept those in her bedroom.)

Warm dark breezes blew through the opened windows, and Rachmaninoff emanated from some unseen stereo, concealed by a gold-latticed trellis. The piano solo dripped its notes, pure as raindrops. From the terrace came the low murmur of comfortable conversation, Pandora and Jeff sounding peaceful and unimpatient.

There were other photographs on the mantelpiece, and Lucilla crossed the floor to inspect these more closely. Old Lady Balmerino, resplendent in a feathered tam-o'-shanter, apparently opening a village fête. A snapshot of Archie and Edmund Aird, two very young men sitting in the boat at the edge of the loch with their rods and their creels stowed on the thwarts. Finally, a studio portrait of herself and Hamish, Lucilla in smocked Liberty lawn and Hamish a fat baby on her knee. Archie must have sent that one to Pandora with one of his letters and she had framed it in silver and set it in the place of honour. Tucked into this silver frame was an invitation whose format was instantly familiar.

Pandora Blair

Mrs. Angus Steynton

At Home

For Katy

Lucilla's first thought was, how nice. And then, how ridiculous. A waste of a card, a waste of a stamp, because there was not the slightest possibility that Pandora would accept. She had gone from Croy when she was eighteen and never returned. Resisted all pleading, first from her parents, and then from her brother, and stayed resolutely away. It was scarcely likely that Verena Steynton, of all people, would achieve what Pandora's own family had so abjectly failed to do.

"Lucilla!"

"Coming . . ."

"What are you doing?"

Lucilla, bearing the wineglasses, joined them on the terrace. "Sorry. I've been snooping round that beautiful room. And listening to the music . . ."

"Oh, darling, don't you love Rachmaninoff? It's one of my most favourites. I know it's a bit hackneyed, but I seem to go for hackneyed things."

"I'm just the same," Lucilla admitted. "Songs like 'Oh, Lovely Moon' and 'The Barcarolle' leave me quite weak-kneed. And some of the old Beatles records. I've got them all at home at Croy. And if I'm feeling *really* blue, I've got a tape of a Fiddlers' Rally in Oban and I play it and I can feel my spirits rise visibly, like mercury in a thermometer when you've got a temperature. All those dear old men and little boys in their kilts and their shirt-sleeves, and an endless round of jigs and reels, as though they didn't know how to stop and didn't want to anyway. I usually end up dancing all by myself and leaping around the room like an idiot."

Jeff said, "I've never seen you do that."

"Well, if you hang around long enough, you probably will. But seriously, Pandora, this is the most beautiful place you've got. And our guest-house is perfection."

"It is rather sweet, isn't it? I was so lucky

to snap it all up. The people who lived here before had to go back to England; I was looking for somewhere to live and it seemed that it was just waiting for me. Jeff, you're meant to be pouring champagne . . ."

"And the furniture? Is that all yours too?"

Pandora laughed. "Oh, darling, I haven't got any furniture, just little bits and pieces that I've gathered on my travels and cart about with me. Most of the furniture here I took over with the house, but of course I've changed almost everything. The sofas were the most hideous blue, and there was a carpet with swirls on. Got rid of that pretty sharpish. I took Seraphina over with the house as well, and she's got a husband who does the garden. All I'm missing out on is a little doggie, but doggies in Majorca are inclined to get shot by youths with airguns, or else they get ticks, or they get stolen, or run over. So there's not really much point." All the glasses were now brimming full. Pandora raised hers.

"Here's to you both, and what heaven it is to have you here. Lucilla, Jeff's been telling me all about your journey down through France. How fascinating it must have been.

And you got to see Chartres, such an experience. I'm longing to hear more, get all the details; but first, and most important, I want to be told all about home, and my precious Archie and Isobel and Hamish. Hamish must be enormous now. And Isobel, with those tedious Americans to stay. I hear all about them in Archie's letters, when he isn't telling me about the latest grouse-bag, or the size of the salmon he caught last week. It's a miracle he's able to do so much with that terrible leg. Tell me how the poor leg is."

"He can't actually do that much," Lucilla told her bluntly. "He just writes you positive letters because he doesn't want you to be upset. And his leg isn't anything. It's tin, full stop. It can't get any better, and we all pray it'll never get any worse."

"Poor darling. Beastly, beastly IRA. How they dare to do such things, and to Archie, of all people."

"They weren't necessarily gunning for *him*, Pandora. They were waiting, over the border, to blast off at a lot of British jocks, and he happened to be one of them."

"Did he know they were there? Or was it an ambush?"

"I don't know. And if I asked, he wouldn't tell me. He won't talk about it. He won't talk about it to anybody."

"Is that a good thing?"

"I don't suppose it is, but there's not much we can do about it."

"He was never a great talker. The most darling man, but even as a little boy he always kept everything to himself. We never even knew he was courting Isobel, and when he told our mother that he wanted to marry her, Mama nearly dropped dead with astonishment because she'd got him lined up for some entirely different female. Never mind, she made the best of it. Just as she always made the best of everything. . . ." Her voice faded. She fell silent, then swiftly emptied her glass. "Jeff, is there any more left in that bottle, or shall we open another?"

But the bottle was not yet empty and Jeff refilled Pandora's glass, and then topped up Lucilla's and his own. Lucilla was now beginning to feel not only light-hearted but light-headed as well. She wondered how much Pandora had already consumed before they joined her. Perhaps the champagne was why she seemed to be talking so much.

"Now tell me . . ." She was off again. "What are the two of you going to do next?"

Jeff and Lucilla looked at each other. Making plans was not one of their strong points. Doing things on the spur of the moment was half the fun.

It was Jeff who replied. "We don't really know. Only thing is, I have to go back to Australia at the beginning of October. I've a flight booked with Qantas on the third."

"Where do you fly from?"

"London."

"So, sometime, you'll have to go back to England."

"Right."

"Is Lucilla going with you?"

Again they looked at each other. "We haven't discussed it," Lucilla said.

"So you're free. Free as air. Free to come and go as you wish. The world is your oyster." She made an expansive gesture with her hand and spilled some of her champagne.

"Yes," Jeff agreed cautiously, "I suppose it is."

"Then let us make plans. Lucilla, would you like to make plans with me?"

"What sort of plans?"

"When you were snooping, as you put it, around my drawing-room, did you notice that large and pretentious copperplate invitation on my mantelpiece?"

"From Verena Steynton? Yes, I did."

"Have you been asked?"

"Yes. Dad sent my invitation on to me and I got it in Ibiza."

"Are you going?"

"I . . . I hadn't actually thought about it."

"*Might* you go?"

"I don't know. Why?"

"Because . . ." She laid down her glass. "I think that I shall go."

The shock of this announcement stunned Lucilla out of her delightful tipsiness and into a state of cold sobriety. She stared at Pandora in total disbelief, and Pandora stared back, her grey eyes with their huge black pupils bright with a strange elation, as though delighting in the expression of blank incredulity she had brought to Lucilla's face.

"You'd go?"

"Why not?"

"Back to Scotland?"

"Where else?"

"For Verena Steynton's *dance?*" It did not make sense.

"It's as good a reason as any."

"But you've never come before. Dad asked you and begged you, and you've never come. He told me."

"There has to be a first time. Perhaps now is the right time." All at once she stood up and walked away from them to stand looking out over the garden. She stayed there for an instant, quite still, silhouetted against the light that shone upwards from the pool. Her dress, her hair moved in the breeze. Then she turned to face them, leaning against the balustrade. She said, and she spoke now in quite a different voice, "I've been thinking so much about Croy. Just lately, I've been thinking so much about it. I'd dream about it, and wake up, and start remembering things I hadn't thought of in years. And then the invitation came. Like yours, Lucilla, forwarded on from Croy. And it brought back a million memories of the fun we used to have at those ridiculous dances and hunt balls. And house parties, and the hills ringing with the crack of guns, and every evening an enormous dinner party. How my poor mother coped with us all, I cannot imagine." She smiled at Lucilla, and then at Jeff. "And you two arriving. Phoning from Palma and turning up out of the blue, and Lucilla so like Archie. Omens. Do you believe in omens, Lucilla?"

"I don't know."

"Neither do I. But I'm certain, with the Highland blood that courses through our veins, that we should." She came back to her chair and sat on the foot-rest, her face close to Lucilla's. Beneath the beauty, Lucilla could discern the years stamped on Pandora's lovely features: the lines around her eyes and mouth, the papery skin, the sharp angle of her jaw-bone. "So, let us make plans. Will you both make plans with me? Would you mind if I asked you to do that thing?"

Lucilla looked across at Jeff. He shook his head. She said, "We wouldn't mind."

"Then this is what we'll do. We'll stay here for a week, just the three of us, and you shall have the time of your lives. And then we'll take my car, and we'll catch the ferry to Spain. And we'll drive through Spain and France, taking our time and making a pleasure of the journey. When we get to Calais, we'll cross over to England. And we'll head

north, and we'll go to Scotland, and we'll go
home. Back to Croy. Oh, Lucilla, say you
think it's a wonderful idea."

"It's certainly totally unexpected," was all
Lucilla could come up with, but if Pandora
noticed a certain lack of enthusiasm in her
voice, she gave no indication of doing so.
Swept along on her own excitement, she
turned to Jeff. "And you? How does it sound
to you? Or do you think I'm out of my
mind?"

"No."

"You wouldn't mind coming to Scotland
with us?"

"If that's what you and Lucilla want, I'd
be delighted."

"Then it's all settled!" She was triumphant. "We'll all stay at Croy with Isobel and
Archie, and we'll all go to the Steyntons'
lovely party."

"But Jeff hasn't been asked," Lucilla
pointed out.

"Oh, that's no problem."

"And he won't have anything to wear."

Pandora dissolved into laughter. "Darling,
you do disappoint me. I thought you were an
unworldly artist, and all you seem to do is

worry about clothes! Don't you see, clothes don't matter. Nothing matters. The only thing that matters is that we're going back home, together. Just think what fun we're going to have. And now we must celebrate!" She sprang to her feet. "The perfect moment to open that second bottle of champagne!"

SEPTEMBER

1

Thursday the Eighth

ISOBEL BALMERINO, at her sewing-machine, stitched the last name-tape, HAMISH BLAIR, onto the last new handkerchief, cut the thread, folded the handkerchief, and laid it on top of the pile of clothes that stood on the table beside her. All done. All that remained were those garments which required that the name-tapes be hand-sewn . . . rugger stockings, an overcoat, and a grey polo-necked pullover, but these could be done at leisure, in the evening, and by the fireside.

She had not had such a session of name-tapes since Hamish first went to Templehall, four years ago, but he had grown during the summer holidays to such an alarming extent that she had been forced to wheel him into Relkirk, school-clothes list in hand, and start all over again. The expedition, as she had known it would be, had been both painful and expensive. Painful because Hamish did not want to think about going back to school, hated shopping, hated new clothes, and miserably resented being done out of a single day of his holiday freedom. And expensive because the regulation uniform could only be purchased at the most up-market and costly shop in the town. The overcoat, the polo-necked sweater, and the rugger stockings were bad enough, but five new pairs of enormous leather shoes were almost more than Isobel, and her bank balance, could take.

With some idea of cheering Hamish up, she had bought him an ice-cream, but he had devoured this morosely and without joy, and they had returned to Croy in an uncommunicative and mutually unfriendly silence. Once home, Hamish had immediately taken himself off, armed with his trout rod, and wearing an expression which implied that he had been grossly mistreated. Isobel was left to hump the parcels and boxes upstairs, where she had slung them into the foot of his wardrobe and firmly shut the door, then made her way to the kitchen to boil a kettle for a cup of tea and start preparing dinner.

The horrible experience of spending vast quantities of money that she could not afford left her feeling quite sick, and Hamish's patent ingratitude did not help. Peeling potatoes, she said a silent goodbye to any dreams of buying herself a new dress for the Steyntons' dance. The old navy taffeta would have to do. Letting herself feel martyred and ill done by, she toyed with the notion of freshening it up with a touch of white at the neck.

But that had all happened two weeks ago, and now September was here. That made everything better, and for a number of reasons. The most important was that, until next May, she was finished with the business of paying guests. Scottish Country Tours had shut up shop for the winter, and the last lot of Americans, complete with baggage, souvenirs, and tartan bonnets, had been waved away. The tiredness and depression that had dogged Isobel all summer was dissolved almost instantly by her sense of freedom and the knowledge that, once more, she and Archie had Croy to themselves.

But this was not all. Born and bred in Scotland, she experienced each year this lifting of the spirits as August slipped away, off the calendar, and one could stop pretending that it was summer. Some years, it was true, there came seasons like the old days, when the lawns grew dry from lack of rain and golden evenings were spent watering the roses and sweet peas and the rows of young lettuces in the vegetable garden. But too frequently the months of June, July, and August were nothing but a long and soggy endurance test of frustration and disappointment. Grey skies, chill winds, and dripping rain were enough to dampen the enthusiasm of a saint. The worst were those dark and muggy days when, in desperation, one eventually retreated indoors and lit a fire, whereupon the sky instantly cleared and the late afternoon sun dazzled out over the sodden garden, tantalizingly too late to be of use to anybody.

This summer, in particular, had been specially disappointing, and with hindsight Isobel realized that the weeks of dark clouds and sunlessness had done much to contribute to her low spirits and physical exhaustion. The first snap of frost was actually welcome, and she was able to put away her cotton skirts and shirts with some satisfaction and revert once more to friendly old tweeds and Shetland pullovers.

But even after splendid summers, September in Relkirkshire was special. Those first light frosts cleared the air, so that the colours of the countryside took on a stronger and richer hue. The deep blue of the skies was reflected in loch and river, and with the harvest safely in, the fields stood golden with stubble. Harebells grew in wayside ditches, and the scented heather, coming into full bloom, stained the hills with purple.

And then, most important of all, September meant fun. A packed season of socializing before the darkness of a long winter closed in on them all, when the bitter weather and snow-packed roads isolated scattered communities and precluded any form of contact. September meant people. Friends. For this was when Relkirkshire came truly into its own.

By the end of July, the last of the annual invasion of holiday-makers had, by and large, left; tents were packed up and caravans towed away, as the tourists headed for home. In their stead, August brought the vanguard of a secondary immigration from the south, regular visitors who returned each year to Scotland for the sport and the parties. Shooting lodges that had stood forlornly empty for most of the year were once more opened up, and their owners, driving north up the motorway in Range Rovers loaded to the gunwales with rods, guns, small children, teenagers, friends, relations, and dogs, took happy and grateful repossession.

As well, local households swelled, not with Americans nor paying guests but with the young families who belonged to these establishments and had, by necessity, moved south to London to live and work, saving their yearly vacations to return home at just this time. All bedrooms were occupied, attics turned into temporary accommodation for gangs of grandchildren, and sparse bathrooms worked overtime. Huge quantities of food were produced, cooked, and eaten every day at dining-room tables elongated by extra leaves.

And then, September. In September, all at

once, everything came to life, as though some celestial stage-manager had made his countdown and pulled the switch. The Station Hotel in Relkirk was transformed from its customary Victorian gloom to a cheerful, crowded meeting-place for old friends, and the Strathcroy Arms, taken over by the syndicate of businessmen who paid Archie reassuring sums of money for the privilege of shooting grouse over his moor, fairly buzzed with activity and sporting talk.

At Croy, the invitations stood stacked on the mantelpiece in the library, and covering every type of convivial occasion. Isobel's contribution to the general jollity was an annual buffet lunch party before the Strathcroy Games. Archie was Chieftain of these Games and led the opening parade of village worthies, their stride tactfully slowed to match his halting gait. For this important ceremony, he wore his regimental balmoral and carried a drawn sword. He took his responsibilities with great solemnity and, at the end of the day, presented prizes, not only for piping and Highland dancing but also for the sweater most expertly knitted from handspun wool, the lightest of sponge cakes, and the winning pot of home-made strawberry jam.

Isobel kept her sewing-machine in the old linen room at Croy, mostly for reasons of convenience but also because it was her favourite and most private retreat. Not large, but quite spacious enough, it had windows facing west, out over the croquet lawn and the road that led up to the loch, and on bright days was always filled with sunshine. The curtains were white cotton, the floor brown linoleum, and the walls were lined with large white-painted cupboards in which were stowed all the household sheets and towels and spare blankets and fresh bed-covers. The solid table on which stood the sewing-machine was also useful for cutting out and dressmaking, and the ironing-board and the iron stood ready for instant use. As well, there was always a comforting nursery smell of laundered linen and the lavender bags that Isobel tucked in with her crisp piles of pillowcases, and this contributed in no small

way to create an extraordinary aura of timelessness and tranquillity.

Which was why, with the name-tapes finished, she made no immediate effort to move
but stayed, sitting on the hard chair, with her
elbows on the table and her chin in her
hands. The view beyond the open window
led, up beyond the trees, to the first gentle
summits of the hills. All was washed in
golden sunlight. The curtains stirred in the
breeze, and that same breath of air shivered
through the branches of the silver birches
that stood on the far side of the lawn.

A leaf dropped, drifting like a tiny kite.

It was half past three and she was alone in
the house. Indoors all was still, but from the
farmyard she heard distant hammering and
the barking of one of the dogs. For once in
her life she had time to herself, there being
no commitment nor person urgently requir-
ing her attention. She could scarcely remember when she had last found herself in such a
situation, and her thoughts drifted back to
childhood and youth and the lazy, aimless
joys of empty days.

A floor creaked. Somewhere a door
slammed shut. Croy. An old house with a

heartbeat all its own. Her home. But she remembered the day, over twenty years ago,
when Archie had first brought her here. She
was nineteen and a tennis party had been arranged, with afternoon tea served in the dining-room. Isobel, the daughter of an Angus
solicitor, and neither beautiful nor assured,
had found herself overwhelmed by the size
and grandeur of the place, and as well by the
glamour and sophistication of Archie's other
friends, all of whom seemed to know each
other frighteningly well. Already hopelessly
in love with Archie, she could not imagine
why he had bothered to include her in the
general invitation. Lady Balmerino appeared
to be equally perplexed, but had been kind,
making certain Isobel sat next to her at the
tea-table, and taking pains to see that she was
not left out of any conversation.

But there was another girl, long-legged
and blonde, who seemed already to have
claimed Archie for her own, and made this
very clear to the assembled company, teasing
him, and catching his eye across the table as
though they shared a million private secrets.
Archie, she was telling them all, belonged to

her, and no other person would be permitted to take possession.

But, at the end of the day, Archie had made up his own mind to marry Isobel. His parents, once they had got over their astonishment, were patently delighted and welcomed Isobel into the family not as Archie's wife but as another daughter. She was fortunate. Gentle, funny, hospitable, unworldly, and totally charming, the Balmerinos were adored by everybody and Isobel was no exception.

From the farm, she heard one of the tractors starting up. Another leaf fluttered to the ground. It occurred to Isobel that now could be an afternoon that had happened long ago, as though time had slipped backwards. The sort of afternoon when dogs sought for shade, and cats basked on window-sills, their furry bellies turned to the sun. She thought of Mrs. Harris, with one of the younger maids in tow, emerging from the kitchen and headed for the walled garden, there to fill a bowl with the last of the raspberries, or reach for the bloomy Victoria plums, capturing their sweetness before the wasps got at them.

All of Croy the way it once had been. No-

body had gone away. Nobody had died. They
were still alive, those two dear old people;
Archie's mother out with her roses, snipping
away at the dead heads and finding time to
chat with one of the gardeners while he raked
the dusty gravel; and Archie's father in the
library, stealing a little snooze with his silk
handkerchief spread across his face. Isobel
only had to go and find them. She imagined
doing this, making her way down the stairs,
crossing the hall to stand at the open front
door. She saw Lady Balmerino in her straw
gardening hat coming in from the garden,
carrying the basket filled with snippings and
faded rose petals. But when she looked up
and saw Isobel, she would frown and show
some confusion because the middle-aged
Isobel would be unfamiliar to her as a
ghost. . . .

"Isobel!"

The voice, raised, impinged upon her
daydreams. Isobel was aware that it had already called, more than once, but she had
scarcely heard. Who was wanting her now?
Reluctantly she collected herself, pushed
back the chair and got to her feet. Perhaps to
be left alone for more than five minutes was

too much to expect. She went out of the
room and down the nursery passage to the
head of the stairs. Leaning over the bannister, she saw below her the foreshortened view
of Verena Steynton standing in the middle of
the hall, having walked into the house
through the open front door.

"Isobel!"

"I'm here."

Verena tilted her head and looked up. "I
was beginning to think there was nobody in."

"Only me." Isobel started down the stairs.
"Archie's taken Hamish and the dogs to the
Buchanan-Wrights' cricket match."

"Are you busy?" Verena did not look as
though she had been busy. As usual, she was
immaculately and suitably turned out, and
surely had just been to the hairdresser.

"I've been sewing Hamish's name-tapes
for school." Instinctively, Isobel put a hand
to her hair, as though the casual gesture
might improve her own tousled head. "But
I've finished now."

"Can you spare me a moment?"

"Of course."

"I've got lots to tell you and two favours to
ask. I meant to phone but I've been in

Relkirk all day and then, driving home, I thought it much simpler and nicer just to call in."

"Do you want a cup of tea?"

"In a moment. No hurry."

"Let's go and be comfortable." Isobel led her visitor into the drawing-room, not with any intentions of grandeur but simply because it was full of sunlight, and the library and the kitchen, at this time of day, were inclined to be gloomy. The windows stood open, the room felt cool, and a mass of sweet peas, which Isobel had picked that morning and arranged in an old soup tureen, filled the air with their fragrance.

"Heaven." Verena sank into a corner of the sofa and stretched out her long and elegantly shod legs. "What a day for the cricket match. Last year it bucketed with rain and they had to pull stumps in the middle of the afternoon because the pitch was flooded. Are those your own sweet peas? What colours! Mine were a bit of a failure this year. Do you know I really hate Relkirk on a warm afternoon? The pavements were banked three deep with fat girls in jeans pushing babies in buggies. And all the babies seemed to be howling."

"I know the feeling. How's everything going?"

She had already made up her mind that Verena wanted to talk about the dance and she was not mistaken.

"Oh . . ." Verena, for a moment, became quite dramatic, groaning as though in pain and closing her eyes. "I'm beginning to wonder why I ever *thought* about throwing a party. Do you know half the invitations haven't even been answered yet? People are so thoughtless. I think they leave them curling on mantelpieces, waiting to die of old age. It makes trying to arrange dinner parties and find beds for everybody quite impossible."

"I wouldn't worry." Isobel tried to sound soothing. "I'd let them make their own arrangements."

"But that would mean utter chaos."

Isobel knew that it wouldn't, but Verena was a perfectionist. "Yes, I suppose so. It must be awful." She added, almost afraid to ask, "Has Lucilla replied yet?"

"No," Verena told her bluntly.

"We did send your invitation on, but she's travelling so she may not even have got it. She sent us a rather vague address in Ibiza, but we haven't heard from her since she was in Paris. She thought she might go and see Pandora."

"I haven't heard from Pandora either."

"I'll be surprised if you do. She never answers anything."

"But Alexa Aird's coming, and bringing a boyfriend. Did you know that Alexa has found herself a man?"

"Vi told me."

"Extraordinary. I wonder what he's like."

"Virginia says he's dishy."

"Can't wait to see him."

"When is Katy arriving?"

"Next week sometime. She called last night. Which is one of the favours that I have to ask you. Have you got a houseful of people staying over the dance?"

"So far, nobody. Hamish will be back at school and I don't know whether Lucilla will be here or not. . . ."

"Well, could you be an angel and have a stray man to stay? Katy told me about him last night. She met him at some dinner party, and liked him. He's an American—a lawyer, I think—but his wife's just died, and he's come over here for a bit of a holiday. He's coming to Scotland anyway to stay with some people who live in the Borders, and she thought it would be friendly to send him an invitation. We can't put him up at Corriehill because I'm full, with all Katy's friends, and Toddy Buchanan hasn't a room free at the Strathcroy Arms, so I thought you could give him a bed? Would you mind? I don't know anything about him except the bit about his wife dying, but if Katy liked him I don't suppose he'd be *dreadfully* heavy weather."

"Poor man. Of course he can come."

"And you'll bring him to the party? You are sweet. I'll ring Katy tonight, and tell her to tell him to get in touch with you."

"What's his name?"

"Something funny. Plucker. Or . . . Tucker. That's it. Conrad Tucker. Why do you suppose Americans always have such peculiar names?"

Isobel laughed. "They probably think Balmerino's pretty odd. What else is happening?"

"Nothing really. We've persuaded Toddy Buchanan to do the catering and run the bar, and produce some sort of a breakfast. For some reason, Katy's generation are always ravenously hungry around four in the morning. And darling Tom Drystone is organizing the band."

"Well, it wouldn't be a party without our whistling postman up on the platform. Are you having a disco?"

"Yes. A young man from Relkirk is doing that. He produces everything. A sort of job lot. Flashing lights and amplifiers. What the noise is going to be like, I dread to think. And we're going to have fairy lights all the way up the drive. I thought it would look festive, and if it's a miserably dark evening, it'll help people find the way."

"It'll look wonderful. You've thought of everything."

"Except flowers. That's the other favour I've got to ask you. Would you help with the flowers? Katy will be there, and I've press-ganged one or two others, but nobody does flowers the way you do, and I'd be endlessly grateful if you'd help."

Isobel felt flattered. It was nice to think

that there was something that she could do better than Verena, and gratifying to be asked.

"The thing is," Verena went on before Isobel had a chance to speak, "I can't think how to decorate the marquee. The house isn't so difficult, but the marquee presents something of a problem because it's so enormous and ordinary flower arrangements would simply be dwarfed. What do you think? You're always full of bright ideas."

Isobel searched for a bright idea but drew a blank. "Hydrangeas?"

"They'll be over by then."

"Hire some potted palms."

"Too depressing. Like the ballroom of some provincial hotel."

"Well, why not make it really countrified and seasonal? Sheaves of ripe barley and branches of rowan. Lovely red berries and those pretty leaves. And the beeches will be turning as well. We can soak the stems in glycerine and simply cover the tent-poles, make them look like autumn trees. . . ."

"Oh, a brainwave. You're brilliant. We'll do it all the day before the party. The Thursday. Will you write it down in your diary?"

"It's Vi's birthday picnic that day, but I can give that a miss."

"You're a saint. What a weight off my mind. The relief of it." Verena stretched luxuriously, swallowed a yawn, fell silent.

The clock on the mantelpiece ticked gently, and the quiet of the room closed in on the two women. Yawns were catching. And it was a mistake ever to sit down in the middle of the afternoon because you didn't feel like ever getting up again. Summer afternoons and nothing in particular to do. Once more Isobel drifted back into that illusion of timelessness in which she had been lost before Verena's interruption. She thought again of old Lady Balmerino, who used to sit here, as she and Verena sat, reading a novel or peacefully sewing her tapestry. Everything now as once it had been. Perhaps in a moment there would come a discreet tap on the door and Harris the butler would enter, pushing before him the mahogany trolley laid with the silver teapot and the eggshell china cups; the covered dishes of scones, fresh from the oven, the bowl of cream, the strawberry jam, the lemon sponge-cake, and the dark, sticky gingerbread.

The clock, with silvery notes, struck four, and the illusion dissolved. Harris was long gone and would never return. Isobel yawned again and then, with some effort, pulled herself to her feet. "I'll go and put the kettle on," she told Verena, "and we'll have that cup of tea."

〄 2 〄

Friday the Ninth

". . . THAT WAS THE YEAR my cousin
Flora had her bairn. Did you know her parents? Uncle Hector was my father's brother,
much younger, of course, and married to a
girl from Rum. Met her when he was a po-
liceman; she was always a shiftless creature,
lost all her teeth when she was scarcely out
of her twenties. When my granny heard, she
was up to high doh, didn't want any candle-
bearing Catholics in the family; she'd been
brought up Wee Free. I knitted a matinee
coat for the bairn. Pink silk with a fern pattern, but she put it in the boiler with the
sheets, it just about broke my heart. . . ."

Violet stopped listening. It didn't seem
necessary to listen. One just nodded, or said
"Oh, yes," every time Lottie paused for

breath, and then she was away again on some other confusing tack.

". . . went into service when I was four-teen, over in a big house in Fife; I cried buckets, but my mother said I had to go. I was the kitchen maid and the Cook was a bisom; I've never been so tired in my life, up at five o'clock in the morning and slept in the attic with a moose."

This at least caught Violet's attention. "A *moose*, Lottie?"

"I think it was a moose. One of those stuffed heads. On the wall. Too big for a stag. Mr. Gilfillan had been in Africa, a mission-ary. You wouldn't have thought a missionary would have gone round killing mooses, would you? Christmas they had roast goose, but all I got was a bit of cold mutton. Mean. Wouldn't give you the drippings off their noses. The attic was that damp, my clothes were wringing wet, caught pneumonia. The doctor came, Mrs. Gilfillan sent me home, never been so glad to get back. Had a cat at home. Tammy Puss. He was that quick. Open the larder door and in with the cream; once we found a dead mouse in the cream. And Ginger had a litter of kittens, half-wild, scratched the skin off my mother's hands . . . she was never good with animals. Hated my father's dog. . . ."

They sat, the two elderly ladies, on a bench in the big park in Relkirk. Before them, the river flowed, heavy with flood-water and stained brown with peat. A fisherman, up to his hips in water, flogged his salmon rod. So far he did not seem to have had so much as a nibble. Across the river stood large Victorian houses, deep in spacious gardens with lawns that ran down to the water. One or two had little boats moored. There were ducks on the water. A man, passing with his dog, threw crusts and the ducks came gobbling, squabbling, to snatch the crusts up.

". . . the doctor said it was a stroke, said she'd got nerves. I wanted to go and be a volunteer, with the war on and everything, but if I'd gone there'd be no one to stay with my mother. My father was a worker out of doors, he grew lovely turnips, but indoors, sit down and take off his boots and that was it . . . never seen a man who could eat so much. He was never a talker, some days never said a word. Trapped rabbits. Ate a lot of rabbits, we did. Course that was before mixamy-toasties. Filthy things now . . ."

Violet, having made her promise to Henry that she would take Lottie off Edie's hands for an afternoon, had suffered an uneasy conscience until she had finally decided to take the plunge and get it over, and had invited Lottie to come shopping with her in Relkirk and to have high tea. She had duly collected Lottie from Edie's cottage, packed her into the car, and driven her into the town. For the occasion Lottie had dressed in her best, a beige Crimplene coat and a hat the shape of a cottage loaf. She carried a huge handbag and wore her tottery high-heeled shoes. From the moment she got into the car, she had not stopped talking. She had talked as they made their way around Marks and Spencer, talked as they waited in the queue to buy fresh vegetables, talked as they searched the crowded streets for what Lottie insisted on calling a haberdasher's.

"I don't think there are any haberdasher's any longer, Lottie. . . ."

"Oh, yes, a little one down that street . . . or was it the next? Mother always came for her knitting wool."

Never believing they would find it, Violet allowed herself to be led around in circles, getting more hot and footsore by the moment, and was torn between annoyance and relief when Lottie finally ran the shop to earth. It was very old and dusty, and crammed with a collection of cardboard boxes containing crochet hooks, faded embroidery silks, and out-of-date knitting patterns. The old woman behind the counter looked as though she had just managed to make it out of a geriatric home, and it took her fifteen minutes to find what Lottie wanted, which was a yard of boiling knicker elastic. Finally, however, it was produced from a drawer filled with odd buttons, put shakily into a paper bag, and paid for. They stepped out onto the pavement, and Lottie was triumphant. "Told you so," she crowed to Violet. "Didn't believe me, did you?"

With their shopping over and it not yet being time for tea, Violet had suggested a walk in the park. They had made their way back to her car, dumped their purchases in the boot, and then crossed the wide sward of grass that led to the river. At the first bench, Violet had firmly sat down.

"We'll have a little rest," she told Lottie, and so here they were, side by side in the golden sunshine, and Lottie still with plenty to say.

"That's the Relkirk Royal, that's where I was, you can just see it through the trees. Nice enough place, but I couldn't stand the nurses. The doctor was good enough, but no more than a young student, don't imagine he knew anything, although he pretended he did. Lovely gardens, though, just as nice as the Cremmy. I wanted Mother cremated, but the minister said she wanted to lie by my father in the churchyard at Tullochard. Though I don't know how he should know more than me."

"I expect your mother told him. . . ."

"More likely made it up himself, always liked to interfere."

Violet looked across the river to where the Relkirk Royal stood high on the hill, its red stone turrets and gables scarcely visible through the leafy trees that surrounded it. She said, "The hospital certainly has a lovely position."

"That's doctors for you. They can pay for anything."

Casually, "What was he called, the young doctor who took care of you?"

"Dr. Martin. There was another, Dr. Faulkner, but he never came near me. It was Dr. Martin who said I could go and live with Edie. I wanted a taxi but it was an ambulance."

"Edie is very kind."

"*She's* had a good enough life, some people have all the luck. Different living in a village to being stuck away up the hill."

"Perhaps you could sell your parents' house and move into a village?"

But Lottie ignored this sensible suggestion and went on, full flood, as though Violet had never made it. It occurred to Violet then that Lottie was more astute than any of them suspected. "Worry about her being so fat, it's a heart attack she'll have one morning, carrying all that flab around with her. And always flying out of the house, off to your house or Virginia's, never sits down for a bit of peace or a chat or to watch the telly. Ought to think of herself sometimes. She told me that Alexa's coming up for Mrs. Steynton's party. Bringing a friend. That's nice, isn't it? But you'll need to watch, men are all the same, after what they can get their hands on. . . ."

"What do you mean, Lottie?" Violet was sharp.

Lottie turned dark round eyes upon her. "Well, she's no pauper, is Alexa. Old Lady Cheriton was never short of sixpence. I read the newspapers, know all about *that* family. Nothing like a bit of cash to start a man leering at a young girl."

Violet found herself assailed by a helpless rage that seemed to surge up from the soles of her feet and, reaching her cheeks, burn them red. Rage at Lottie's impertinence, and helplessness because Lottie was, after all, only voicing what all Alexa's family, obscurely, feared.

She said, "Alexa is very pretty and very dear. The fact that she is also independent has nothing to do with the friends she chooses."

But Lottie either ignored or missed the snub. She gave a little laugh, tossing her head. "I wouldn't be too sure about that. And coming from London, too. Lot of money grubbers. Yuppies," she added with some force, saying the word as though it were dirty.

"Lottie, I don't think you know what you're talking about."

"All these girls are the same. Always were, see a handsome man and they're away like a bitch in heat." She shivered suddenly, as though the excitement of the thought had reached every nerve-end of her gangling frame. Then she put out a hand and closed it over Violet's wrist. "That's another thing. Henry. See him about the place. He's small, isn't he? Comes to Edie's and never says a word. Looks funny to me sometimes. I'd worry if I were you. Not like other little boys . . ."

Her bony fingers were strangely strong, the grip viselike. Violet, repelled, knew an instant of panic. Her immediate instinct was to prize the fingers loose, get to her feet and escape, but just then a girl walked by pushing a child in a buggy, and common sense came to Violet's rescue. The panic, the annoyance faded. It was, after all, just poor Lottie Carstairs, to whom life had not been kind, letting her sad, sexual frustrations and her rambling imagination run away with her. And if Edie could stand having her cousin to live with her, surely Violet could cope calmly for a single afternoon.

She smiled. She said, "It's good of you to be concerned, Lottie, but Henry is a very ordinary little boy and sound as a bell. Now . . ." She shifted slightly, glancing at her watch, and felt Lottie's fingers loosen their manic grip and slip away. Violet, unhurried, reached for her handbag. ". . . I think it's time we went and found somewhere pleasant to have our tea. I'm feeling quite peckish. I fancy fish and chips. How about you?"

⚜ 3 ⚜

As ISOBEL, WORN OUT WITH the daily demands of her busy life, retreated from time to time to the linen room, so her husband found solace in his workshop. This was in the basement of Croy, an area of stone-flagged passages and dimly lighted cellars. The old boiler lived down here, a brooding, smelly monster that looked large enough to drive a liner, and demanded constant and regular attention and enormous quantities of coke. As well, one or two other rooms were still employed—to store unused china, unwanted items of furniture, the coal and the logs, and a much-diminished wine cellar. But mostly, the basement stood deserted, hung with cobwebs and invaded each year by families of field mice.

The workshop was next door to the boiler room, which meant that it was always pleasantly warm, and it had large windows, barred like a jail's, which faced south and west and let in sufficient light for cheerfulness. Archie's father, neat with his hands, had set it all up, with heavy benches, racks for tools, vises, and clamps. And it was here that the old man had liked to potter, repairing his children's damaged toys, dealing with various inevitable breakages that occurred about the house, and concocting his own salmon flies.

After he died, the workshop had stood empty for some years, unused, neglected, and gathering dust. But when Archie came back to Croy after his eight months in hospital, he painfully made his way down the stone stairs, limped the length of the echoing passage, and took repossession. The first thing he saw as he entered the room was a broken balloon-back chair, its back legs shattered by the weight of some corpulent occupant. It had been brought down to the workshop before old Lord Balmerino died. He had made a start on its repair but never finished the job, and the chair had been left, forgotten and untended, ever since.

Archie stood and looked at the forlorn

piece of furniture for some time. Then he shouted for Isobel. She came. She helped him sweep away the dirt and the cobwebs and the mouse droppings and the drifts of old sawdust. Scuttling spiders were sent packing, as were solidified pots of glue, piles of yellowed newspapers, ancient tins of paint. Isobel cleaned the windows and somehow forced them open, letting in the sweet fresh air.

Meanwhile Archie, having wiped and oiled all the fine old tools, the chisels and hammers, saws and planes, replaced them in orderly fashion in their racks. With that done, he sat down and wrote out a list of all that he needed, and Isobel went into Relkirk and bought it for him.

Only then was he able to get down to work and finish the job that his father had started.

Now he sat at that same bench, the afternoon sun slanting through the top half of the window, and finished priming the carving he had been working on, from time to time, over the last month or two. It was about ten inches high and depicted the figure of a girl sitting on a boulder with a small Jack Russell terrier leaning against her knee. The girl wore a sweater and a kilted skirt, and her hair was windblown. It was, in fact, Katy Steynton and her dog. Verena had given Archie a photograph of her daughter, taken up on the moor last year, and from this he had made the drawings for the carving. With the primer dry, he would paint it, reproducing as closely as possible the muted colours of the photograph. And then it would be given to Katy as a twenty-first birthday present.

It was done. He laid down the brush and leaned back in his chair to stretch the aches out of his limbs, and assess his creation over the top of his half-moon spectacles. He had never before attempted the complications of a sitting figure, and a female one at that, and was inordinately pleased with the way it had turned out. Girl and dog made a charming composition. Tomorrow he would paint it. He looked forward with some satisfaction to applying the final touches.

From upstairs, he heard the faint sound of the telephone ringing. It was only just audible, and for months he and Isobel had been talking about the sense of installing another bell in the basement so that he could hear the sound more easily, should he be alone in the house. But they had done nothing about this and he was alone in the house now, and wondered how long the telephone had been ringing, and if there was time for him to make his way upstairs and pick up the receiver before the caller, losing heart, hung up. He thought about ignoring it but the ringing continued. Perhaps it was important. He pushed back his chair and made his slow way down the passage and up the stairs to answer the wretched instrument. The nearest receiver was in the kitchen and it was still ringing shrilly as Archie crossed over to the dresser and picked it up.

"Croy."

"Dad!"

"Lucilla!" His heart leaped with joy. He reached for a chair.

"Where were you? The phone's been ringing for hours."

"Down in my workshop." He settled himself, taking the weight off his leg.

"Oh, I'm sorry. Is Mum not there?"

"No. She and Hamish have gone blackberrying. Lucilla, where are you?"

"I'm in *London*. And you'll never guess where I'm ringing from. You'll never guess in a thousand years."

"In that case you'd better tell me."

"The Ritz."

"What the hell are you doing there?"

"Staying the night. And then we're driving up tomorrow. We'll be home tomorrow night."

Archie took off his spectacles; he could feel the grin of delight spreading over his face. "Who's 'we'?"

"Jeff Howland and me. And . . . wait for it . . . *Pandora*."

"Pandora?"

"I thought that would surprise you. . . ."

"But what's Pandora doing with you?"

"She's coming home. She says it's for Verena Steynton's dance, but I suspect it's really to see Croy and all of you again."

"Is she there now?"

"No. She's having a toes-up. I'm phoning from my room. I'm all alone except for Jeff. I've got so much to tell you and Mum, but I won't do it now because it's all so complicated. . . ."

But Archie would not let her off with this excuse. "When did you get to London?"

"This morning. Just before lunch. We've all been driving through Spain and France in Pandora's car. We've had the most amazing time. Then we caught the ferry early this morning and came to London. I was all ready to head north right away, but Pandora wanted to draw breath, so she brought us here. Insisted. And don't worry about the bill because she's footing it. She footed the whole trip, ever since we left Palma. Paid for all the petrol, the hotels, everything."

"How . . ." His voice broke. It was ridiculous, unmanly, to be so emotional. He tried again. "How is she?"

"She's fine. Terribly pretty. Lots of fun. Oh, Dad, you are pleased I'm bringing her home, aren't you? It's not going to be too much for Mum? Pandora's not what you call madly domesticated and I don't suppose she'll ever raise a finger to do anything to help, but she's so excited about seeing you both again. It will be all right, won't it?"

"More than all right, my darling. It's like a miracle."

"And don't forget, I'm bringing Jeff as well."

"We look forward to meeting him."

"See you tomorrow then."

"What time?"

"About five? But don't worry if we're a little late."

"We won't."

"I can't wait."

"Nor me. Drive carefully, my darling."

"Of course." She sent him a kissing noise down the hundreds of miles of wire, and rang off.

Archie was left sitting on the hard kitchen chair and holding the buzzing receiver in his hand. Lucilla and Pandora. Coming home.

He replaced the receiver. The buzzing ceased. The old kitchen clock ticked slowly. For a few moments he sat where he was, and then got to his feet and went out of the kitchen and down the passage to his study. Sitting at his desk, he opened a drawer and took out a key. Using this key, he opened another, smaller drawer. From this he withdrew an envelope, yellowed with the years and addressed in Pandora's large and immature scrawl to himself, at the Headquarters of The Queen's Loyal Highlanders, in Berlin. The date of the postmark was 1967. It contained a letter, but he did not take this letter out to read because he knew it by heart. Which meant that there was no reason why he had never torn it to shreds, nor flung it on a fire, except that he could not bring himself to destroy it.

Pandora. Coming back to Croy.

From the distance came the sound of a car, growing louder, approaching the house, up the hill from the main road. The noise of its engine was unmistakable. Isobel and Hamish returning in the minibus from their blackberrying expedition. Archie put the envelope back into its drawer, locked it away, disposed once more of the key, and went to meet them.

Isobel had driven the minibus around the back of the house and parked it in the yard and, by the time Archie returned to the kitchen, they were there, his wife and his son, flinging open the door and staggering triumphantly through it, each weighed down by two huge baskets brimming with dark fruit.

After a session in the bramble thickets they were both disreputable, dirty, and mud-stained, and looked, Archie decided fondly, no better than a pair of tinkers.

Every time he set eyes on Hamish, he knew a small shock of surprise, because the boy, these summer holidays, had grown like a young tree, getting taller and larger by the day. At twelve, he now topped his mother, and his out-at-elbow sweater was strained across a pair of muscular shoulders. His shirt hung out of his jeans, purple juice stained his hands and mouth, and his abundant corn-coloured hair was sorely in need of a cut. Archie, eyeing him, was filled with pride.

"Hi, Dad." Dumping the baskets onto the kitchen table, Hamish groaned. "I'm starving."

"You're always starving."

Isobel, too, set down her load. "Hamish, you've been eating blackberries all afternoon." She wore her baggy corduroys and a shirt that Archie had long since discarded. "You can't be hungry."

"I am. Blackberries don't fill you up." Hamish was headed for the dresser where the cake tins were stacked. He removed a lid with a clatter and reached for a knife.

Archie admired their harvest. "You've done frightfully well."

"We must have picked about thirty pounds. I've never seen so many. We went over to the other side of the river where Mr. Gladstone grows his turnips. The hedgerows around those fields are groaning with fruit." Isobel pulled out a chair and sat down. "I'd die for a cup of tea."

Archie said, "I have news for you."

She looked up quickly, always fearing the worst. "Good news?"

"The best," he told her.

"But when did she call? What did she say? Why didn't she let us know before?" Isobel, alight with excitement, gave Archie no time to answer any question. "Why didn't they call us from Palma, or France, and give us more notice? Not that I need a moment's notice, it doesn't matter; all that matters is that they're coming. And staying at the *Ritz*. I

don't think that Lucilla's ever stayed in a hotel in the whole of her life. Pandora is ridiculous. They could easily have gone somewhere
a little less grand. . . ."

"Pandora probably doesn't know anywhere else."

"And they're staying over the dance? And
she's bringing the sheep-farmer? Do you suppose she actually persuaded Pandora to
come? It's so extraordinary, after all these
years, that it's taken *Lucilla* to persuade her.
I'll have to get all the bedrooms ready. We'll
be quite a house party because we've got that
American friend of Katy's coming as well.
And food. I think there are still some pheasants in the deep-freeze. . . ."

They were, by now, sitting around the table and drinking tea. Hamish, in famished
desperation, had put the kettle on and made
this. While his parents talked, he had set the
table with three mugs, the tins that contained
the cakes and biscuits, and a loaf of bread on
its wooden board. As well, he had found butter and a jar of Branston Pickle. Hamish had,
just now, a passion for Branston Pickle and
spread it on everything. He was, at this moment, engaged in concocting a sandwich, the

dark pickle oozing out between two enormous doorstops of bread.

". . . did she tell you about Pandora? Did she say anything at all about her?"

"Not very much. Just sounded pleased with life."

"Oh, I wish I'd been here to talk to her."

"You can talk to her tomorrow."

"Have you told anyone else they're coming?"

"No. Just you."

"I'll have to call Verena and tell her she's got three more people coming to her party. And I must tell Virginia. And Vi."

Archie reached for the teapot and refilled his mug.

"I was thinking. Perhaps it would be a good idea to ask all the Airds for lunch on Sunday? What do you say? After all, we don't know how long Pandora's going to be staying, and next week's going to be like a three-ring circus with one thing and another. Sunday might be a good day."

"That's a brilliant idea. I'll ring Virginia. And I'll order a sirloin from the butcher."

Hamish said "Yum yum" and reached for another slice of gingerbread.

". . . and if it's a fine day we can play croquet. We haven't played croquet all summer. You'll have to cut the grass, Archie." She set down her mug, businesslike. "Now. I've got to make bramble jelly, and I'll have to get all the bedrooms ready. But I mustn't forget to ring Virginia. . . ."

"I'll do that," said Archie. "You can leave that to me."

But Isobel, with the great jelly-pan set on the Aga and the blackberries simmering, knew that if she did not share her exciting news with somebody, she would burst, and so found time to call Violet. At first there was no reply from Pennyburn, so she hung up and called again half an hour later.

"Hello."

"Vi, it's Isobel."

"Oh, my dear."

"Are you busy?"

"No, I'm sitting down with a drink in my hand."

"But, Vi, it's only half past five. Have you taken to the bottle?"

"Temporarily. I've had the most exhausting day of my life, wheeling Lottie Carstairs around Relkirk and giving her tea. Never mind, it's all over now and I've done my good deed for the week. But I did feel I deserved a large whisky and soda."

"You certainly do. Or even *two* large whiskies and soda. Vi, something really exciting has happened. Lucilla rang from London and she's coming home tomorrow and she's bringing Pandora with her."

"She's bringing *who?*"

"Pandora. Archie's over the moon with delight. Just think. He's been trying to get her back to Croy for the past twenty-one years and now she's actually coming."

"I can't believe it."

"Incredible, isn't it? Come for lunch on Sunday and see them all. We're asking all the other Airds as well, you can come with them."

"I'd love to do that. But . . . Isobel, why did she suddenly decide to come? Pandora, I mean."

"No idea. Lucilla said something about the Steyntons' party, but it seems a fairly feeble excuse."

"How extraordinary. I . . . I . . . wonder what she will look like?"

"No idea. Probably smashing. Except that she's thirty-nine now, so there are bound to be a few wrinkles. Anyway, we'll soon see for ourselves. I must go, Vi. I'm making bramble jelly and it's just about to boil over. See you Sunday."

"So kind. And I'm thrilled about Lucilla . . ."

But the brambles claimed Isobel. " 'Bye, Vi." And she rang off.

Pandora.

Vi put down her receiver, took off her spectacles, and rubbed her aching eyes. She had been tired before, but Isobel's news, delivered with such joy, left her with the sensation that she was being beleaguered. As though impossible demands were about to be made of her, and vital decisions to be made.

She lay back in her chair and closed her eyes, wished that Edie were here, her oldest and dearest friend, so that she could confide, and discuss, and be comforted. But Edie was in her cottage, lumbered with Lottie, and even a telephone call was out of the question, with Lottie listening to every word and drawing her own dangerous conclusions.

Pandora. Now thirty-nine, but because Violet had not seen her since she was eighteen, she had stayed, in Violet's mind, perpetually that enchanting teenager. Like a person already dead. People who had died never aged, just stayed in the memory the way they had once been. Archie and Edmund had matured to middle age, but not Pandora.

Which was ridiculous. Everybody grew older at the same speed, like people at airports being carried along by those moving walkways. Pandora was thirty-nine and had lived a life, if all accounts were to be believed, that was anything but quiet and peaceful. Experience would have left its mark, drawing lines, wrinkling skin, dulling the bright lustre of that amazing hair.

But it was almost impossible to imagine. Violet sighed, opened her eyes, reached for her drink. This would not do. She must pull herself together. The implications of the situation had nothing to do with her. She would make no decision because there was none to be made. She would simply continue to do what she had always done, which was to observe, disregard, and keep her counsel.

Edmund Aird, returning home to Balnaid from Edinburgh at seven o'clock in the evening, walked through his front door just as the telephone started to ring. Standing in the hall, he paused, but when no one immediately answered the call, he laid his brief-case down on the table and went to the library, to sit at his desk and pick up the receiver.

"Edmund Aird."

"Edmund. Archie here."

"Yes, Archie."

"Isobel asked me to call you. She wants you and Virginia and Henry to come for lunch on Sunday. We've asked Vi as well. Can you make it?"

"How very kind of Isobel. I think so . . . just a moment . . ." He reached in his pocket for his diary, laid it on the blotter, turned the pages. "As far as I'm concerned, that would be fine, but I'm only just back and I haven't spoken to Virginia yet. Do you want me to go and find her?"

"No, don't bother. You can ring me if you can't come, and if we don't hear, we'll expect you all at about a quarter to one."

"We look forward to it." Edmund hesitated. "Is this for some occasion we should know about, or just a routine invitation?"

Archie said, "No." And then said, "Yes. I mean, it is an occasion. Lucilla's coming home tomorrow. . . ."

"That's great news."

"She's bringing some Australian with her."

"The sheep-farmer?"

"That's right. And she's bringing Pandora."

Edmund, with some deliberation, closed his diary. It was bound in navy-blue hide, with his initials in gold in one corner. It had been in his stocking last Christmas, a present from Virginia.

"Pandora?"

"Yes. Lucilla and the sheep-farmer went to stay with her in Majorca. They've all come back together, driving through Spain and France. Got to London this morning." Archie paused, as though waiting for some comment from Edmund. But Edmund did not speak and, after a bit, Archie went on. "I forwarded an invitation from Verena Steynton, so I suppose she thought it might be fun to come home for the party."

"It's as good a reason as any."

"Yes." Another pause. "Sunday then, Edmund?"

"Yes, of course."

"Unless we hear from you."

"We look forward to it. Thank you for calling."

He rang off. The library, the house were silent. It occurred to him that perhaps Virginia and Henry were out somewhere, and he was totally alone. This sense of solitude grew, became oppressive. He found himself straining his ears, needing the reassurance of a raised voice, the clatter of dishes, the bark of a dog. Nothing. Then, from beyond the open window, came the long, bubbling call of a curlew, flying low over the fields beyond the garden. A cloud covered the sun, and the cool air stirred. He put the diary back in his pocket, smoothed his hair with his hand, straightened his tie. He needed a drink. He got up from the chair, left the room, and went in search of his wife and his son.

⚘ 4 ⚘

Saturday the Tenth

LUCILLA SAID, "I've never come home in such style before."

"How did you come before?" Jeff was driving. He had been at the wheel the whole of their long journey north.

"In trains from school. Or driving a ratty little car from Edinburgh. Once I flew from London, but that was in the days when Dad was still a soldier and the War Office paid my fare."

It was half past three, a Saturday afternoon, and now there were only twenty miles to go. They had made good time. The motorway was behind them, Relkirk bypassed, and the winding road comfortingly familiar, leading them to Strathcroy and home. The river kept them company, and ahead lay the hills. The air was clear, the sky enormous, and the fresh breeze, sweeping in through opened windows, sweet and heady as young wine.

Lucilla could scarcely believe their good fortune. It had been raining in London and pouring in the Midlands, but as they crossed the Border, she had watched the clouds disintegrate, disperse, roll away to the east, and Scotland welcomed them with a blue sky and trees just on the point of turning gold. Lucilla thought that this was extremely obliging of her native country and felt as pleased as if she, personally, had stage-managed the miraculous transformation, but deliberately made no comment on either their luck or the stunning scenery. She had known Jeff for long enough to discover that he did not appreciate, and was even embarrassed by, over-effusion.

They had set off at ten o'clock this morning, checking out of the Ritz, and watching the majestic porters load Pandora's dark-red Mercedes with her impressive array of matched luggage, along with their own humble backpacks. Pandora had forgotten to tip the porters, so Lucilla had had to do it for her. She knew that she would never get it back, but after a night of total luxury with dinner and breakfast thrown in, she felt that it was the least she could do.

To begin with, Pandora had sat in the front of her magnificent car, cosy in her mink, because after the nailing heat of a Majorcan August, she felt in need of its opulent comfort. The cold and the rain were not what she had expected. While Jeff drove them out of the city, jousted with traffic, achieved the motorway, she kept up an endless stream of inconsequential chat. Later, she fell silent, gazing out of the window at the grey and dull countryside through which they swept, in the fast lane, at eighty miles an hour. The windscreen wipers worked flat out, immense juggernauts sent up blinding, muddy showers of spray, and even Lucilla had to admit that it was all thoroughly disagreeable.

"Goodness, it's ugly." Pandora snuggled deeper into her fur.

"I know. But it's just this bit."

For lunch, they stopped at a Motorway Service Station. Pandora wanted to leave the motorway and go in search of some wayside pub, preferably thatched, where they could sit by an open fire and drink cheering concoctions like whisky and ginger ale. But Lucilla knew that if they allowed themselves to be so diverted, they would never get back to Croy.

"There isn't time. This isn't Spain, Pandora. It isn't France. We've no time to waste on frivolities."

"Darling, hardly a *frivolity*."

"Yes, it is. And you'd get talking to the barman and we'd be there forever."

So the Motorway Service Station it was, which proved just as unenjoyable as Lucilla feared it would be. Queuing with trays for sandwiches and coffee; and then sitting on orange plastic chairs at a Formica table, hemmed in by irritable families with fractious children, punky youths in pornographic T-shirts, and muscular truck drivers, all seemingly content to wrap themselves around mind-boggling platefuls of fish and chips, evilly coloured trifles, and cups of tea.

After lunch, Pandora and Lucilla had changed places; Pandora had made herself comfortable on the back seat and fallen instantly asleep. She had been asleep ever since, which meant that she had missed the dramatic crossing of the Border, the clearing of the sky, and the miraculous excitement of actually coming home.

They drove through a small country town. "Where's this?" Jeff asked.

"Kirkthornton."

The pavements were crammed with Saturday-afternoon shoppers, the municipal gardens bright with dahlias. Old men sat on benches enjoying the kindly warmth. Children licked ice-creams. A bridge curved high over a tumbling river. A man fished. The road led on up the hill. Pandora, bundled in mink, was curled up like a child, her head supported by Jeff's jacket rolled into a pillow. A lock of bright hair fell across her face, her lashes lay black on her jutting cheek-bones.

"Do you think I should wake her up?"

"Up to you."

This had been her pattern, her routine, all through the long journey from Palma, through Spain and France. Spurts of immense energy, activity, conversation, much laughter, and sudden impetuous suggestions.

We really should see that cathedral. It's only ten kilometers out of our way.

Look at that delicious river. Why don't we

stop for a moment and have a skinny-dip? There's no one to see.

You know, we've just passed the most enchanting café. Let's turn round and go back and have a drink.

But the drink would spin out into a long and leisurely lunch, with Pandora falling into conversation with any person who happened to be within earshot. Another bottle of wine. Coffee and cognac. And then . . . out. Sleep. She could catnap anywhere, and though this was sometimes embarrassing, it meant, at least, that she stopped talking, and Lucilla and Jeff had learned to be grateful for these respites. Without them Lucilla was not certain whether they would have survived the passage. Travelling with Pandora was a little like travelling with an ebullient child, or a dog—entertaining and companionable but as well quite dauntingly draining.

The Mercedes crested the slope. At the summit, the countryside opened and the views were magnificent. Beeches, fields, scattered farms, grazing sheep, the river far below them, the far-away hills bloomy and purple as ripe plums.

"If I don't wake her now she'll still be

asleep when we get home. It's only about ten minutes away."

"Then wake her."

Lucilla stretched out her arm, laid her hand on the soft fur of Pandora's shoulder and gave her a little shake.

"Pandora."

"Um."

"Pandora." Another shake. "Wake up. We're almost there. We're almost home."

"What?" Pandora's eyes fluttered open. They stared blankly, disorientated, confused. She closed them again, yawned, stirred, stretched. "What a lovely sleep. Where are we?"

"Heading for Caple Bridge. Almost home."

"Almost home? Almost at Croy?"

"Sit up and you'll see. You've missed the best bit of the drive, snoring away on the back seat."

"I wasn't snoring. I never snore." But after a bit she made an effort and did sit up, pushing her hair out of her eyes, gathering her furs around her as though chilled. She yawned again, stared from the window.

Blinked. Her eyes brightened. "But . . . we're nearly *there!*"

"I told you."

"You should have woken me hours ago. And the rain's gone. It's all sunshiny. And the green. I'd forgotten such greenness. What a welcome. 'Caledonia, stern and wild, fit nurse for a poetic child.' Who wrote that? Some stupid old fool. It's not stern and wild, it's just utterly beautiful. How perfectly sweet of it to be looking so lovely." She groped for her bag, her comb; tidied her hair. A mirror, some lipstick. A generous splash of Poison. "I must smell good for Archie."

"Don't forget about his leg. Don't expect him to come running to sweep you up in his arms. If he sweeps you up in his arms, he'll probably fall flat on his back."

"As if I'd suggest such a thing." She looked at her tiny diamond watch. "We're early. We said we'd be there at five and it's not four o'clock yet."

"We've made fantastic time."

"Dear Jeff." Pandora gave his shoulder an appreciative thump, as though she were patting a dog. "What a clever driver."

Now they were running downhill. At the

bottom of the incline, they took the steep hump of Caple Bridge, turned left, and were at the start of the glen. Pandora leaned forward in her seat. "But it's amazing. Absolutely nothing seems to have changed. Some people called Miller used to live in that cottage. They were terribly old. He'd been a shepherd. They must be dead by now. They used to keep bees and sell jars of heather honey. Oh dear, I'm getting so fraught, I think I might have to stop for a pee. No, of course I don't want to. Just imagination." She gave Jeff another thump on his shoulder. "Jeff, you're doing your silent act again. Can't you think up one small word of appreciation?"

"Sure," he grinned. "It's great."

"It's more than that. It's *our* country now. The Balmerinos of Croy. Really heart-stirring, like a roll of drums. And we're coming home. We should be wearing feathers in our bonnets, and there should be a piper playing somewhere. Why didn't you think of that, Lucilla? Why didn't you arrange it? After twenty years, surely it's the least you could have done for me."

Lucilla laughed. "I'm sorry."

Now the river once more ran alongside the road, its banks verdant with green rushes, the pastures on the other side grazed by peaceful herds of Friesian cows. Harvested fields were carpets of gold in the sunlight. The Mercedes swept around the curve of the road and the village of Strathcroy came into view. Lucilla saw the cluster of grey stone houses, smoke rising straight from chimney-pots, the tower of the church, the pleasing groups of ancient and shady beeches and oaks. Jeff slowed down to a prudent speed and they passed the War Memorial, the small Episcopal church, and were into the long, straight main street.

"The supermarket's new." Pandora sounded quite accusing.

"I know. It's run by people called Ishak. They're Pakistanis. Now, Jeff, it's here . . . turn right . . . up through the gates. . . ."

"But the park's gone! It's not parkland any more. It's all ploughed up."

"Pandora, you knew that happened. Dad wrote and told you."

"I suppose I forgot. But it does look strange."

Up the back drive. The hill reared ahead of them, the tumbling waters of the Pennyburn splashed and tumbled down under the little stone bridge. Then the avenue . . .

"We're here," said Lucilla, and leaned across Jeff to put the heel of her hand on the horn.

At Croy, Lucilla's family filled in the long waiting hours of the afternoon. Isobel was upstairs seeing to the final details of the visitors' bedrooms, checking clean towels and arranging flowers for dressing-tables and mantelpieces. Hamish had decided to take the dogs for a walk, disappeared after lunch and had not been seen since. And Archie, Lord Balmerino, was in the dining-room laying the table for dinner.

He had been finally forced into doing this. Waiting for anything or anybody was not his strong point, and as the day wore on, he had become increasingly restless, impatient, and anxious. He hated the thought of his loved ones belting up the murderous miles of the motorway, and his imagination had no difficulty at all in presenting hideously detailed pictures of pile-ups, mangled metal, and dead bodies. He had spent much time looking at his watch, going to the window at the faintest sound of a car engine, and was patently unable to settle for a moment. Isobel had suggested that he mow the croquet lawn but he had turned this down because he wanted to be certain of being on the spot when the car actually drew up in front of the house. Retreating to his study, he had sat down with *The Scotsman* but could not concentrate either on the news or the crossword. He tossed the paper aside and started prowling again.

At last Isobel, who had enough to do without her husband getting under her feet, lost her patience.

"Archie, if you can't sit still, then make yourself useful. You can lay the table for dinner. The clean mats and the napkins are on the sideboard." And she had gone upstairs quite crossly, and left him to it.

Not that he minded laying tables. In the old days, Harris used to perform the task, so there could be nothing unmanly about it. And when the American paying guests stayed, laying the table for dinner was always Archie's job, and he got certain pleasure from doing it with military thoroughness, knives and forks precisely aligned, and napkins folded into mitres.

The wineglasses looked slightly dusty, so he had found a tea-towel and was engaged in giving them a bit of a polish when he heard the car coming up the hill. His heart lurched. He looked at the clock, which told him four o'clock. Too early surely. He set down the glass and the cloth. It could not be. . . .

The blast of the car horn, a long continuous blare, tore the quiet afternoon and his own uncertainty into shreds.

Lucilla's traditional signal.

He could not move fast, but he moved as fast as he could. Down the length of the dining-room, through the door.

"Isobel!"

The front door stood open. He was crossing the hall as the car appeared, a thundering great Mercedes scattering gravel beneath its wheels.

"Isobel! They're here."

He got to the door but no farther. Pandora was quicker than he, out of the car almost before it had drawn to a halt, running across the gravel towards him. Pandora with that same bright hair flying all over the place and those same long spindly legs.

"Archie!"

She wore a fur coat that reached almost to her ankles but that did not stop her bounding two at a time up the steps, and if he could no longer lift her off her feet and whirl her around the way he used to when she was a child, there was nothing the matter with his arms, and his arms were ready and waiting for her.

Isobel . . . dear, uncomplicated, hospitable, unchanging Isobel . . . had allocated Pandora the best spare bedroom. This was in the front of the house, with tall sash windows facing south down the hill and over the glen and the river. It was furnished much as Pandora remembered it in her mother's day. Twin brass bedsteads, high off the ground, each wide as a small double bed. A faded carpet patterned with roses and an ornate dressing-table with many small drawers and a swing-mirror.

The old curtains, however, were gone, and heavy cream linen draperies hung in their place. The refurbishment had probably been planned with all the paying guests in mind. They would scarcely appreciate threadbare chintz with sun-rotted linings. For them as well, the adjoining dressing-room had been converted into a bathroom. Not that it looked very different, because Isobel had simply installed a bath and a basin and a lavatory, and left the rugs, the laden bookshelves, and the comfortable armchair where they were.

Pandora was meant to be unpacking. "Unpack and make yourself comfortable," Isobel had told her. She and Jeff, between them, had humped all Pandora's luggage upstairs. (Archie, of course, could not hump luggage on account of his leg. Pandora decided not to think about Archie. His grey hairs had shocked her, and she had never seen a man so thin.) "Have a bath if you want. There's gallons of hot water. Then come down and have a drink. We'll eat about eight o'clock."

But that was fifteen minutes ago and Pandora had got no farther than carrying her dressing-case into the bathroom and putting a few bottles out on the marble wash-stand. Her pills and potions, her Poison, bath-oil, creams and cleansers. Later she would have a bath. Not now.

Now, she still had to convince herself that she was really home. Back at Croy. But it was difficult because in this room she did not feel as though she belonged. She was a guest come to stay, a bird of passage. Abandoning her bottles, she went back to the bedroom, to the window, to lean out with her elbows on the sill, to gaze at the oft-remembered view and be quite, quite certain that it was not all a dream. This took some time. But what had happened to her own room, the room that had been Pandora's since babyhood? She decided to go and have a nose-around.

She went out of the room, went to the top of the stairs, paused. From the direction of the kitchen came cheerful domestic sounds and muted voices. Lucilla and Isobel busy with preparations for dinner and probably talking about Pandora. They were bound to talk. It did not matter; she did not mind. She crossed the landing and opened the door of what had been her parents' room, and was now Archie and Isobel's. She saw the huge double bed, the chaise longue at the foot of it with a sweater of Isobel's flung down, a pair of shoes, carelessly discarded. She saw the family photographs, the silver and crystal on the dressing-table, bedside books. There was the smell of face-powder and eau-de-cologne. Sweet and innocent scents. She closed the door and went on down the passage. She found the room that had been Archie's, swept and garnished with Jeff's backpack and his jacket set down in the middle of the carpet. The next room . . . Lucilla. Still filled with all the cherished flotsam of a schoolgirl . . . posters thumbtacked to the walls, china ornaments, a tape player, a guitar with a broken string.

And finally her own room. Her old room. Perhaps Hamish slept here? She had not yet met Hamish. Cautiously she turned the knob and pushed the door open. Not Hamish. Not anybody. Empty of any personal possession. New furniture, new curtains. No trace of Pandora.

What had they done with her books, her records, clothes, diaries, photographs . . . her *life?* All probably swept upstairs to some attic when the room was stripped and emptied, repainted, re-wallpapered, and given that beautiful new, blue, fitted carpet.

It was as though Pandora had ceased to exist, was already a ghost.

There was no point in asking why, because it was patently obvious. Croy belonged to Archie and Isobel, and to keep the place going as a viable proposition, every room must be put to good use. And Pandora had given up any claim to it by the simple act of going away and never coming back.

Standing there, she thought of those last miserable weeks when she had been beyond herself with an unhappiness that she was not allowed to talk about. Misery had made her cruel, and she was cruel to the two people she loved most in the world; snapping at her father, ignoring her mother, sulking for days on end and generally making their lives a misery.

In this room, she had spent hours lying face downwards on her bed with her record player churning out, over and over again, the saddest songs she knew. Matt Monro telling some female to "Walk Away." And Judy Garland tearing her guts out with "The Man That Got Away."

The road gets tougher,
It's lonelier and rougher,
With hope you burn up,
Tomorrow he will turn up . . .

Voices.
Darling, do come and eat some lunch.
I don't want any lunch.
I wish you'd tell me what's troubling you.
I just want to be left alone. It wouldn't be
any good telling you. You'd never under-
stand. . . .

She saw again her mother's face, confused
and dreadfully hurt. And was ashamed. At
eighteen, I should have known better. I
thought that I was adult and sophisticated,
but the truth was that I knew less about life
than a child. And it took me too long to find
out.

Too long, and too late. All over. She closed
the door and went back to her unpacking.

Dinner was over. They had sat, the six of
them, around the candle-lit table, and eaten

their way through Isobel's lovingly prepared celebratory meal. If she had not exactly killed a fatted calf, she had gone to great pains to produce a suitable feast. Cold soup, roast pheasant, *crème brûleé,* and a splendid Stilton, all washed down by the best wine that Archie could bring up from his father's depleted cellar.

Now it was nearly ten o'clock, and Isobel, with Pandora in attendance, was in the kitchen dealing with the last of the washing-up—the pots and pans, the ivory-handled knives and vegetable dishes too large to fit into the dishwasher. Pandora was meant to be helping, but after drying up a knife or two and putting three saucepans into the wrong cupboard, she had laid aside the tea-towel, made herself a mug of Nescafé, and sat down to drink it.

Conversation during dinner had been non-stop, for there was much to hear and much to tell. The adventure of Lucilla and Jeff's bus journey down through France from Paris; their Bohemian sojourn in Ibiza; and at last the bliss of Majorca and the Casa Rosa. Isobel's mouth had watered, hearing Lucilla's description of the garden there.

"Oh, I would love to see it."

"You should come. Lie in the sun and do nothing."

Archie laughed at this. "Isobel lie in the sun and do nothing? You must be mad. Before you could blink, she'd be bottoms up in the flower-beds, tearing at weeds."

"I haven't got any weeds," said Pandora.

And then, home news. Pandora was avid for every scrap of gossip. The latest on Vi, the Airds, the Gillocks, Willy Snoddy. Did Archie still hear from Harris and Mrs. Harris? She listened with some dismay to the saga of Edie Findhorn and her cousin Lottie.

"Heavens! That ghoul. Don't say she's come back into our lives. I'm glad you warned me. I shall take pains to cross the road if I see her coming."

She was told about the Ishak family, exiled from Malawi and arriving in Strathcroy with scarcely a penny between them.

". . . but they had some relations in Glasgow who'd already managed to do quite well for themselves, and with a bit of financial help from them, they managed to take over Mrs. McTaggart's newsagent's shop. You wouldn't recognize the place. It's a proper supermarket. We didn't think they'd last, but we were all mistaken. They're as industrious as ants, never seem to close their shop, and business booms. As well, we like them. They're all so helpful and kind."

And so on to the Balmerinos' slightly grander neighbours, which meant anybody living within a radius of twenty miles: the Buchanan-Wrights, the Ferguson-Crombies, the new people who had come to live at Ardnamoy; whose daughter had married; whose unlikely son had become a money-broker in the City and was coining millions.

No detail was unimportant. The only topic that was never brought up, as though by tacit agreement, was Pandora and what she had been doing with herself for the past twenty-one years.

She did not mind. She was back at Croy and for the moment that was all that mattered. The wayward years faded into unreality, like a life that had happened to another person, and surrounded by family she was happy to consign them to oblivion.

Sitting at the kitchen table, she sipped coffee and watched Isobel at the sink, scouring the roasting pan. Isobel wore red rubber gloves and a blue-and-white apron tied over her tidy dress, and it occurred to Pandora that she was an exceptional woman, peacefully labouring away and quite unresentful of the fact that the rest of her family had taken themselves off, and she was left to clear up the detritus of the meal by herself.

For, after dinner, the others had all dispersed. Archie, excusing himself, had gone down to his workshop. Hamish, with the promise of financial reward, had agreed to take advantage of the long evening light and mow the croquet lawn. He had gone to do this with good grace, and Pandora was much impressed. What she did not realize was how impressed Hamish had been by her. An aunt to stay was not an exciting prospect. Hamish had visions of a Vi-type person with grey hair and laced-up shoes, and had received the shock of his life when he was introduced to Pandora. A stunner. Like a film star. Over his pheasant, he entertained fantasies of showing her off to the other seniors in his class at Templehall. Perhaps Dad would bring her over to watch some match or other. Hamish's stock with schoolmates would go sky-high. He wondered if she liked rugger.

"Isobel, I do love Hamish."

"I'm quite keen on him myself. I just hope he doesn't grow too enormous."

"He's going to be divinely handsome." She took another mouthful of coffee. "Do you like Jeff?"

Jeff, predictably sated by two weeks of female company and unaccustomed gracious living, had wheeled Lucilla down to the Strathcroy Arms for a restoring jar of Foster's lager downed in comfortably masculine surroundings.

"He seems really nice."

"Terribly kind. And all through that long drive, he never once lost his patience. A bit laconic, though. I suppose all Australians are strong and silent. I wouldn't really know. Never met any others."

"Do you think Lucilla's in love with him?"

"No, I don't think so. They're just . . . that awful phrase . . . very good friends. Besides, she's terribly young. You don't want to start thinking about permanent relationships when you're only nineteen."

"You mean marriage."

"No, darling. I don't mean marriage."

Isobel fell silent. Pandora decided that she had, perhaps, said the wrong thing and cast about for a more amusing and less touchy topic. "Isobel, I know who you haven't told me about. Dermot Honeycombe and Terence. Are they still running the antique shop?"

"Oh dear." Isobel turned from the sink. "Didn't Archie tell you in one of his letters? So sad. Terence died. About five years ago."

"I don't believe it. What did poor Dermot do? Find himself another nice young man?"

"No, never. He was heart-broken, but faithful. We all thought he might leave Strathcroy, but he stayed; all by himself. Still running the antique shop, still living in their little cottage. Every now and then he asks Archie and me over for a meal, and gives us tiny helpings of frightfully dainty food with amusing sauces. Archie always comes home starving and has to be given soup or corn-flakes before he goes to bed."

"Poor Dermot. I must go and see him."

"He'd love that. He's always asking after you."

"I can buy some trinket from him to give Katy Steynton for her birthday. We haven't talked about that either. The dance, I mean." Isobel, finished at last, pulled off her rubber gloves, laid them on the draining-board, and came to sit down with her sister-in-law. "Are we going to be a huge house party?"

"No. Just us. No Hamish because he'll be back at school. And some sad American Katy met in London and took pity on. Verena hasn't got space for him, so he's coming here."

"Goodness! How nice. A man for me. Why is he sad?"

"His wife's just died."

"Oh dear, I hope he's not too gloomy. Where's he going to sleep?"

"In your old bedroom."

Which settled that question. "And what about the night of the party? Where are we having dinner?"

"Here, I think. We could ask the Airds to join us, and Vi. They're coming for lunch tomorrow; I thought I'd speak to Virginia then."

"You never said."

"What, that they're coming for lunch?

Well, I've told you now. That's why Hamish is cutting the croquet lawn."

"Lovely afternoon entertainment, all laid on. What are you going to wear for the dance? Have you got a new dress?"

"No. I've run out of money. I had to buy Hamish five new pairs of shoes for school. . . ."

"But, Isobel, you *must* have a new dress. We'll go and find one for you. Where shall we go? To Relkirk. We'll have a day out . . ."

"Pandora, I told you . . . I really can't afford it."

"Oh, darling, the least I can do is stand you a little gift." The back door opened and Hamish appeared, having finished his mowing just before darkness fell, and once again in his usual state of ravenous hunger. "We'll talk about it later."

Hamish collected his snack. A bowl of Weetabix, a glass of milk, a handful of chocolate biscuits. Pandora finished her coffee, set down the mug. She yawned. "I think I must go to bed. I'm bushed." She got to her feet. "Good night, Hamish."

She did not attempt to kiss him and Hamish was torn between relief and disappointment.

"Will I find Archie in his workshop? I'll just pop down and have a word." She stooped and kissed Isobel. "And good night to you, darling. Heaven to be here. Delicious dinner. See you all in the morning."

In the basement, Archie, absorbed and concentrated, worked by a strong bulb with a wide shade that threw a bright circle onto his work-bench. Painting the carving of Katy and her dog was both tricky and fiddly. The muted check of the skirt, the texture of the sweater, the subtle, varying streaks of colour in the hair, each presented a challenge and took all his dexterity to accomplish.

He laid down one sable brush and took up another, then heard Pandora approach. Her step was unmistakable, descending the stone stair that led down from the kitchens, as was the sharp tap of her high heels down the ill-lighted stone-flagged passage. He paused in his work to look up and saw the door open and Pandora's head come around the edge of it.

"Am I interrupting?"

"No."

"Goodness, it's gloomy. I couldn't find the light switch. Like a dungeon. But I must say, you're quite cosy in here." She found a chair and sat beside him. "What are you doing?"

"Painting."

"I can see that. What a charming little statue. Where did you get it?"

He told her, not without pride. "I made it."

"You made it? Archie, you are brilliant. I never knew you were so handy."

"It's for Katy's birthday. It's her. With her dog."

"What a lovely idea. You didn't used to be able to make things. It was always Pa who glued our toys together and mended broken china. Did you go to classes or something?"

"I suppose I did. After I was wounded . . ." He corrected himself. "After my leg was shot off and when I was finally discharged from hospital, I got sent to Headley Court. That's the Forces rehabilitation centre for chaps who've been disabled.

Dismembered in some way. That's where they fit the artificial limbs. Legs, arms, hands, feet. Anything that you are missing is supplied for you. Within, of course, reason. And then they give you months of bloody hell until you've learned to use it properly."

"It doesn't sound very nice."

"It was all right. And there was always some poor bugger worse off than yourself."

"But you were alive. You weren't dead."

"True."

"Is it very horrible, having a tin leg?"

"Better than none at all, which seems to be the alternative."

"I never heard how it happened."

"Better not."

"Was it a nightmare?"

"All violence is a nightmare."

Forbidden ground. She backed off. "I'm sorry . . . go on telling me."

"Well . . . once I . . ." He had lost the thread of what he had been saying. He took off his spectacles, rubbed his eyes with his fingers. "Once . . . I was more or less ambulant, they taught me how to use a treadle jigsaw. Occupational therapy and good exercise for the leg. And from that, it sort of snowballed. . . ."

It was all right. The dangerous moment was safely over. If Archie did not want to talk about Northern Ireland, then Pandora did not want to hear.

"Do you mend things, like Pa used to?"

"Yes."

"And that dear little figure. How do you start to make something like that? Where do you begin?"

"You start with a block of wood."

"What kind of wood?"

"For this one, I used beech. Beech from Croy, a windblown branch from years back. I squared it off into a block with the chain-saw. Then I made two drawings from the photograph, a front view and a side view. Then I transferred the front elevation onto the face of the block, and the side elevation onto the side of the block. Are you with me?"

"All the way."

"Then I cut it out on the band-saw."

"What's a band-saw?"

He pointed. "That's the band-saw. It's electrically operated and lethally sharp, so don't start fiddling."

"I wasn't going to. What do you do then?"

"Start carving. Whittling."

"What with?"

"Wood-carver's chisels. A penknife."

"I'm amazed. Is this the first you've done?"

"By no means, but this was more difficult because of the composition. The girl sitting and the dog. That was quite difficult. Before, they've been standing figures. Soldiers mostly, in various regimental uniforms. I get the details of the uniforms from a book of plates I found up in Pa's library. It was that book that gave me the idea. They make quite good wedding presents if the bridegroom happens to be in the Army."

"Have you got any to show me?"

"Yes. There's one here." He pulled himself out of his chair, went to a cupboard, took out a box. "I didn't actually give this one away because I wasn't quite satisfied with it, so I made another. But it'll give you an idea. . . ."

Pandora took the figure of the soldier from him and turned it in her hands. It was a replica of an officer in the Black Watch, every detail perfect—from brogues, to kilt, to the red hackle in his khaki bonnet. She thought it perfect and was filled with wordless admiration for Archie's unsuspected talent, his precision, his undeniable artistry.

Also incredulous. "Do you mean to say you *give* these away? Archie, you're dotty. They're beautiful. Unique. Visitors from overseas would snap up just such a souvenir. Have you ever tried selling them?"

"No." He seemed quite surprised at the idea.

"Have you ever thought of it?"

"No."

She knew a burst of sisterly irritation. "You are hopeless. You always were a laid-back old stick, but this is ridiculous. There's Isobel slaving away, trying to keep everything going by having strings of Americans to stay, and you could be churning these things out and making a fortune."

"I doubt that. Anyway, it's not a case of churning. They take a lot of time."

"Well, get someone to help you. Get two people to help you. Start a little home industry."

"I haven't the space down here."

"What about the stables? They're empty. Or one of the barns?"

"It would mean reconstruction, equipping, electricity laid on, safety regulations, fire precautions."

"So?"

"So it would cost money. Which is a commodity pretty thin on the ground."

"Could you get a grant?"

"Grants, as well, are thin on the ground just now."

"You could *try* for one. Oh, don't be so hopeless, Archie. Be a bit more enterprising. I think it's the most wonderful idea."

"Pandora, you were always full of wonderful ideas." He took the soldier from her and laid him back in his box. "But you're right about Isobel. I do what I can to help, but I know she's got far too much on her plate. Before Northern Ireland, I thought about trying to get some sort of a job . . . as a factor, or something. I don't know who'd have employed me but I didn't want to leave Croy, and it seemed the only sort of work I could do. . . ." His voice, ruminating, trailed to silence.

"But now you've learned a new trade. All

this. Hidden talents have sprung to life. All you need is a little enterprise and a lot of determination."

"And a lot of money."

"Archie"—she spoke quite crossly—"whether you have one leg or two, you can't just shed responsibility."

"Are you speaking from experience?"

"*Touché.*" Pandora laughed and shook her head. "No. I'm the last to preach. Just talking off the top of my head." Abruptly, she abandoned the argument, yawned and stretched, reached upwards, spreading her fingers. "I'm tired. I came to say good night. I'm going to bed."

"I hope you have sweet dreams."

"What about you?"

"I want to get this finished and done with. Then, every spare moment I have I shall be able to spend with you."

"Dear man." On her feet, she stooped to kiss him. "I'm glad I came home."

"Me too."

She went to the door, opened it, hesitated, and turned back.

"Archie?"

"What is it?"

"I've often wondered. Did you get that letter I sent you in Berlin?"

"Yes."

"You never replied."

"By the time I'd decided what I was going to say, you'd gone to America and it was too late."

"Did you tell Isobel?"

"No."

"Did you . . . speak to anybody?"

"No."

"I see." She smiled. "The Airds are coming for lunch tomorrow."

"I know. I asked them."

"Good night, Archie."

"Good night."

The evening slipped into night. The house settled as the momentum of another busy day wound itself down. Hamish watched television for a bit and then made his way upstairs. Isobel, in the kitchen, laid the table for breakfast—the last chore of the day—and then let the dogs out for their last sniff around the dark garden, alert for scents of marauding rabbit. Lights were turned off, and she too headed for bed. Later still Jeff and Lucilla returned from the village. They let themselves in through the back door. Archie heard their voices above him in the hall. And then silence.

Past midnight, and he was finally finished. Another day and the enamel would be dry. He tidied up, put lids on small paint-pots, cleaned his brushes, turned off the light and closed the door. Slowly he made his way down the shadowy passage and up the stairs to do his nightly rounds, which he called putting the house to bed. He checked locks on doors and snibs on windows, fire-guards and electrical plugs. In the kitchen, he found the dogs asleep. He filled a tumbler with water and drank it. Finally he trod up the stairs.

But he did not go immediately to his own bedroom. Instead he walked down the passage and saw the shaft of light, still burning, beneath the door of Lucilla's room. He tapped and opened the door and found her in bed, reading by lamplight.

"Lucilla."

She looked up, marked her page and laid her book aside. "I thought you'd gone to bed hours ago."

"No. I've been working." He came to sit

on the edge of her bed. "Did you have a good evening?"

"Yes, it was fun. Toddy Buchanan in his usual good form."

"I wanted to say good night, and I wanted to say thank you."

"What for?"

"Coming home. Bringing Pandora."

His hand lay on her eiderdown. She laid her own on top of it. Isobel's night-gowns were white lawn trimmed with lace, but Lucilla slept in a green T-shirt with "Save the Rain Forests" printed across the chest. Her long dark hair was spread like silk on her pillow, and he was filled with love for her.

"You're not disappointed?" she asked him.

"Why should I be disappointed?"

"Often when you've looked forward to something for years, you feel a bit let down when it actually happens."

"I don't feel let down."

"She is beautiful."

"But dreadfully thin, don't you think?"

"I know. There's nothing of her. But she's so hyper that she burns everything up."

"What do you mean?"

"Just that. She sleeps a lot, but when she's awake she's charging on every cylinder. Super-charging, I would say. Being with her all the time is really quite exhausting. And then she passes out as though sleep is the only thing that's going to top up her batteries."

"She was always like that. Mrs. Harris used to say, 'That Pandora. Either up in the clouds or doon in the midden.'"

"Manic-depressive."

"Surely not as bad as that."

"Tending that way."

He frowned. And then asked the question that had been niggling around at the back of his mind all evening. "You don't think she's on drugs?"

"Oh, Dad."

He immediately wished that he had not mentioned his fears. "I only ask you because I imagine you know more about these things than I do."

"She's certainly not a junkie. But perhaps she does take something to bubble her along. A lot of people do."

"But she's not addicted?"

"Oh, Dad, I don't know. But worrying

about Pandora isn't going to do any good.
You've just got to accept her for what she is.
The person she's turned into. Have fun with
her. Lots of laughs."

"In Majorca . . . do you think she's
happy?"

"She seems to be. And why not? A heavenly house, a garden, a pool, lots of
money . . ."

"Does she have friends?"

"She has Seraphina and Mario, who take
care of her . . ."

"That wasn't what I meant."

"I know. No, we didn't meet her friends,
so I don't know if she has any or not. We
didn't really meet anybody. Except one man.
He was there the day we arrived, but after
that we never saw him again."

"I thought she would have a resident
lover."

"I think probably he was her lover and the
reason he didn't come back was because we
were there." He said nothing to this, and
Lucilla smiled. "It's a different world out
there, Dad."

"I know that. I know."

She put her arms around his neck and

pulled him down and kissed him. She said, "You mustn't worry."

"I won't."

"Good night, Dad."

"Good night, my darling. God bless you."